6G Urban Innovation

6G Urban Innovation

AI and Digital Twin for Next-Gen Sustainable Cities

Edited by

Ashu Taneja
Abhishek Kumar
Suresh Vishnudas Limkar
Mariya Ouaissa
Mariyam Ouaissa

iSTE

WILEY

First published 2025 in Great Britain and the United States by ISTE Ltd and John Wiley & Sons, Inc.

ISTE Ltd
27-37 St George's Road
London SW19 4EU
UK

www.iste.co.uk

John Wiley & Sons, Inc.
111 River Street
Hoboken, NJ 07030
USA

www.wiley.com

Library of Congress Control Number: 2025939935

British Library Cataloguing-in-Publication Data
A CIP record for this book is available from the British Library
ISBN 978-1-83669-065-8

The manufacturer's authorized representative according to the EU General Product Safety Regulation is Wiley-VCH GmbH, Boschstr. 12, 69469 Weinheim, Germany, e-mail: Product_Safety@wiley.com.

Contents

Preface

This book presents the 6G-powered integration of artificial intelligence (AI) and digital twin (DT) technology for sustainable smart cities. In the context of smart cities, 6G, AI and DT hold enormous potential for transformation by boosting city infrastructure and planning, streamlining healthcare facilities, and improving transportation. 6G offers high-speed and low-latency seamless transfer of vast amounts of data, which, when analyzed with sophisticated AI models, enhance the decision-making capabilities for smart city infrastructure and urban planning. Through continuous monitoring and virtual modeling of urban ecosystems, DT technology enables predictive maintenance for energy distribution, water management and waste management in smart city landscapes for environmental sustainability.

This book covers the technological innovations, trends and concerns associated with 6G, as well as practical challenges encountered in the implementation of AI and DT for transforming smart cities for a sustainable future.

The book also addresses a comprehensive convergence of 6G, AI and DT for various use case scenarios of sustainable smart cities. It reveals how to effectively integrate a collection of keys enabling technologies (KET) into a single system for network management, resource control, data sensing, automation and decision-making. Technological convergence is advantageous for real-time applications that use a large number of devices. Through the innovative integration of 6G, AI and DT, the concept of intelligent transportation, including connected cars and roadside units, can become a reality. This convergence also plays a crucial role in smart healthcare, enabling patients to receive remote treatment or monitoring through telemedicine or telesurgery thanks to the intelligent interconnectivity

Chapter written by Ashu TANEJA, Abhishek KUMAR, Suresh Vishnudas LIMKAR, Mariya OUAISSA and Mariyam OUAISSA of devices. For sustainable development, energy-efficient communication is made possible through the resource control mechanism. This book provides a comprehensive guide, from the technological background to the real-time implementation across various use-case scenarios.

July 2025

1

AI-Enabled Energy Management in Mobile Wireless Sensor Network for 6G Internet-of-Things (IoT)

Mobile wireless sensor networks (MWSNs) within the Internet-of-Things (IoT) are undergoing a significant transformation with the advent of sixth generation (6G) technology, which prioritizes low-latency, high-speed communication, and efficient energy management. This chapter explores the artificial intelligence (AI)-driven strategies that enhance the performance of 6G-enabled MWSNs while optimizing energy consumption and extending network lifespan. The roles of federated learning, deep learning and reinforcement learning are highlighted in addressing energy efficiency challenges. Additionally, innovative approaches for intelligent and sustainable energy management in next-generation wireless networks are introduced, leveraging neuromorphic computing and quantum-inspired algorithms to achieve smarter and more eco-friendly operations. The integration of edge computing and blockchain further strengthens security and data privacy while minimizing energy overhead. Future advancements in 6G MWSNs will continue to rely on AI-driven optimizations to ensure seamless, scalable, and energy-efficient network operations.

1.1. Introduction

Wireless communication and the Internet-of-Things (IoT) are witnessing rapid transformation with the advent of sixth generation (6G) technologies (Mao et al. 2020). The function of mobile wireless sensor networks (MWSNs) becomes ever more important as we move toward this next generation of connection. Comprising many tiny, independent sensors, these networks may gather and broadcast data in many scenarios. However, considering the mobility nature of these sensors and the

---

Chapter written by Bhanu Partap SINGH, Lav SONI and Ashu TANEJA.

low-latency, high-speed requirements of 6G networks, energy management becomes somewhat challenging (Maduranga et al. 2024).

This chapter delves into the challenging field of artificial intelligence (AI)-enabled energy management in MWSNs for applications in 6G IoT (Sodhro et al. 2020; Sefati et al. 2024), exploring how the use of AI and machine learning (ML) could provide methods for optimizing lifetime within such networks and reducing the levels of energy usage and increasing performance in these highly demanding systems.

By the end of this chapter, readers will be fully aware of the existing level of the art, challenges and potential routes in this crucial area of research (Alhammadi et al. 2024).

Generation	Key features	Energy management approach
1st Gen	Static nodes, limited resources	Fixed duty cycling
2nd Gen	Improved hardware, longer range	Adaptive duty cycling
3rd Gen	Mobile nodes, dynamic topology	Mobility-aware protocols
4th Gen (5G)	High speed, low latency	AI-assisted optimization
5th Gen (6G)	Ultra-high speed, massive connectivity	Advanced AI/ML techniques

Table 1.1. *Evolution of wireless sensor networks (WSNs)*

Table 1.1 shows WSN development throughout many generations, therefore stressing the evolving methods of energy management. The complexity of energy management rises as we move toward 6G networks, which calls for the acceptance of powerful AI and ML methods (Manogaran et al. 2021).

1.2. 6G IoT: a new frontier for MWSNs

With unheard-of speeds, ultra-low latency and huge device density, 6G technology promises to bring in a new age of communication. The IoT will be much changed by these developments, allowing a large spectrum of fresh uses and services. In this regard, MWSNs are likely to be rather important in achieving 6G IoT's full possibilities (Zhu et al. 2023).

Expectations for 6G networks include data speeds of up to 1 Tbps, latency as low as 1 microsecond and capacity for up to ten million devices per square kilometer. Among the many fresh uses these features will allow are brain–computer connections, tactile Internet and holographic communications. As the eyes and ears of the 6G IoT ecosystem, MWSNs will be indispensable in gathering the enormous volumes of data needed to enable these uses (Dubey et al. 2023; Abbas et al. 2024).

However, the higher performance standards of 6G networks also provide major difficulties for MWSNs, especially with relation to energy usage. 6G applications' high data rates and low latency will demand sensor nodes to process and transmit data at hitherto unheard-of rates, hence possibly fast depleting energy resources. Moreover, the great device density allowed by 6G networks will lead to higher network complexity, which emphasizes even more effective energy management (Guo et al. 2021).

Figure 1.1 shows the projected growth in IoT devices and the corresponding increase in data generation until 2030.

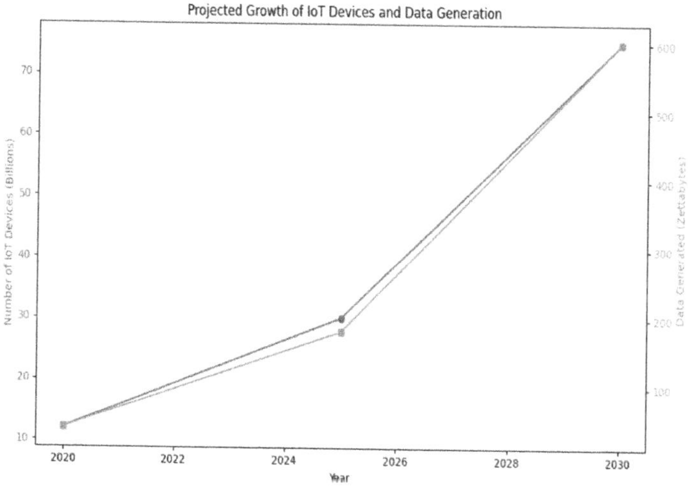

Figure 1.1. *Projected growth of IoT devices and data generation. For a color version of this figure, see: www.iste.co.uk/taneja/6gurban.zip*

This graph shows the predicted exponential expansion in data produced as well as IoT device count. Over 75 billion IoT devices are expected to be running by 2030, producing roughly 600 zettabytes of data yearly (Verma et al. 2020). This enormous scale emphasizes how urgently effective energy management in MWSNs supports the 6G IoT ecosystem (Gera et al. 2023).

The value of MWSNs to 6G IoT transcends simple data collection and dissemination. Difficult tasks such as autonomous decision-making, edge computing and cooperative sensing will fall to these systems. For smart city applications tracking public safety, air quality and traffic flow, MWSNs might be used, for instance. Apart from data collecting, the sensor nodes would localize it, make real-time decisions, and coordinate with other nodes to optimize city operations.

In healthcare environments, MWSNs might be used for remote treatment as well as for ongoing patient monitoring in hospitals (Singh et al. 2024). Wearable sensors would gather vital signs and other health-related data, analyze it at the edge and forward only pertinent information to medical professionals. This method would need advanced energy management to guarantee long-term functioning of the wearable gadgets while preserving the great dependability expected by medical uses (Lv et al. 2021).

Environmental monitoring is another area where MWSNs will be very vital in the 6G IoT ecosystem. Sensor nodes placed in polar areas, seas or forests would have to run for long stretches of time free from human interference. These nodes would gather information on pollution levels, animal migrations or climate change; so, strong energy management techniques would be necessary to live in demanding surroundings and maintain long-term data collecting capacity (Logeshwaran et al. 2024).

Integration of MWSNs with other developing technologies will increase their possibilities in the environment of the 6G IoT. For dynamic 3D sensing and network reconfiguration, for instance, the mix of MWSNs with unmanned aerial vehicles (UAVs) enables their use as mobile base stations or data mules, UAVs gather data from ground-based sensors and convey it to central processing units (Dabas et al. 2024). This hybrid method would provide new dimensions to energy management and call for plans considering the energy limitations of ground sensors and flying vehicles.

Deeper into the 6G era, the distinction between sensing and communication will keep blurring. Ideas such as ambient backscatter communications and combined radar-communication systems will become increasingly frequent (Chen and Okada 2020). Under these conditions, MWSNs will not only detect the surroundings but also use the same signals for communication, thus possibly improving the energy-efficient operations. Realizing these advantages, nevertheless, will depend on advanced energy management strategies able to accommodate the dual character of these systems (Chen et al. 2020).

Furthermore, allowing new paradigms in distributed intelligence and collaborative sensing will be the great connection promised by 6G networks. Large-scale sensing systems will be built on MWSNs, where hundreds or even millions of nodes cooperate to accomplish challenging sensing missions (Xu 2021). By spreading the burden across many nodes, this cooperative strategy might perhaps result in more energy-efficient activities. It does, however, also create fresh difficulties with regard to network coordination and energy balance (Gong et al. 2022).

Examining the following breakdown of energy consumption in a standard MWSN node shown in Figure 1.2 helps us better grasp the energy consumption trends in 6G IoT applications.

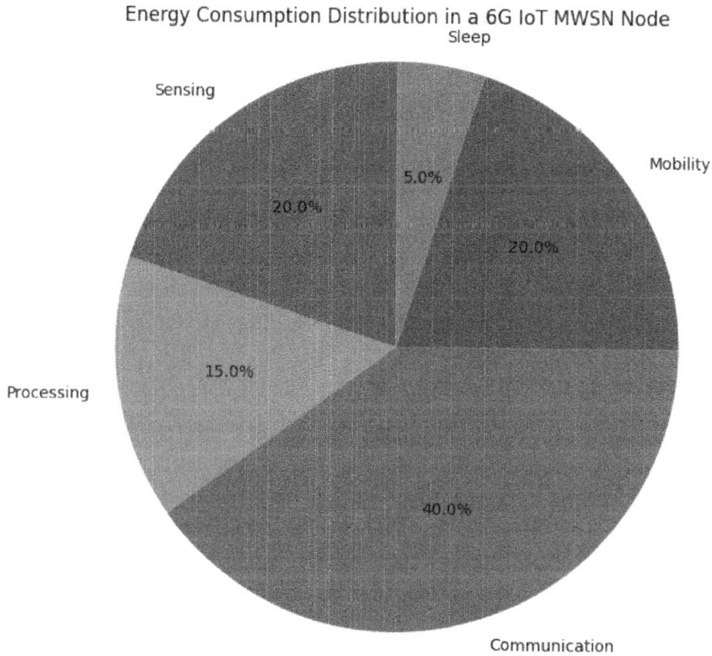

Figure 1.2. *Energy consumption distribution in a 6G IoT MWSN node. For a color version of this figure, see: www.iste.co.uk/taneja/6gurban.zip*

With 40% of the total energy used, Figure 1.2 shows that for MWSN nodes, communication is still the most energy-intensive activity. Sensing and movement, each using 20% of the energy, come next (Letaief et al. 2021). Processing contributes for 15%; the node uses only 5% of its energy in sleep mode. These ratios demonstrate the need for energy management strategies, emphasizing increasing mobility and communication while also improving the efficiency of sensing and processing operations (Kamruzzaman 2022).

Entering the 6G era will make the energy management problems facing MWSNs in IoT devices more challenging. The need to handle ultra-high-speed connections, analyze vast amounts of data and maintain long-term operation in diverse environments will drive current energy management techniques beyond their reach. Here is where solutions offered by AI could assist in changing the energy use in these sophisticated networks (Chataut et al. 2024).

The following sections will look at the particular challenges presented by 6G IoT applications for MWSN energy management, investigate the possibilities of AI and ML approaches in tackling these difficulties and go over innovative research in this sector. Knowing these characteristics will enable us to equip the 6G IoT ecosystem for the energy management requirements of the next wireless sensor networks more effectively.

1.3. Energy management challenges in 6G IoT MWSNs

MWSNs face fresh energy management issues with the shift to 6G IoT. These difficulties result from the special qualities of 6G networks and the increasing demands of IoT applications. Developing practical AI-powered energy management solutions depends on an awareness of these difficulties (Padmapriya et al. 2022).

Ultra-high data rates and low latency

Data speeds up to 1 Tbps and latency as low as 1 microsecond are envisaged in 6G networks. For MWSNs, this entails processing and forwarding enormous volumes of data at hitherto unheard-of rates. The limited power resources of sensor nodes may be rapidly depleted by the energy consumption connected with such high-speed activities. Duty cycling and other conventional energy-saving strategies may not be enough as they might cause unacceptable data transfer delays (Jamshed et al. 2024).

Massive device density

Energy management in MWSNs finds great difficulty, given the capacity of 6G networks to handle up to ten million devices per square kilometer. The complexity of the network architecture and the possibility for interference rise along with the increasing count of devices. As more frequent communications and the need for complex routing systems to properly run the network depend on this density, energy consumption might rise (Du et al. 2020).

Heterogeneous network integration

The convergence of many network technologies including cellular networks, satellite communications and short-range wireless protocols will probably define 6G

IoT ecosystems. MWSNs will have to run smoothly in these varied surroundings, maybe moving between many channels of communication. This adaptability to changing network circumstances and maintaining many radio interfaces comes at higher energy consumption (Taneja et al. 2023).

Enhanced mobility and dynamic topology

The mobile character of MWSNs in 6G IoT systems presents more energy management difficulties. Depending on their closeness to other nodes or base stations, nodes might have to regularly change their location information, adapt to changing network topologies and modify their transmission power. These mobility-related activities have a big influence on energy use (Mittal et al. 2024).

Edge computing and in-network processing

Edge computing will become even more important for 6G IoT applications in order to lower latency and save bandwidth. This moves part of the computing load to the sensor nodes themselves, which must handle increasingly difficult data processing and analysis chores. This raises the energy needs for local computing even when it may lower the energy consumption connected to data transport (Mwashita and Odhiambo 2024).

Quality of service (QoS) requirements

Variations in 6G IoT applications will affect their QoS needs for data throughput, latency, dependability and availability. For MWSNs, meeting these various QoS criteria and optimizing energy usage will be very difficult. Energy management techniques have to be adaptable enough to fit varying application requirements without sacrificing network longevity (Pan et al. 2021).

Energy harvesting and transfer

Energy collecting methods are probably going to become more common if we want MWSNs in 6G IoT applications to survive. Integrating energy collecting features, however, presents fresh difficulties in terms of controlling erratic power sources and best using the acquired energy. Furthermore, wireless power transfer technologies might be used, which call for precise management to distribute energy across the network.

Security and privacy overheads

6G IoT applications' higher data sensitivity and connection need stronger security and privacy protection. Using sophisticated encryption, authentication and privacy-preserving methods might bring major energy overheads for sensor nodes with limited resources (Vaigandla 2022).

Cross-layer optimization

6G IoT-efficient energy management MWSNs call for optimization at many tiers of the network stack. This covers the physical layer, for example, transmission power control MAC layer, channel access mechanism network layer, routing protocols and application layer, and data aggregation. Coordinating these improvements across layers is a difficult task (Mukherjee et al. 2022).

Long-term autonomy

Many 6G IoT applications will need for MWSNs to run autonomously for long stretches, maybe in hostile or inaccessible conditions. This calls for energy management techniques that can adapt to changing circumstances and preserve network performance over extended periods of time, apart from human involvement (Jayadharshini et al. 2024).

Figure 1.3 shows the relative impact of these challenges on energy consumption in 6G IoT MWSNs.

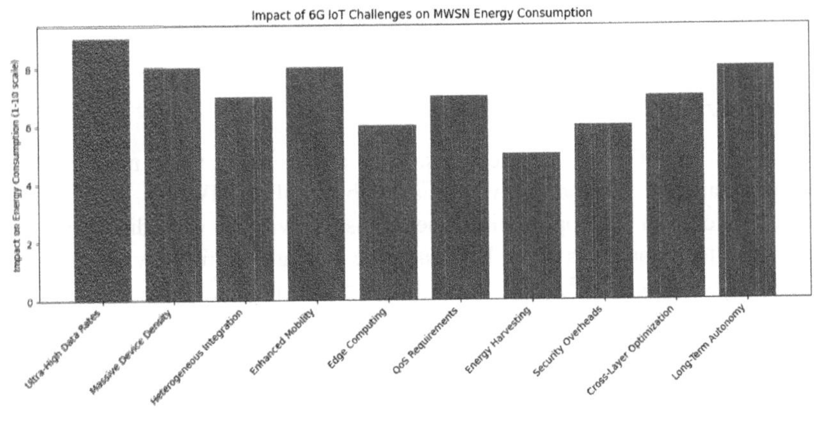

Figure 1.3. *Impact of 6G IoT challenges on MWSN energy consumption*

Rated on a scale of 1–10, this graph shows the relative influence of every obstacle on energy usage in 6G IoT MWSNs. The most important obstacles are ultra-high data rates and great gadget density, closely followed by improved mobility and the necessity of long-term autonomy.

Dealing with these issues calls for a paradigm change in our attitude to MWSN energy management. Conventional approaches stressing single-layer optimizations or stationary energy saving techniques are most likely not suited in the dynamic and complex environment of 6G IoT.

Here is where AI-enabled technology might really transform society and provide the tools to build intelligent, adaptable, all-encompassing energy management systems (Lin and Xiang 2023).

The next section will examine how ML techniques and AI may be used to address challenges and revolutionize 6G IoT MWSN energy management.

1.4. AI and machine learning for energy management in 6G IoT MWSNs

6G IoT applications in MWSNs face complicated energy management challenges that call for creative ideas able to match dynamic settings, govern significant operations and maximize performance across many dimensions.

Among the exciting solutions to these problems are AI and ML technologies, as they let us learn from data, make wise judgments and continuously enhance system performance (Hossain et al. 2023).

This section explores how AI and ML can be applied to various aspects of energy management in 6G IoT MWSNs, highlighting key techniques and their potential benefits.

Reinforcement learning (RL) for adaptive energy management

Energy management in dynamic MWSN systems is fitting for RL. RL algorithms can create perfect policies for duty cycle management, energy allocation and transmission power regulation by means of environmental interaction and feedback in the form of incentives or penalties.

For improving the sensor node's sleep/wake cycles, for instance, we may develop a Q-learning-based method. By changing the node operations depending on variables such as the remaining battery life, network traffic and application needs, the system will learn to balance energy economy with network performance.

Consider Figure 1.4 for a simplified Q-learning process for sleep/wake scheduling.

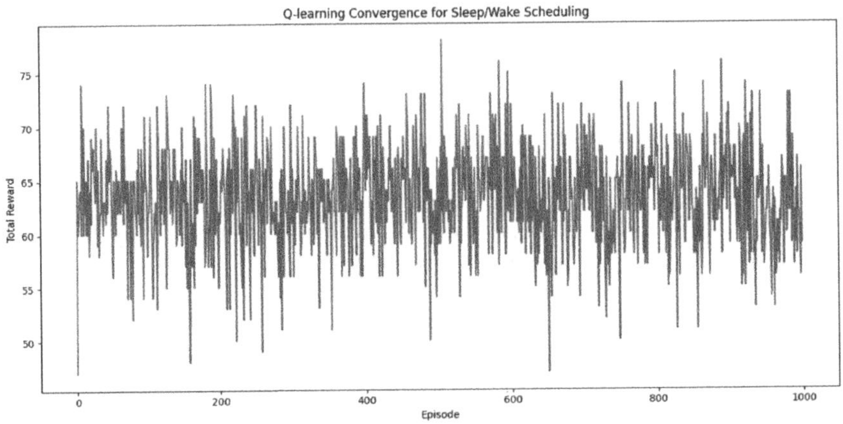

Figure 1.4. *Q-learning convergence for sleep/wake scheduling*

Figure 1.4 shows how a Q-learning system converges over time to an ideal sleep/wake schedule, therefore maximizing the overall reward which, in this instance, relates to network performance and energy economy.

Deep learning for network traffic prediction

Everyone may predict network traffic patterns in 6G IoT MWSNs using deep learning methods, namely the recurrent neural networks (RNNs) and long short-term memory (LSTM) networks. By means of exact traffic prediction, proactive energy management becomes achievable and allows nodes to change their operational settings to reflect expected traffic loads.

To predict future traffic levels, we may teach an LSTM network using past network traffic data. These predictions imply that the network may dynamically modify channel allocation, transmission power and routing choices to maximize energy consumption while also meeting QoS criteria.

Federated learning for distributed energy optimization

Federated learning (FL) provides a practical approach to cooperative energy management for big-scale 6G IoT MWSNs. Instead of raw data, FL allows many nodes or clusters to train ML models locally and exchange only the model updates with a central server. This approach provides anonymity, reduces communication overhead and allows globally optimal energy management strategies to be created (Cai et al. 2022).

A 6G IoT MWSN might make use of FL to optimize data aggregation techniques, transmission power control or routing protocol optimization throughout the network. Every node or cluster would learn from its nearby environment and assist to build a global model reflecting different network conditions and energy constraints.

Genetic algorithms for multi-objective optimization

Genetic algorithms (GAs) may be applied to solve complex, multifarious optimization problems in 6G IoT MWSN energy management. GAs can simultaneously maximize many parameters such as energy consumption, network lifetime, data delivery ratio and latency.

In hierarchical MWSNs, for instance, a GA can be applied to discover optimum configurations for clustering where network coverage and connectivity balance energy efficiency. The method will evolve over many generations to give responses that progressively improve the trade-offs between many objectives.

Figure 1.5 shows a simplified implementation of a GA for cluster head selection.

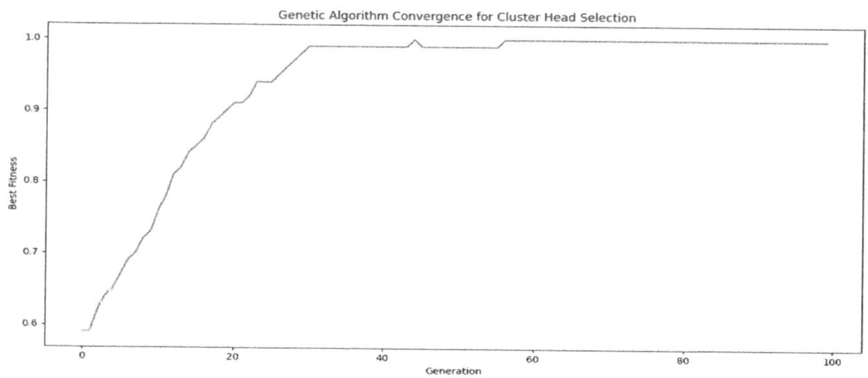

Figure 1.5. *Genetic algorithm convergence for cluster head selection*

Figure 1.5 shows how a GA converges to an optimal solution for cluster head selection in an MWSN, balancing energy efficiency and network performance.

Unsupervised learning for anomaly detection

Unsupervised learning techniques include autoencoders, and clustering algorithms may help to achieve in 6G IoT MWSN anomaly detection. By use of anomalies in network behavior or energy consumption patterns, we might identify security hazards, malfunctioning nodes or perhaps wasteful activities that use energy unnecessarily.

Energy consumption data from sensor nodes may be used in a K-means clustering approach to identify clusters of normal behavior and flag outliers as probable irregularities. This approach might help to identify early energy-draining issues and speedy remedies.

Transfer learning for adaptive energy management

Transfer learning approaches should be very useful in 6G IoT MWSNs put up in numerous environments. Models educated on energy management strategies in one context – for example, urban surroundings – can be fine-tuned and tailored to multiple environments – for example, rural or industrial contexts – even with less additional training data.

This approach may significantly minimize the time and effort required to develop effective energy management strategies for new projects, therefore enabling faster flexibility to changing network conditions or application requirements (Pan et al. 2021).

Deep reinforcement learning for joint optimization

Deep reinforcement learning (DRL) is suitable for demanding, high-dimensional energy management problems in 6G IoT MWSNs by combining the benefits of deep learning with RL. DRL may be used for integrated optimization of many network properties including transmission power, routing and data compression in order to gain optimal energy efficiency.

Current network conditions, energy levels and application demands will let a DRL agent learn, for example, when to transmit data, how much to compress it, which route to use, and at what power level.

Swarm intelligence for distributed energy management

Swarm intelligence algorithms find use in distributed energy management in 6G IoT MWSNs, motivated by the communal behavior of social insects. Distributed allies using techniques such as particle swarm optimization (PSO) or ant colony optimization (ACO) may help tackle complex optimization problems.

ACO might be used, for instance, to find energy-efficient routing patterns in a large-scale MWSN by use of virtual "ants" depositing pheromones on paths determined by their energy efficiency and other performance parameters (Babbar et al. 2023).

Figure 1.6 examines the following comparison to see how various AI and ML approaches could affect energy efficiency in 6G IoT MWSNs.

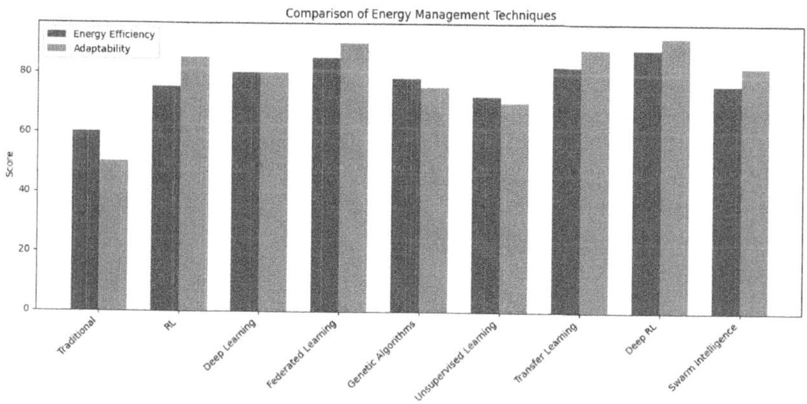

Figure 1.6. *Comparison of energy management techniques. For a color version of this figure, see: www.iste.co.uk/taneja/6gurban.zip*

Figure 1.6 compares the prospective effects on energy efficiency and flexibility in 6G IoT MWSNs of many AI and ML techniques. The results suggest that current techniques including DRL and FL provide major benefits over older approaches in both energy efficiency and flexibility.

Energy management in 6G IoT: applications of AI and ML techniques, great opportunities for improving network performance, extending network lifetime and enabling new types of applications present MWSNs. These approaches do, however, also provide various challenges including increased computational complexity, the need for large amounts of training data and some privacy concerns (Muhammad et al. 2017).

As research in this field develops more sophisticated AI-enabled energy management systems, incorporating multiple technologies to tackle the unique challenges of 6G IoT MWSNs might be predicted. The following section will go over some of the creative paths and evolving trends in this interesting discipline.

1.5. Cutting-edge research and emerging trends

Many innovative research paths and developing trends are influencing the trajectory of the area of AI-enabled energy management for 6G IoT MWSNs. This is a changing subject. This section covers some of the most interesting fields of research along with their expected influence on network performance and energy economy.

Quantum-inspired algorithms for energy optimization

Inspired by concepts of quantum computing, a new class of classical algorithms under development might solve difficult optimization problems more precisely than existing methods. Within the scope of energy management for 6G IoT MWSNs, quantum-inspired algorithms might help effective resource allocation, routing, and scheduling tasks. To identify optimum solutions in large-scale, challenging contexts, quantum-inspired evolutionary algorithms (QIEas) integrate ideas from quantum computing with evolutionary computation. By means of these methods, multi-objective optimization challenges in energy management, such as lowering energy consumption and optimizing network lifespan, can be resolved, thereby extending network lifetime.

Neuromorphic computing for low-power AI

By using neuromorphic computing, which seeks to replicate the structure and operation of organic brain networks in hardware, extreme low-power AI systems are achievable. This might allow the implementation of sophisticated energy management systems based on strong AI to be used on constrained resource-limited sensor nodes.

Major research interest in this field drives development on neuromorphic structures and algorithms to handle challenging tasks in pattern recognition, anomaly detection and minimal energy-consuming decision-making. Including neuromorphic computing in 6G IoT MWSNs could deliver highly distributed intelligence in very effective energy management.

Explainable AI for transparent energy management

As AI systems turn out to be more complex and influence significant decision-making processes, explainable AI approaches are being significantly searched. In the context of an energy management framework of 6G IoT MWSNs, XAI may aid in explaining why and how certain energy-related choices are made.

This field of study aims to provide AI models with perfect prediction and assessment ability along with transparent output explanations. In large-scale IoT devices, transparency might allow us to trust, debug and even improve AI-based energy management algorithms.

Continual learning for adaptive energy management

Continuous learning, or lifetime learning as it is sometimes called, centers on AI systems that can continually gain fresh information and adapt to changing surroundings without losing any previously acquired knowledge. For 6G IoT MWSNs, this method is very pertinent since network conditions and energy consumption may constantly change.

Constant learning research in energy management focuses on techniques to progressively update AI models with fresh data, thereby balancing the retention of useful historical knowledge with the acquisition of new skills. This may lead to somewhat adaptable energy management systems that evolve with time and under various deployment settings.

Federated learning with differential privacy

Although FL offers exciting opportunities for dispersed learning in MWSNs, privacy and data security concerns still create challenges. Research efforts on FL with differential privacy are meant to solve problems by creating techniques that are able to provide strong privacy assurances while preserving the advantages of group learning.

In the framework of energy management, this might enable sensor nodes to participate in global optimization strategies without revealing any private information about their local surroundings or operation. Applications for 6G IoT in sensitive fields such as industrial monitoring or health mostly depend on such a development path.

Energy-aware AI model compression

The computational and energy needs of more sophisticated AI models might become intolerable for deployment on sensor nodes with limited resources. Energy-aware AI model compression research aims to provide methods to minimize AI model computational complexity and size, while additionally preserving their performance.

This covers techniques such as information distillation, quantization and pruning, all tuned with energy economy in mind. The aim is to allow the implementation of advanced AI-based energy management systems, even on the most resource-constrained nodes in a 6G IoT MWSN.

Bio-inspired energy management strategies

Over millions of years, nature has developed effective energy management techniques. Emulating these natural processes is the aim of research into bio-inspired methods for MWSN energy management. These cover finding inspiration from systems such as ecological balance for network-wide energy distribution, animal hibernation for deep sleep modes and photosynthesis for energy harvesting (Zinyongo et al. 2023).

To create neuromorphic computing systems for sensor nodes, for instance, researchers are looking at ways to replicate the energy-efficient information processing in the human brain, therefore drastically lowering energy usage for AI-based activities.

Reinforcement learning with human-in-the-loop

Although completely autonomous energy management systems are the ideal, including human knowledge into the learning process helps to hasten the creation of successful plans. In RL with human-in-the-loop, studies investigate how best to mix AI learning algorithms with human expertise.

Early on in the rollout of 6G IoT MWSNs, this method might be especially helpful as it lets network operators direct the learning process depending on their domain knowledge and individual application needs. The system may get more autonomous over time and yet be able to include human input as necessary.

Edge-cloud collaborative AI for energy management

The interaction of cloud resources and edge computing with 6G networks offers new opportunities for AI-based energy management. Investigating will dynamically distribute the AI tasks across the sensor nodes, edge devices and cloud infrastructure to optimize energy economy and performance.

This would include more intricate analysis at the edge, light preprocessing and decision-making on sensor nodes, and cloud-based big-scale optimization. It is challenging to create algorithms able to make intelligent decisions on the site of execution of different AI pipelines based on present network conditions, energy levels and application demands.

1.6. AI-driven energy harvesting and wireless power transfer

Intelligent management of multiple energy sources becomes increasingly important as wireless power transfer technologies and energy harvesting become more pertinent in 6G IoT MWSNs. This field of research investigates how AI may be used to predict energy availability from ambient sources, maximize timing and energy collecting quantities, and effectively distribute wirelessly broadcast power throughout the network (Esenogho et al. 2022).

This might involve developing deep learning models to anticipate solar energy availability based on weather patterns and past data or RL algorithms setting ideal rules for when to acquire and preserve energy.

Figure 1.7 depicts the prediction to show the possible influence of these newly developing research paths on energy efficiency in 6G IoT MWSNs.

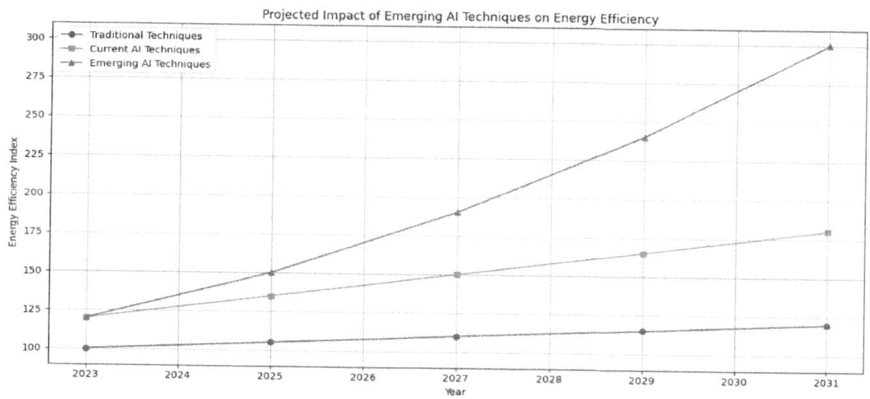

Figure 1.7. *Projected impact of emerging AI techniques on energy efficiency. For a color version of this figure, see: www.iste.co.uk/taneja/6gurban.zip*

Figure 1.7 projects, in contrast to current and traditional AI approaches, the potential impact of emerging AI methods on energy efficiency in 6G IoT MWSNs. The much steeper improvement curve of the novel approaches suggests their ability to alter the energy management in these networks.

These creative research lines and fresh ideas show great promise in addressing the difficult energy management problems in 6G IoT MWSNs. Also, they provide fresh challenges for scholars to handle:

– *Scalability*: given 6G networks allow for large numbers of devices, it becomes essential to ensure that AI-based energy management systems can develop effectively.

– *Robustness*: AI systems have to be able to control the dynamic and sometimes unpredictable nature of IoT environments, preserving performance even in the face of node failures, interference or changing network conditions.

– *Resource constraints*: many IoT devices will remain fairly resource-limited even with hardware improvements. One of the challenges is creating AI techniques able to operate under such limitations.

– *Security and privacy*: given AI systems' increasing entwining with network operations, ensuring their security against attacks and preserving user privacy becomes increasingly more important.

– *Interoperability*: given the diverse ecosystem of 6G IoT devices and applications, AI-based energy management systems must be able to run across various platforms and protocols.

– *Ethical considerations*: ensuring fairness and avoiding unanticipated consequences becomes a big issue when AI systems make more autonomous decisions on network performance and energy allocation.

Overcoming challenges and fully realizing the opportunities of AI-enabled energy management in 6G IoT MWSNs will depend on multidisciplinary collaboration. Researchers in fields such as wireless communications, ML, distributed systems and energy harvesting will develop whole solutions by working together (Basheer and Naik 2021).

Moreover, tight cooperation between academics and business will be crucial to narrow the gap between theoretical developments and actual application. Validating the efficacy of new AI-enabled energy management technologies and pointing out opportunities for future development critically depend on real-world testbeds and pilot installations.

Looking forward, the junction of AI, IoT and 6G technologies promises to bring in a new age of intelligent, energy-efficient wireless sensor networks. These networks will not only be more affordable and environmentally friendly but also allow for new kinds of applications made possible by energy restrictions.

There are many potentially great opportunities arising from smart cities that can dynamically maximize resource use based on real-time data, environmental monitoring systems that can run autonomously for years in far-off locations, and healthcare applications that can provide continuous, personalized monitoring free from frequent battery changes.

Realizing this goal, nevertheless, would herald a need for ongoing research in AI-enabled energy management and innovation. Researchers are following several interesting paths and developing trends, as we have discussed in this chapter. Every one of these fields might help toward the overall objective of building intelligent, adaptable and energy-efficient 6G IoT MWSNs (Taneja et al. 2022).

Finally, the topic of AI-enabled energy management for 6G IoT MWSNs finds itself at a fascinating intersection. Although the obstacles are great, the possible benefits are also huge. Using AI and ML will allow us to design wireless sensor networks that are not just more energy-efficient but are also sophisticated and flexible systems that can transform our interactions with (and knowledge of) our environment.

Research in this area could provide ever more advanced AI-enabled energy management systems combining many approaches to solve the special problems of 6G IoT MWSNs. These developments will not only increase the lifetime and performance of wireless sensor networks but also allow fresh uses and services that we can scarcely imagine today.

The journey toward completely AI-enabled, energy-efficient 6G IoT MWSNs is just starting, and it will provide possibilities as well as difficulties.

To translate the exciting concepts and developing trends covered in this chapter into useful, deployable solutions, researchers, engineers and practitioners working across several disciplines will need to collaborate (Taneja et al. 2022).

Proceeding will assist us in maintaining a balance between expanding the boundaries of what is technically conceivable and ensuring that the solutions we provide are pragmatic, safe and beneficial for society. Not only are better networks going to be developed, but these technologies will also be leveraged to address pragmatic issues and improve a persons quality of life.

6G IoT AI-powered energy management MWSNs could have a great impact in the future. As we keep innovating and stretching the boundaries of what is possible, we are approaching a time when intelligent, energy-efficient wireless sensor networks are ubiquitous, smoothly integrated into our daily lives, and working behind the scenes to produce a more connected, efficient and sustainable world.

New ideas and techniques are continually under development; hence, in this field, we can expect quick improvement in the future. Researchers and practitioners have to remain current with these innovations, continually learning and modifying their approaches to use the most recent findings in AI and energy management (Nassa 2011).

Ultimately, in wireless communications and networking, the junction of 6G, IoT and AI offers a major and exciting area of research. The challenges are significant, but the possible advantages could be massive (Mahmood et al. 2014). Through constant innovation and pushing the boundaries of AI-driven energy management, we can create a future wherein 6G IoT MWSNs not only meet but exceed our expectations, hence launching a new era of intelligent, sustainable and revolutionary applications.

1.7. Conclusion

AI-driven energy management in MWSNs is an essential advancement for enhancing energy efficiency in the 6G Internet future. Using AI methodologies, including ML, deep learning and RL, MWSNs may optimize energy savings, prolong network longevity and augment data transmission dependability. AI-driven predictive analytics provide proactive energy management techniques, reducing energy waste and assuring sustainable network operations. The use of AI in MWSNs for 6G networks provides substantial improvements in intelligent resource allocation, adaptive routing and self-healing functionalities. Nonetheless, issues such as computational complexity, real-time processing limitations and security vulnerabilities must be resolved to optimize the promise of AI-driven energy management. Future study needs to concentrate on creating lightweight AI models, advancing energy-efficient algorithms and strengthening security frameworks to guarantee resilient and sustainable MWSNs. AI-driven energy management will significantly influence the evolution of wireless sensor networks, facilitating the development of intelligent, self-optimizing and energy-efficient 6G communication systems.

1.8. References

Abbas, M.T., Grinnemo, K.J., Ferré, G., Laurent, P., Alfredsson, S., Rajiullah, M., Eklund, J. (2024). Towards zero-energy: Navigating the future with 6G in Cellular Internet of Things. *Journal of Network and Computer Applications*, 230, 103945.

Alhammadi, A., Shayea, I., El-Saleh, A.A., Azmi, M.H., Ismail, Z.H., Kouhalvandi, L., Saad, S.A. (2024). Artificial intelligence in 6G wireless networks: Opportunities, applications, and challenges. *International Journal of Intelligent Systems*, 2024(1). doi: 10.1155/2024/8845070.

Babbar, H., Rani, S., Bouachir, O., Aloqaily, M. (2023). From massive IOT toward IOE: Evolution of energy efficient autonomous wireless networks. *IEEE Communications Standards Magazine*, 7(2), 32–39.

Basheer, P. and Naik, R.P. (2021). Cutting-edge algorithm for seamless void-free routing in wireless sensor networks. *Networks*, 2(12) [Online]. Available at: https://www.ijeasm.com/PublishedPaper/2Vol/Issue12/2021IJEASM220211685a-67f64c61-eebd-4693-9aff-0d08e65e0c4036679.pdf.

Cai, Z., Chen, Q., Shi, T., Zhu, T., Chen, K., Li, Y. (2022). Battery-free wireless sensor networks: A comprehensive survey. *IEEE Internet of Things Journal*, 10(6), 5543–5570.

Chataut, R., Nankya, M., Akl, R. (2024). 6G networks and the AI revolution – Exploring technologies, applications, and emerging challenges. *Sensors*, 24(6), 1888.

Chen, N. and Okada, M. (2020). Toward 6G Internet of Things and the convergence with RoF system. *IEEE Internet of Things Journal*, 8(11), 8719–8733.

Chen, J., Li, S., Xing, J., Wang, J., Fu, S. (2020). Multiple nodes access of wireless beam modulation for 6G-enabled Internet of Things. *IEEE Internet of Things Journal*, 8(20), 15191–15204.

Dabas, D., Mehra, P.S., Chawla, D., Sharma, J., Jamshed, A. (2024). 6G for intelligent Internet of Things. In *Network Optimization in Intelligent Internet of Things Applications*, Batra, P.K., Mehra, P.S., Tanwar, S. (eds). Chapman and Hall/CRC Press, Boca Raton, 19–36.

Du, J., Jiang, C., Wang, J., Ren, Y., Debbah, M. (2020). Machine learning for 6G wireless networks: Carrying forward enhanced bandwidth, massive access, and ultrareliable/low-latency service. *IEEE Vehicular Technology Magazine*, 15(4), 122–134.

Dubey, P.K., Singh, B., Kumar, V., Dubey, A.K. (2023). Applications of wireless, 5G, 6G, and Internet of Things technologies. In *AI-Aided IoT Technologies and Applications for Smart Business and Production*, Khang, A., Misra, A., Gupta, S.K., Shah, V. (eds). CRC Press, Boca Raton, 61–83.

Esenogho, E., Djouani, K., Kurien, A.M. (2022). Integrating artificial intelligence Internet of Things and 5G for next-generation smartgrid: A survey of trends challenges and prospect. *IEEE Access*, 10, 4794–4831.

Gera, B., Raghuvanshi, Y.S., Rawlley, O., Gupta, S., Dua, A., Sharma, P. (2023). Leveraging AI-enabled 6G-driven IoT for sustainable smart cities. *International Journal of Communication Systems*, 36(16). doi: 10.1002/dac.5588.

Gong, Y., Yao, H., Wang, J., Li, M., Guo, S. (2022). Edge intelligence-driven joint offloading and resource allocation for future 6G industrial Internet of Things. *IEEE Transactions on Network Science and Engineering*. doi: 10.1109/TNSE.2022.3141728.

Guo, F., Yu, F.R., Zhang, H., Li, X., Ji, H., Leung, V.C. (2021). Enabling massive IoT toward 6G: A comprehensive survey. *IEEE Internet of Things Journal*, 8(15), 11891–11915.

Hossain, M.A., Xiang, A., Kiani, A., Saboorian, T., Kaippallimalil, J., Ansari, N. (2023). AI-assisted E2E network slicing for integrated sensing and communication in 6G networks. *IEEE Internet of Things Journal*, 11(6), 10627–10634.

Hosseinzadeh, M., Hemmati, A., Rahmani, A.M. (2022). 6G-enabled Internet of Things: Vision, techniques, and open issues. *CMES-Computer Modeling in Engineering & Sciences*, 133(3), 509–556.

Jamshed, M.A., Ayaz, F., Kaushik, A., Fischione, C., Ur-Rehman, M. (2024). Green UAV-enabled Internet-of-Things network with AI-assisted NOMA for disaster management. In *2024 IEEE 35th International Symposium on Personal, Indoor and Mobile Radio Communications (PIMRC)*, 1–6.

Jayadharshini, P., Kamalam, G.V., Abirami, T. (2024). Future 6G approaches: Integrating intelligent security, sensing, and communication into a green network's architecture. In *Intelligent Wireless Sensor Networks and the Internet of Things*, Chander, B., Anoop, B., Guravaiah, K., Kumaravelan, G. (eds). CRC Press, Boca Raton, 86–106.

Kamruzzaman, M.M. (2022). Key technologies, applications and trends of Internet of Things for energy-efficient 6G wireless communication in smart cities. *Energies*, 15(15), 5608.

Letaief, K.B., Shi, Y., Lu, J., Lu, J. (2021). Edge artificial intelligence for 6G: Vision, enabling technologies, and applications. *IEEE Journal on Selected Areas in Communications*, 40(1), 5–36.

Lin, Z. and Xiang, W. (2023). Wireless sensing and networking for the Internet of Things. *Sensors*, 23(3), 1461.

Logeshwaran, J., Patel, S.K., Kumar, O.P., Al-Zahrani, F.A. (2024). Hybrid optimization for efficient 6G IoT traffic management and multi-routing strategy. *Scientific Reports*, 14(1), 30915.

Lv, Z., Lou, R., Li, J., Singh, A.K., Song, H. (2021). Big data analytics for 6G-enabled massive Internet of Things. *IEEE Internet of Things Journal*, 8(7), 5350–5359.

Maduranga, M.W.P., Tilwari, V., Rathnayake, R.M.M.R., Sandamini, C. (2024). AI-enabled 6G Internet of Things: Opportunities, key technologies, challenges, and future directions. *Telecom*, 5(3), 804–822.

Mahmood, A., Ismail, A., Zaman, Z., Fakhar, H., Najam, Z., Hasan, M.S., Ahmed, S.H. (2014). A comparative study of wireless power transmission techniques. *Journal of Basic and Applied Scientific Research*, 4(1), 321–326.

Manogaran, G., Baabdullah, T., Rawat, D.B., Shakeel, P.M. (2021). AI-assisted service virtualization and flow management framework for 6G-enabled cloud-software-defined network-based IoT. *IEEE Internet of Things Journal*, 9(16), 14644–14654.

Mao, B., Kawamoto, Y., Kato, N. (2020). AI-based joint optimization of QoS and security for 6G energy harvesting Internet of Things. *IEEE Internet of Things Journal*, 7(8), 7032–7042.

Mittal, A., Pandey, H., Arsh, M., Soni, M., Goyal, H.R., Sharma, S. (2024). Advancements and applications of Artificial Intelligence in various sectors: From Internet of vehicles to 6G and healthcare. In *2024 4th International Conference on Pervasive Computing and Social Networking (ICPCSN)*. IEEE, Salem, 107–112.

Muhammad, Z., Saxena, N., Qureshi, I.M., Ahn, C.W. (2017). Hybrid artificial bee colony algorithm for an energy efficient Internet of Things based on wireless sensor network. *IETE Technical Review*, 34(sup1), 39–51.

Mukherjee, A., Goswami, P., Khan, M.A., Manman, L., Yang, L., Pillai, P. (2020). Energy-efficient resource allocation strategy in massive IoT for industrial 6G applications. *IEEE Internet of Things Journal*, 8(7), 5194–5201.

Mukherjee, A., Panja, A.K., Obaidat, M.S., De, D. (2022). *6G Based Green Mobile Edge Computing for Internet of Things (IoT)*. Springer, Berlin.

Mwashita, W. and Odhiambo, M.O. (eds) (2024). 6G and D2D as enablers of the convergence of Artificial Intelligence (AI) and Internet of Things (IoT). In *From Internet of Things to Internet of Intelligence*. Springer, Berlin, 21–41.

Nassa, V.K. (2011). Wireless communications: Past, present and future. *Dronacharya Research Journal*, 50.

Nguyen, D.C., Ding, M., Pathirana, P.N., Seneviratne, A., Li, J., Niyato, D., Poor, H.V. (2021). 6G Internet of Things: A comprehensive survey. *IEEE Internet of Things Journal*, 9(1), 359–383.

Padmapriya, T., Salameh, A.A., Wildan, M.A., Kishore, K.H. (2022). AI enabled-6G: Artificial Intelligence (AI) for integration of 6G wireless communications. *International Journal of Communication Networks and Information Security*, 14(3), 372–379.

Pan, Q., Wu, J., Zheng, X., Yang, W., Li, J. (2021). Differential privacy and IRS empowered intelligent energy harvesting for 6G Internet of Things. *IEEE Internet of Things Journal*, 9(22), 22109–22122.

Sefati, S.S., Haq, A.U., Nidhi, Craciunescu, R., Halunga, S., Mihovska, A., Fratu, O. (2024). A comprehensive survey on resource management in 6G network based on Internet of Things. *IEEE Access*, 12, 113741–113784.

Singh, S.P., Kumar, N., Kumar, G., Balusamy, B., Bashir, A.K., Al-Otaibi, Y.D. (2024). A hybrid multi-objective optimisation for 6G enabled Internet of Things (IoT). *IEEE Transactions on Consumer Electronics*. 71(1). doi: 10.1109/TCE.2024.3411037.

Sodhro, A.H., Pirbhulal, S., Luo, Z., Muhammad, K., Zahid, N.Z. (2020). Toward 6G architecture for energy-efficient communication in IoT-enabled smart automation systems. *IEEE Internet of Things Journal*, 8(7), 5141–5148.

Taneja, A., Rani, S., Alhudhaif, A., Koundal, D., Gündüz, E.S. (2022). An optimized scheme for energy efficient wireless communication via intelligent reflecting surfaces. *Expert Systems with Applications*, 190, 116106.

Taneja, A., Rani, S., Raza, S., Jain, A., Sefat, S.M. (2023). Energy efficient IRS assisted 6G network for Industry 5.0. *Scientific Reports*, 13, 12814.

Vaigandla, K.K. (2022). Communication technologies and challenges on 6G networks for the Internet: Internet of Things (IoT) based analysis. In *2022 2nd International Conference on Innovative Practices in Technology and Management (ICIPTM)*. IEEE, Greater Noida, 27–31.

Verma, S., Kaur, S., Khan, M.A., Sehdev, P.S. (2020). Toward green communication in 6G-enabled massive Internet of Things. *IEEE Internet of Things Journal*, 8(7), 5408–5415.

Xu, L. (2021). Application of wearable devices in 6G Internet of Things communication environment using artificial intelligence. *International Journal of System Assurance Engineering and Management*, 12(4), 741–747.

Zhu, G., Lyu, Z., Jiao, X., Liu, P., Chen, M., Xu, J., Zhang, P. (2023). Pushing AI to wireless network edge: An overview on integrated sensing, communication, and computation towards 6G. *Science China Information Sciences*, 66(3), 130301.

Zinyongo, D., Kumar, S., Rajpoot, A.K. (2023). A comprehensive review on energy efficient Internet of Things based wireless sensor network. In *2023 International Conference on Computing, Communication, and Intelligent Systems (ICCCIS)*. IEEE, Greater Noida, 19–25.

2

Security Solutions for Smart Cities Using Digital Twin

The concept of "smart cities" emerged from the way fast cities are expanding and their use of modern technology. To ensure that municipal operations run well and to improve the quality of life for the residents, these cities use modern technology such as artificial intelligence (AI), the Internet of Things (IoT) and big data analytics. Protecting smart cities becomes even more crucial as municipal infrastructure grows more complex. This chapter investigates ways to improve smart city security using digital twin technologies. Digital twins replicate actual systems and procedures virtually. This allows real-time simulation, analysis and monitoring of metropolitan environments. Cities can forecast probable hazards, identify weak points and respond quickly to thwart security breaches by integrating IoT sensors and data analytics into digital twin models. The chapter demonstrates how public places, transit systems, energy grids and critical infrastructure may be monitored using digital twins. By simulating various security scenarios, digital twins enable legislators, security personnel and city planners to create pre-emptive strategies to handle internet threats, physical attacks and environmental hazards. Digital twins may also help to organize emergency response activities and make people more catastrophe ready by providing real-time data and predictive analytics. Digital twins combined with AI and machine learning algorithms improve security measures constantly. This guarantees that the smart city can manage fresh challenges and risks. Apart from supporting security management, digital twins may assist in resource optimization, cost reduction and decision-making by means of their ability to identify the ideal approach of use. This chapter provides a thorough analysis of how digital twins could be a transforming tool for creating more flexible and secure smart cities.

2.1. Introduction

The concept of "smart cities" has emerged as a radical means to use technology to enhance living in cities as more and more people migrate to them. These towns

Chapter written by Sulakshana MALWADE, SHIKHA, Mandeep KAUR, Vibhuti REHALIA, Kimmi VERMA, Anupma GUPTA and Mohammad Alamgir HOSSAIN.

want to leverage cutting-edge digital technologies such as the Internet of Things (IoT), artificial intelligence (AI), machine learning, big data and cloud computing to better use resources, improve public services and make the cities safer, more sustainable and more efficient for the local residents. Now that digital technologies have been included, safety and security in smart cities are particularly crucial as they increase the vulnerability of cities to both online and physical risks. The hazards of infrastructure failures, hacking, natural catastrophes and even terrorism attacks increase as cities use increasingly integrated systems. This emphasizes even more the need for developing sensible security measures. The digital twin is now a transforming approach to handle these challenges. A digital twin is a computer simulation of a genuine system or process that behaves and resembles the actual one perfectly. It does this in real time (Seyedrezaei et al. 2023). Digital twins let us see, study, and simulate cities in real time by collecting data from IoT cameras, geographic information systems (GIS) and other tracking tools. When talking about smart cities, digital twins let you make digital copies of whole cities, which can include important structures, transport networks, energy grids, information systems and public areas. These virtual models help city planners, managers and security staff keep an eye on, analyze and guess possible security risks. This way, actions can be taken quickly to stop events or lessen their effects. When digital twins are used in urban security systems, they provide many important benefits (Mouratidis 2021). These virtual models collect and analyze data from physical assets all the time. This lets different urban systems be watched in real time, which helps find weak spots and risks before they become full-scale security events. Figure 2.1 shows how digital twin technology can be used to make smart towns safer.

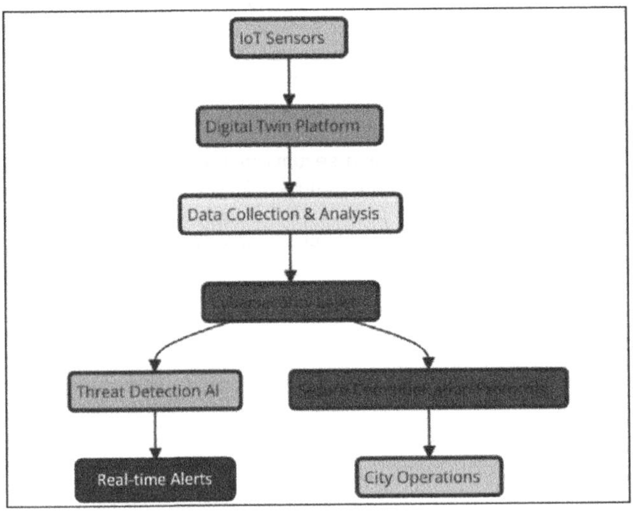

Figure 2.1. *Security solutions for smart cities using digital twin. For a color version of this figure, see: www.iste.co.uk/taneja/6gurban.zip*

Whether they monitor assaults on communication networks, keep a watch on dubious activity in public spaces or identify potential issues in significant networks such as water, electricity or transportation, digital twins provide a more proactive approach to managing urban security. They also allow us to develop thorough simulations of various security scenarios. This allows municipalities to experiment in a safe virtual environment on how they would manage various conceivable hazards or issues. By integrating AI and machine learning techniques capable of identifying patterns, forecasting future hazards and recommending the best course of action, digital twins enhance security choices (Debrah et al. 2022). These systems function alongside real-time tracking and modeling. In cities especially, where security issues may be complex and change rapidly and need a high degree of situational awareness and adaptability, this ability is very helpful. When machine learning algorithms are coupled with digital twins, for example, they may identify patterns of crime, transportation congestion or even natural calamities such as floods and earthquakes. By analyzing prior data and simulating many probable outcomes, these systems may provide forecasts that let security personnel make better decisions and more effective use of resources. Furthermore, facilitating the cooperation among the many agencies in charge of maintaining city safety is easier using digital twins (Sadri et al. 2023). Cities nowadays must cooperate to handle security concerns, which usually include many diverse organizations such as police, fire fighters, public agencies and business sector partners. Digital twins act as a central hub where everyone may exchange information, collaborate on security projects and rapidly and successfully address events. This group effort is necessary for handling big events such as terrorist attacks or natural disasters that affect many people. In these situations, quickly making decisions and combining data are key to limiting damage. Another great thing about using digital twins for smart city security is that they can help people be better prepared for and respond to disasters (Piras et al. 2024). Digital twins help city officials try and improve emergency reaction plans by modeling different types of emergencies, such as fires, medical situations and hacks. The purpose of these models is not only to find holes in the current security system, but also to show how resources such as medical services or police officers can be successfully used in emergency situations. Digital twins can also provide real-time information during a real crisis, which helps officials keep track of what is happening and change their plans as needed.

2.2. Understanding digital twin technology

2.2.1. *Definition and basic principles of digital twins*

A digital twin is a computerized copy of a real thing, system or process that lets you watch, simulate and analyze it in real time. This computer copy gives a full picture of the real thing, showing all of its features, actions and interactions with its surroundings. The main purpose of a digital twin is to help us understand the real system better by showing, studying and guessing how it will work in different situations. Digital twins connect the real and digital worlds by using data from sensors, IoT devices and other tracking technologies to keep the digital model and the real thing in sync at all times (Alnaser et al. 2024). The idea behind a digital twin is that the real item and its digital copy are always exchanging data with each other. The flow of data lets the virtual model adjust and improve itself as things change in the real world. In the case of a smart city, for example, sensors built into infrastructure such as buildings, traffic systems or energy grids collect data that is then sent to the digital twin, which acts and behaves such as the physical system. This contact helps find problems before they happen, improves speed and creates situations that show how processes will work in the future. IoT, cloud computing, AI, machine learning and big data analytics are some of the new technologies that digital twins use to improve their abilities (Elmousalami 2020a). By combining these technologies, digital twins can model and guess what will happen, which helps businesses make choices based on data. In smart cities, digital twins help city planners, security staff and infrastructure managers understand urban systems better. This helps them make better decisions and improves safety, efficiency and sustainability.

2.2.2. Components and architecture of a digital twin system

A digital twin system is made up of several important parts that work together to make a virtual model of a real thing or system that is correct and changes over time. These elements encompass devices that receive facts, systems for handling facts, analytics and modeling equipment, and the remarks loop that keeps the real and digital worlds in sync. The first important part is collecting records. That is usually accomplished with IoT monitors, smart tech and other tracking tools that get data from the real element in actual time. These gadgets accumulate a variety of statistics, consisting of information approximating the surroundings, overall performance and state reviews. In a smart metropolis, devices may monitor things such as air quality, visitor developments or energy use. The information is sent to the processing system, which is generally a cloud platform, after it has been amassed. There, it is saved and organized in order that it may be analyzed. Cloud computing is a key part of handling the huge quantities of facts that digital twins create, making it feasible to scale up or down and get actual-time statistics quickly. The following essential component is the analytics and modeling tools, which take in records and system and analyze them (Zayed et al. 2023). This equipment uses AI models, machine learning algorithms and prediction analytics to locate tendencies, spot outliers and play out possible results. For instance, these can be used to anticipate network traffic disruptions and their impact on the critical infrastructure. This makes it less complicated to expect feasible dangers and make better decisions. Eventually, the remarks method ensures that the digital dual stays in sync with the actual gadget. As the real-world gadget adjusts or grows, updates are made in real time to the digital version. This lets the gadget be constantly monitored and progressed (Kharchenko et al. 2020). This actual-time data glide ensures that the virtual dual is a dependable and correct copy of the actual device. This makes it a very useful tool for handling complicated systems such as healthcare systems, smart cities or industrial processes.

2.2.3. *Applications of digital twins in various industries*

A lot of different types of businesses are using digital twin technology because it can model, predict and improve the way systems and processes work. One of the most well-known uses is in industry, where digital twins are used to make production lines run more smoothly and tools work better. Manufacturers make digital copies of their tools and production processes. This lets them keep an eye on performance in real time, find broken equipment and plan repair needs before they cause costly downtimes (Elmousalami and Elaskary 2020). This makes operations run more smoothly and cuts down on unexpected output stops. Digital twins are used to improve the performance of power plants and energy grids in the energy business. Operators can keep an eye on energy flow, predict breakdowns and boost efficiency by making virtual models of engines, electrical lines and other parts. Digital twins can also help with adding green energy sources because they let grid workers test and find the best way to distribute energy based on changing factors such as demand and weather trends. Digital twin technology has also helped the healthcare field, especially when it comes to personalized treatment and patient care. Data from medical records, imaging tools and smart tech can be used to make digital twins of each patient. These computer models can show doctors how different treatments will work on a patient's body, which helps them make better decisions (Elmousalami 2020b). Digital twins are also used to keep an eye on and improve the performance of medical devices such as ventilators and MRI machines. Table 2.1 shows a summary of the uses, results, trends and effects of digital twin technology. This makes repair plans better and makes sure that the devices are working properly.

Application	Key finding	Future trend	Impact
Real-time traffic monitoring	Improved traffic flow and reduced congestion	Integration with autonomous vehicles and smart infrastructure	Reduced traffic-related accidents and improved public safety
Predictive maintenance in infrastructure	Proactive identification of system failures and reduced downtimes	Integration with AI-powered predictive analytics	Increased infrastructure lifespan and cost savings

Application	Key finding	Future trend	Impact
Smart energy grid management	Enhanced efficiency and resilience of energy grids	Integration with renewable energy systems and real-time demand forecasting	Improved energy efficiency and reduced operational costs
Urban surveillance systems (Zade et al. 2024)	Increased monitoring capabilities and quicker responses to incidents	Use of advanced AI and machine learning for threat detection and response	Increased public safety and enhanced crime prevention
Public safety and emergency response	Faster emergency response and resource optimization	Use of AI for predictive analytics and real-time response	Improved resource allocation during emergencies and faster response times
Water and wastewater management	Enhanced resource management and reduced wastage	Integration of IoT and AI for water quality monitoring and system optimization	Increased sustainability and efficient use of resources
Critical infrastructure protection	Improved system reliability and protection from cyber threats	Integration with AI to enhance system robustness and automated threat detection	Enhanced resilience of critical systems and reduced vulnerability
Smart parking systems (Xu et al. 2023)	Reduced parking congestion and optimized space utilization	Use of smart sensors and AI to automate parking management	Increased urban mobility and convenience for citizens
Cybersecurity in smart cities	Enhanced detection and prevention of cyberattacks on critical infrastructure	Development of autonomous cybersecurity systems	Improved protection of critical assets and reduced attack surface
Disaster risk management	Improved preparedness and reduced impact of natural disasters	Use of AI-driven models to simulate and predict disaster scenarios	Improved disaster preparedness and reduced human and material losses
Smart health monitoring	Continuous health monitoring and better healthcare resource allocation	Integration of real-time health data and predictive models for proactive care	Improved healthcare outcomes through real-time monitoring
Smart lighting systems (Murthy et al. 2022)	Reduced energy consumption and optimized city-wide lighting systems	Use of AI and IoT for energy-efficient systems	Improved energy conservation and reduced city-wide costs

Application	Key finding	Future trend	Impact
Waste management optimization	Increased waste collection efficiency and reduced environmental impact	Integration of smart sensors and IoT to optimize waste collection routes	Optimized waste collection, improved hygiene and environmental benefits

Table 2.1. *Summary of understanding digital twin technology*

2.3. Security challenges in smart cities

2.3.1. *Overview of security threats in smart cities*

As cities become more "smart", they depend increasingly on technologies that work together to improve services, make cities more environmentally friendly and make people's lives better. These technologies have a lot of good points, but they also make security more difficult in many ways. Because smart cities have linked infrastructure, huge amounts of data flow and automated systems, there are many ways that they could be attacked. Threats include hacking of important assets and real security holes in cities that are used by criminals (Elmousalami et al. 2024a). One big worry about security in smart cities is that systems that are tied to each other can be hacked. When IoT devices, sensors and digital platforms are used together in areas such as transportation, healthcare and energy sources, they make it easier for malicious people to attack. When thousands of endpoints send and collect data, the chance of someone getting in without permission and taking advantage of it grows. Smart towns also depend on complicated networks and services from outside sources, which means that problems can happen one after another. One thing broken part, such as a water treatment plant or traffic light system, can cause a lot of problems and even put people's safety at risk (Attaran et al. 2024). Physical dangers to security are another way that smart cities can be broken. Automated public transport systems or smart building structures can be taken over or messed with, which can cause crashes or bad things to happen. Drones, robots and other self-driving systems that are used to run cities could also be used for bad things, such as spying, stealing data or attacking important infrastructure.

2.3.2. *Cybersecurity risks in connected infrastructure*

A smart city's linked infrastructure is what makes it work. IoT devices, sensors and networks are used a lot to keep an eye on, run and improve different city systems. But because so many things in these places are linked, they are also open to a lot of hacking risks. Most parts of a smart city are linked to each other and often work on their own, so if there is a break in one part of the system, it can cause other parts to stop working as well, hurting important services such as transport, healthcare and energy management.

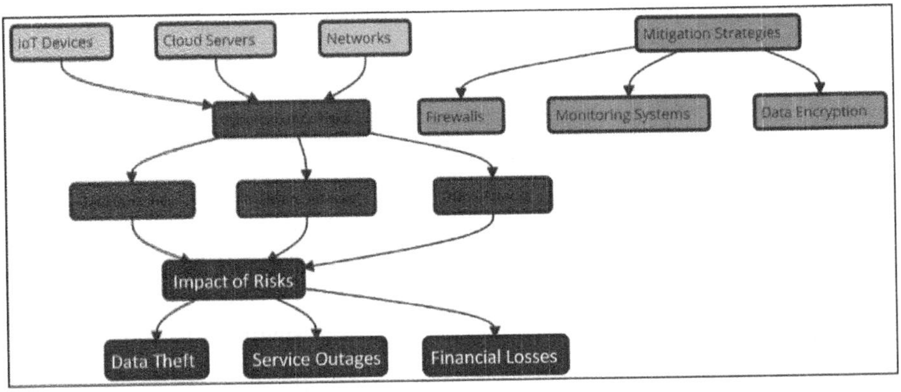

Figure 2.2. *Cybersecurity risks in connected infrastructure. For a color version of this figure, see: www.iste.co.uk/taneja/6gurban.zip*

One major safety risk in smart cities is that these linked networks could be accessed by unauthorized people. Figure 2.2 shows the hacking risks that come with critical systems and networks that are linked together. IoT devices are very important to smart towns, but they are often not well protected, with weak or default passwords, old software and not enough security. These holes can be used by attackers to take control of gadgets or systems. For instance, a hacker could take over systems that control traffic and reroute it, which could lead to accidents or traffic jams (Jacoby and Usländer 2020). DDoS attacks on important infrastructure, such as city-wide communication networks or emergency services, could make it hard for the government to handle situations properly, which could put people in danger.

2.3.3. *Privacy concerns in data collection and processing*

One of the biggest problems with smart cities is that they gather, handle and analyze huge amounts of personal data all the time. This can be seen as an invasion of privacy. The main job of smart cities is to use data to make urban systems work better. To do this, they often need to collect private data from people, such as their health data, social contacts and even behavior trends. This information is necessary to make services and infrastructure better, but it makes people very worried about their safety and privacy. A big privacy risk in smart towns is all the different kinds of data that are being collected. IoT monitors, cameras and mobile apps constantly create data that can be linked back to specific individuals (Elmousalami et al. 2024b).

This makes people worry about privacy and the possibility of personal data being misused. Putting all of this information together could cause profiling, which is when personal habits, tastes or even political views are drawn from the information without the person's knowledge. This could lead to discrimination or abuse. Without the right protections, hackers, government agencies or private companies could get to this info without permission, putting people's privacy at risk. The centralization of data handling and storing brings up another problem. People may not have much control over their own data in smart cities because they usually use cloud platforms and third-party service providers to store and analyze it. Because everything is in one place, there is a higher chance of data breaches and unauthorized access.

2.4. Integrating digital twin for security solutions

2.4.1. *Using digital twin for real-time monitoring of infrastructure*

Real-time tracking of infrastructure is one of the best ways that digital twin technology can be used to make smart towns safer. Many IoT sensors and other linked devices collect a lot of data that can be used to create a digital twin of urban systems such as transportation networks, energy grids, water supply systems and public buildings that is always changing and adapting. These digital copies make it possible to see how the city's actual infrastructure is working and how it connects to other parts of the city in real time. Real-time tracking lets you find any strange behavior or possible security holes in the system. For example, a digital twin can keep an eye on the state of important parts of the infrastructure, such as power lines, lifts in public buildings and water pipes, at all times. If a sensor finds a problem or something out of the ordinary, such as a traffic light that is not working right or the water pressure changing in a way that does not make sense, this information is immediately updated in the digital twin. This lets security staff and city managers fix the problem before it gets worse.

2.4.2. *Enhancing situational awareness through digital replicas*

By making real-time, live digital copies of actual places, systems and equipment, digital twin technology makes it much easier to know what is going on in smart cities. These virtual models give security teams, city leaders and emergency response units a full and changing picture of what is going on. This makes it easier to judge the state of cities and act quickly and effectively on risks. Situational awareness is the skill of noticing, understanding and predicting possible problems or dangers in the surroundings. This is very important for handling safety in cities. For instance, during a security breach, a digital twin of the city's public transport system could show blocked routes, crowded areas and weak entry points. This would allow police and first responders to change their plans accordingly. Digital twins also make it easier for different groups and partners, such as police, fire services, healthcare providers and energy companies, to work together.

2.5. Applications of digital twin in smart city security

2.5.1. *Intelligent traffic management and accident prevention*

Intelligent traffic control and accident prevention is one of the most important ways that digital twin technology is used to make smart cities safer. Unsafe and slow traffic flow, crashes and traffic jams are big problems in modern cities that affect both safety and the city's general usefulness. Digital twins are a strong answer because they make virtual models of transport networks that are constantly updated with new information from sensors, cameras and other IoT devices spread all over the city. These computer models give a full, changing picture of traffic conditions, which helps city planners and security staff keep an eye on traffic trends, spot possible dangers and act quickly when something goes wrong. Figure 2.3 shows methods for managing traffic that are smart enough to stop accidents.

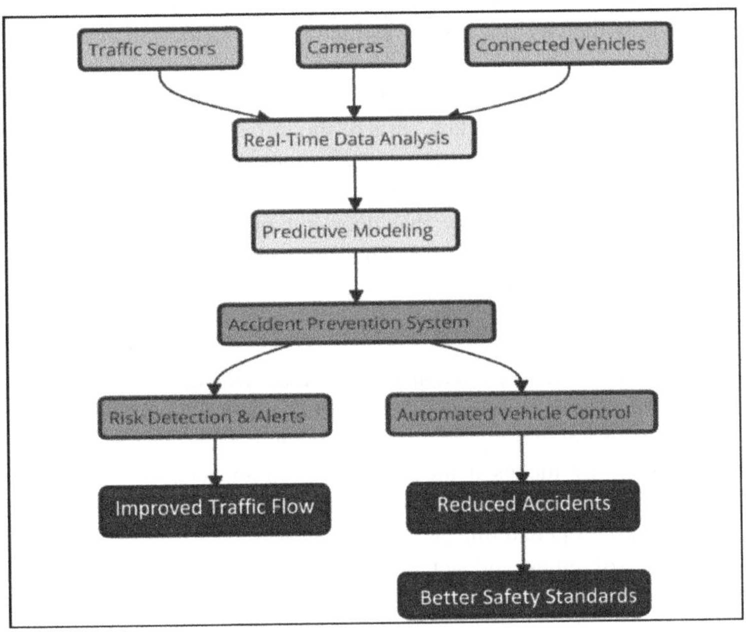

Figure 2.3. *Intelligent traffic management and accident prevention. For a color version of this figure, see: www.iste.co.uk/taneja/6gurban.zip*

Traffic management systems can mimic real-time conditions, find the best times for traffic lights and automatically move cars to avoid crashes or traffic jams. For instance, if there is an accident at a busy crossing, the digital twin can quickly find the blockage and offer different paths that will have less of an effect on the areas around it. This real-time feature not only helps clear up traffic jams, but it also cuts down on the time it takes for emergency workers to get to the spot, which makes the public safer overall. Digital twins also make prediction analytics possible, which lets you guess when traffic will be bad or where accidents are likely to happen by using both past data and real-time inputs. For example, the system can look at trends in traffic, weather and time of day to figure out where crashes are most likely to occur. By finding these "hotspots", the government can take steps to lower the risk of an accident before it happens, such as adding more police officers, changing the way traffic lights work or putting up warning signs. This cautious method to traffic control makes cities much safer, cuts down on crashes and makes transportation networks work better.

2.5.2. *Surveillance and public safety enhancement*

Public safety and surveillance are very important in smart cities because combining different systems such as transportation, public areas and infrastructure makes the environment complicated and open to security risks. This is where digital twins really shine: they give us real-time, highly interactive digital models of cities that are correct in space and time. These models can be used to improve public safety and monitoring. Digital twins can constantly watch public areas such as streets, parks and shopping malls by combining IoT devices, security cameras and social media feeds. The virtual copy shows these areas in real time, so security staff can keep an eye on things and figure out what is going on from one central screen. For instance, if cameras or sensors pick up on a public disturbance or something strange, the system instantly sends a warning to officials along with a detailed map of where the event is happening and a live video feed. This lets people respond faster because police or security teams can be sent straight to the scene with the most up-to-date information. Digital twins also help with predictive spying, which lets you look at patterns and trends over time. Security teams can find high-risk places and send resources there by looking at past crime or event data in certain areas. For example, based on past trends and social conditions, digital twins can tell police where crimes such as theft and mischief are most likely to occur so they can take steps to stop them.

2.5.3. *Critical infrastructure protection*

Protecting critical infrastructure is an important part of smart city security. Digital twin technology is a key part of protecting important urban systems such as power lines, water supply networks and communication networks. These systems are what hold modern towns together, and if they break down or are disrupted, terrible things can happen, such as losing power, drinking water becoming contaminated or the whole system failing. Digital twins provide a real-time, virtual copy of these complicated systems, which lets them be constantly managed and monitored to make sure they are safe and reliable. In the energy industry, digital twins of power lines let workers keep an eye on the health of equipment, keep track of how energy is distributed and guess when problems might happen. Digital twins can find early signs of wear or failure by combining real-time data from smart meters, transformers and power lines. This ensures the repair is carried out before problems get worse. This ability to predict repair helps keep the power grid steady, even during times of high demand, and avoids costly breakdowns. Digital twins can also mimic events such as a hack or a natural disaster. This lets us test how the grid would react and make changes to how infrastructure is built or how emergency reaction plans are made. Digital twins can also be used to mimic the flow of water through pipes and treatment plants in water supply systems. This way, leaks, contamination or changes in pressure can be checked for.

2.6. Privacy and ethical considerations

2.6.1. *Data privacy issues with digital twin data collection*

While using digital twin technology in smart cities can help keep an eye on infrastructure and make city systems work better, it also raises serious privacy issues. To work, digital twins need to constantly gather and handle huge amounts of data from many sensors and devices that are built into real systems such as public places, transportation networks and utilities. Concerns have been raised about monitoring and the possible abuse of personal data because this data can include private information about people's movements, behaviors and contacts with city infrastructure. When a city is smart, it collects a lot of data that can be used to identify people. This data can be about anything, from traffic trends to health information.

2.6.2. *Ethical challenges in implementing surveillance systems*

The safety and protection of smart cities depend on surveillance systems, but putting them in location brings up important social questions. While digital twins are blended with monitoring technologies such as cameras, drones, and sensors, they could provide a complete image of towns in real time, which makes them safer and better able to manage emergencies. However, the huge use of this tracking equipment could make people worry about their rights, their privacy and the way the authorities could possibly abuse them. Finding the right mix between privateness and security is one of the most crucial social issues. Surveillance systems can help find illegal interest, prevent terrorism and help people get help quickly in an emergency, but they can also be too much of a good thing and violate a human being's right to privacy. Surveillance might be common in public regions of a smart metropolis, making people feel like they are constantly being watched. This can make people much less unsure about being able to act freely. This ethical hassle makes us think about how much tracking is needed and whether or not it is okay to do this for the sake of public protection. Also, if they are not carefully controlled, monitoring structures that use digital twins could cause unfair or biased behavior.

2.6.3. *Strategies for securing personal and sensitive data*

As digital twins become more important for controlling and keeping an eye on smart city infrastructure, keeping personal and private data safe becomes very important. Because of the huge amounts of data that come from many places, such as IoT devices, cameras and monitoring systems, it is important to set up strong data protection plans that protect people's privacy while still letting digital twins work. Encryption is one of the most important ways to keep personal information safe. Cryptography makes sure that private information is sent and kept in a way that cannot be read by unauthorized people. Cities can make it much less likely that data will be stolen or accessed without permission by encrypting both data that is in motion (such as data sent between IoT devices and central computers) and data that is at rest (such as data that is stored). Additionally, end-to-end encryption is very useful when collecting personal or health-related data because it makes sure that only authorized individuals can access and understand the data. A second important approach is to keep data as simple and anonymous as possible. It is safer for towns to collect personally identifiable information (PII) if they anonymize the data before they handle or analyze it. Anonymization gets rid of information that can be used to identify a person, so the data cannot be linked to specific users.

2.7. Technological challenges and solutions

2.7.1. *Integration of diverse technologies*

Certainly one of the largest problems with putting digital twin structures into smart cities is getting all the different technologies to work together. These encompass gadgets, the Internet of Things (IoT) and AI. Each of these technologies is crucial to the infrastructure of smart cities, but they all work on extraordinary structures, protocols and requirements, which makes it difficult to integrate them and ensure smooth interoperability. IoT gadgets, such as sensors and smart devices, are what collect real-time information from things such as public places, power grids and transportation networks in cities. Both of these technologies can also use a lot of one of a kind security measures, connection methods and information paperwork, which makes it tougher to combine them into a single digital twin gadget. AI algorithms are frequently used to handle the large amounts of information that IoT devices produce. They do this using predictive analytics, making choices and optimizing things. The trouble comes when AI models process real-time raw data from IoT devices while ensuring data security and minimizing latency.

AI systems need a lot of computing power and complex models, and they must be able to operate seamlessly with existing infrastructure. To cope with these problems, interoperability equipment and software program answers can be created to ensure that records from distinct resources can be handled and shared correctly. Standardized conversation strategies and interfaces, like MQTT or CoAP, make this feasible by letting devices transmit and receive data efficiently and with low latency. Edge computing can also be used to reduce the delay and ensure that information is processed in actual time. This accelerates decision-making and reduces the burden on centralized systems. So in order for IoT, AI and devices to work collectively in digital twin structures, these technological problems have to be solved. The device also needs to be able to work with new technologies and react to them.

2.7.2. *Data interoperability and standardization*

For instance, IoT devices made by different companies might use different data forms, which make it hard to combine data streams into a single digital twin model that makes sense. In the same way, third-party service providers, private companies and public sector organizations may all use different software and systems, which makes integrating data even harder. To fix these problems, we need to create standard data formats and methods that make it easy for data from different systems to be sent to and handled by each other. The Open Geospatial Consortium (OGC) and other groups have made progress in building standards for spatial data. Other groups are working on making global APIs and data models. Also, systems for data control must be set up to make sure that data is gathered, handled and shared in a way that follows protection laws and industry rules. Smart cities can make their digital twin systems more efficient, secure and useful by making sure that data can be shared and is standardized. This will let them use all of the benefits of linked urban data.

2.7.3. *Scalability of digital twin systems for large cities*

Scalability is one of the most difficult things about setting up digital twin systems for big cities. It is important for digital twin systems to be able to adapt to the growing amount of data and exchanges between urban parts as cities get bigger and more complicated. Large towns have a lot of infrastructure, from public transit and electricity to healthcare systems and other public services. This makes system speed, data management and computing power more difficult. As more parts are added to the virtual model, the large-scale digital twin system gets more complicated. For example, there will be a lot more IoT devices and sensors spread out across a city. This will create a huge amount of data that needs to be handled and analyzed right away. To handle this much data, you need a strong cloud system and powerful computer tools that can handle the constant flow of data without slowing down or losing dependability. Coordinating between different groups, such as city leaders, utility companies and police, also needs tools to be able to talk to each other and work together without any problems. To solve these problems with scaling, cities can use flexible and decentralized systems that spread the work of computing across many nodes. Edge computing, in which devices handle data locally instead of using a central computer, can also help cloud technology work better and speed things up. Also, using cloud-native technologies such as apps and containerization makes it possible for digital twin systems to grow as cities do. Smart cities can make sure that their digital twin systems stay effective and can handle the complexity of big cities while also being able to grow in the future by using infrastructure solutions that are easy to expand.

2.8. Results and discussion

Using digital twin technology in security solutions for smart cities has shown a lot of promise. IoT devices that are used to monitor infrastructure in real time have made it easier to find weak spots in important systems such as energy lines and transportation systems. More security is added by predictive analytics, which finds possible risks such as traffic jams or cyberattacks before they happen. Being able to model different security situations has made it easier to respond to emergencies and use resources more efficiently.

Table 2.2 gives an in-depth look at four important security solutions that are used in smart cities with digital twin technology: monitoring infrastructure in real time, using predictive analytics to find threats, simulating security situations and protecting data privacy. Figure 2.4 measures the effectiveness, difficulty and cost of different security methods.

Security solution	Effectiveness (%)	Implementation difficulty (%)	Cost estimate ($ millions)
Real-time infrastructure monitoring	90	44	2.5
Predictive analytics for threat detection	85	60	3
Simulated security scenarios	80	52	1.8
Data privacy safeguards	75	78	4.2

Table 2.2. *Security solution evaluation*

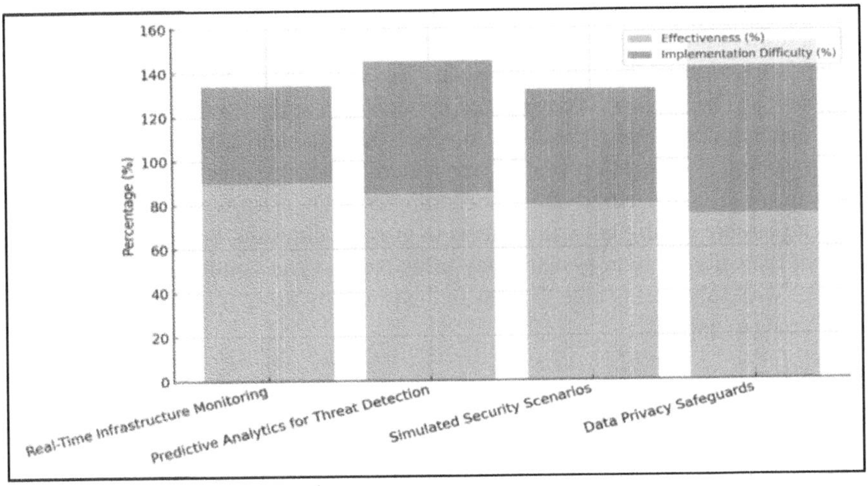

Figure 2.4. *Effectiveness and implementation overlap across security solutions. For a color version of this figure, see: www.iste.co.uk/taneja/6gurban.zip*

At 90%, real-time infrastructure monitoring is the most efficient, which shows how important it is for making sure that vital infrastructure keeps running. The low difficulty level (44% of application) and estimated cost of $2.5 million of this solution make it a very good choice for cities that want to improve security without spending a lot of money.

Figure 2.5 shows how different methods relate in terms of how well they work and how hard they are to implement.

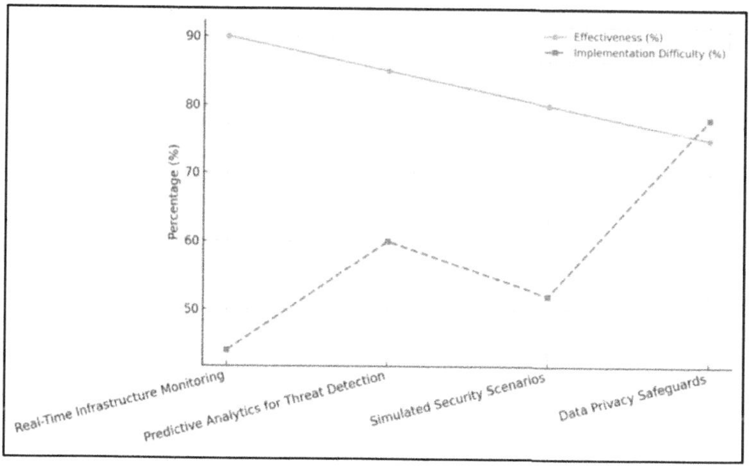

Figure 2.5. *Comparison of effectiveness and implementation difficulty across solutions. For a color version of this figure, see: www.iste.co.uk/taneja/6gurban.zip*

By monitoring in real time, cities can quickly find problems or breaches, reducing the chance of problems and raising public safety. With an 85% grade, predictive analytics for threat detection also works well. Figure 2.6 shows how effective ideas are, how hard they are to put into action and how much they are expected to cost.

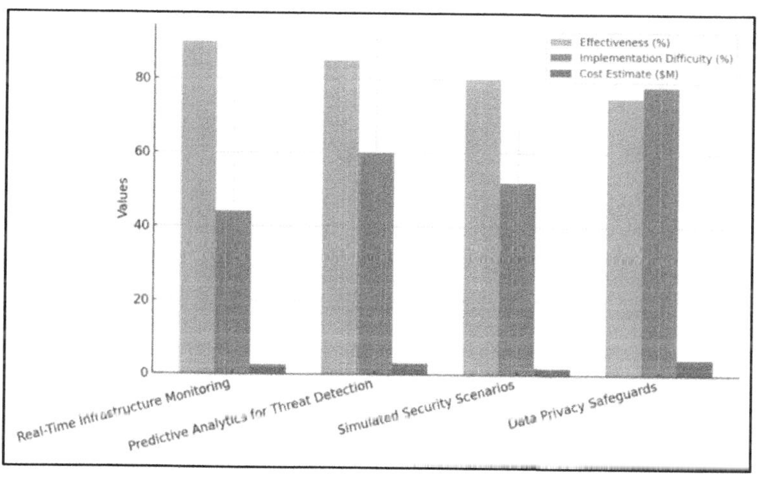

Figure 2.6. *Effectiveness, implementation difficulty and cost estimates for security solutions. For a color version of this figure, see: www.iste.co.uk/taneja/6gurban.zip*

However, the fact that it is 60% harder to implement and is expected to cost $3 million shows that putting these kinds of systems in place needs more advanced technology and resources. Even though it is complicated, its ability to predict the future helps find possible threats before they happen, so steps can be taken ahead of time to lower risks. With an 80% efficiency rate, simulated security scenarios give useful information about possible security breaches through scenario modeling. With a middling challenge level of 52% and a lower cost estimate of $1.8 million, it seems like it would be a good way for towns to try out different security measures and get better prepared without spending a lot of money.

Threat type	Mitigation efficiency (%)	Response time (minutes)	Resource allocation efficiency (%)
Cyberattack prevention	92	15	88
Physical infrastructure failure	89	10	85
Traffic congestion	78	30	80
Natural disasters	85	20	87
Public safety threats	90	25	90

Table 2.3. *Threat mitigation efficiency comparison*

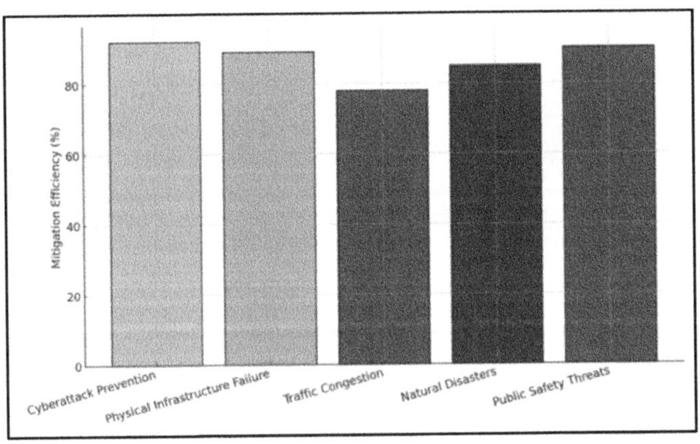

Figure 2.7. *Threat mitigation efficiency across various threat types. For a color version of this figure, see: www.iste.co.uk/taneja/6gurban.zip*

Table 2.3 shows how well different security problems in smart cities are dealt with in terms of threat mitigation efficiency. It focuses on three key performance metrics: response time, resource allocation efficiency and threat mitigation efficiency.

With a 92% success rate, cyberattack prevention is the most effective way to stop attacks, showing how important it is for protecting important digital systems. Figure 2.7 shows how well different types of threats can be stopped. At 15 minutes, the response time is pretty quick, so hacking can be stopped quickly. It also has an 88% resource allocation efficiency, which means that it makes good use of the resources it has for hacking defense. This answer is very important for stopping online dangers that can stop the city from doing many things and put privacy and safety at great risk.

Physical infrastructure failure comes in second with an 89% reduction efficiency. This shows that tracking systems are good at keeping important infrastructure such as transportation, energy lines and water supply systems from failing.

Figure 2.8 shows how different types of threats relate in terms of how well they work.

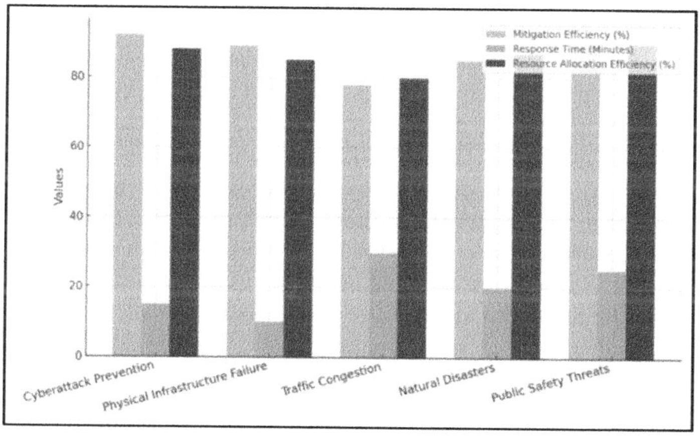

Figure 2.8. *Comparison of efficiency metrics for different threat types. For a color version of this figure, see: www.iste.co.uk/taneja/6gurban.zip*

Cities can quickly deal with and solve problems before they get worse with a response time of just 10 minutes. The fact that resource sharing efficiency is 85% shows that resources are being used well to keep and fix infrastructure. At 78%, traffic congestion has the lowest reduction efficiency, which shows how hard it is to manage movement in cities. Even so, its reaction time of 30 minutes is still doable, and its resource sharing efficiency of 80% means that the city can use its resources to help relieve traffic. But traffic jams are still something that could be better, especially in places with a lot of people. With scores of 85% and 90%, respectively, for prevention effectiveness, natural disasters and public safety threats do very well. Both methods show fast reaction times and good use of resources, which makes sure that cities are ready for emergencies and public safety events.

2.9. Conclusion

Putting digital twin technology to use in smart cities could completely change how safe they are and how well their infrastructure works. Digital twins make virtual copies of important systems that can be monitored in real time, used for predictive analytics and simulated scenarios. These instruments let us detect and stop security risk much more easily. Digital twins gather sophisticated data from IoT sensors and use AI-driven analytics to provide us with valuable insights that enable us to use resources more effectively, lower hazards before they start and make smarter choices. These abilities are crucial for managing large cities full of security concerns such as traffic congestion, damaged infrastructure and internet attacks capable of causing great harm. Using digital twin technology in smart cities still presents challenges even if the advantages are evident. Particularly when gathering and managing vast volumes of private personal data, solid control systems and rigorous encryption policies help to address issues of data privacy. Combining many technologies such as IoT, AI and gadgets, we also need compatibility rules to ensure that every system may interact without any issues. Big cities notably have scalability issues as they produce so much data and need a lot of processing capability to manage it. To get around these problems, cities need to spend money on full security systems that cover both the technical and moral issues of using digital twins. For cooperation and scaling to go more smoothly, the public and private sectors should work together to create uniform data standards and use decentralized systems such as edge computing. Also, informing people and being open about how data is used will be very important for building trust and making sure that tracking and monitoring systems are used in a decent way.

2.10. References

Alnaser, A.A., Ali, A.H., Elmousalami, H.H., Elyamany, A., Mohamed, A.G. (2024). Assessment framework for BIM-digital twin readiness in the construction industry. *Buildings*, 14, 268.

Attaran, S., Attaran, M., Celik, B.G. (2024). Digital twins and industrial Internet of Things: Uncovering operational intelligence in industry 4.0. *Decis. Anal. J.*, 10, 100398.

Debrah, C., Chan, A.P., Darko, A. (2022). Artificial intelligence in green building. *Autom. Constr.*, 137, 104192.

Elmousalami, H.H. (2020a). Artificial intelligence and parametric construction cost estimate modeling: State-of-the-art review. *J. Constr. Eng. Manag.*, 146, 03119008.

Elmousalami, H.H. (2020b). Comparison of artificial intelligence techniques for project conceptual cost prediction: A case study and comparative analysis. *IEEE Trans. Eng. Manag.*, 68, 183–196.

Elmousalami, H.H. and Elaskary, M. (2020). Drilling stuck pipe classification and mitigation in the Gulf of Suez oil fields using artificial intelligence. *J. Pet. Explor. Prod. Technol.*, 10, 2055–2068.

Elmousalami, H., Elmesalami, H.H., Maxi, M., Farid, A.A.M., Elshaboury, N.A.T. (2024a). A comprehensive evaluation of machine learning and deep learning algorithms for wind speed and power prediction. *Decis. Anal. J.*, 13, 100527.

Elmousalami, H.H., Elshaboury, N.A.T., Maxi, M.M.I., Ibrahim, A.H., Elyamany, A.H. (2024b). Bayesian optimized ensemble learning system for predicting conceptual cost and construction duration of irrigation improvement systems. *KSCE J. Civ. Eng.*, 100014.

Jacoby, M. and Usländer, T. (2020). Digital twin and Internet of Things – Current standards landscape. *Appl. Sci.*, 10, 6519.

Kharchenko, V., Illiashenko, O., Morozova, O., Sokolov, S. (2020). Combination of digital twin and artificial intelligence in manufacturing using industrial IoT. In *Proceedings of the 2020 IEEE 11th International Conference on Dependable Systems, Services and Technologies*, Kyiv, 14–18 May, 196–201.

Mouratidis, K. (2021). Urban planning and quality of life: A review of pathways linking the built environment to subjective well-being. *Cities*, 115, 103229.

Murthy, A., Irshad, M., Noman, S.M., Tang, X., Hu, B., Chen, S., Khader, G. (2022). Internet of Things, a vision of digital twins and case studies. In *IoT and Spacecraft Informatics*, Yung, K.L., Ip, A.W.H., Xhafa, F., Tseng, K.K. (eds). Elsevier, Amsterdam, 101–127.

Piras, G., Agostinelli, S., Muzi, F. (2024). Digital twin framework for built environment: A review of key enablers. *Energies*, 17, 436.

Sadri, H., Yitmen, I., Tagliabue, L.C., Westphal, F., Tezel, A., Taheri, A., Sibenik, G. (2023). Integration of blockchain and digital twins in the smart built environment adopting disruptive technologies – A systematic review. *Sustainability*, 15, 3713.

Seyedrezaei, M., Becerik-Gerber, B., Awada, M., Contreras, S., Boeing, G. (2023). Equity in the built environment: A systematic review. *Build. Environ.*, 245, 110827.

Xu, H., Wu, J., Pan, Q., Guan, X., Guizani, M. (2023). A survey on digital twin for industrial Internet of Things: Applications, technologies and tools. *IEEE Commun. Surv. Tutor.*, 25, 2569–2598.

Zade, N.J., Lanke, N.P., Madan, B.S., Katariya, N.P., Ghutke, P., Khobragade, P. (2024). Neural architecture search: Automating the design of convolutional models for scalability. *Panamerican Mathematical Journal*, 34(4), 178–193. doi: 10.52783/pmj.v34.i4.1877.

Zayed, S.M., Attiya, G.M., El-Sayed, A., Hemdan, E.E.-D. (2023). A review study on digital twins with artificial intelligence and internet of things: Concepts, opportunities, challenges, tools and future scope. *Multimed. Tools Appl.*, 82, 47081–47107.

3

Security Solutions for Smart Cities Using Digital Twin: A DevOps Approach in the Era of 6G Powered Ultra-Smart Cities

The rapid advancements in artificial intelligence and digital twin technology have opened new levels of innovations in the smart city sector, supporting sustainable development in the future. AI-driven digital twins are set to revolutionize city planning, optimize resource utilization and facilitating decision-making in ultra-intelligent cities. Using real-time data, predictive analytics and autonomous systems, 6G-enabled digital twins create more integrated, resilient and sustainable cities. This chapter discusses the main issues, technological innovations and future scope of work for developing AI and digital twin integration into future smart cities.

3.1. Introduction

3.1.1. *Overview of digital twin technology*

The rapid adoption of 5G technology is enhancing current systems by enabling high-speed internet connectivity, which in turn drives innovation in IoT-based smart city solutions. The fast-paced evolution of technology is encouraging users to transition to 5G, benefiting from improved network efficiency and performance. This accelerated development has triggered a competitive race among private companies to overcome 5G limitations and capitalize on the commercial potential of building smarter cities. This chapter outlines the principal directions and scope of sixth-generation (6G) technologies, such as digital twins, which, if implemented in cities already equipped with 5G infrastructure, could significantly contribute to the transformation into smarter cities.

Chapter written by C.V. Suresh BABU and Logapadmini B.

3.1.2. *The role of 6G in ultra-smart cities*

According to Dangi et al. (2023), while 5G networks are still in their early stages, the groundwork for 6G wireless technology is already being laid. Although 6G connectivity may not be immediately available everywhere, upgrading to the 6G system is considered a natural progression. A cellular network is typically divided into different geographical regions called cells. Compared to earlier generations, 6G networks are expected to support more advanced applications that go beyond typical human use. These include large-scale manufacturing, smart transportation systems, intelligent home setups and immersive virtual reality (VR) experiences. Each of these verticals comes with unique Quality of Service (QoS) requirements, making the impact of 6G both diverse and far-reaching (Dangi et al. 2023).

3.1.3. *The need for security solutions in smart cities*

The quick implementation of smart city technologies has greatly enhanced urban living through increased efficiency, sustainability and public services. The added connectivity comes with enormous security challenges that call for strong solutions. Due to the extensive use of IoT devices, cities are exposed to cyber-attacks, unauthorized access and data leaks. Moreover, the large volume of personal data harvested creates concerns regarding privacy and abuse. Critical infrastructures such as energy networks and transportation systems are also vulnerable to cyber-attacks, which can result in extreme disruptions. In order to counter such threats, smart cities need to implement security-by-design concepts so that security features are built in from the development phase. Monitoring and real-time response to threats are crucial to identify and contain cyber risks. In addition, vigorous privacy protection regulations need to be implemented in order to counter data collection with users' security. As cities become more advanced, security solutions must be prioritized in order for them to remain resilient and sustainable against emerging dangers (Elmaghraby and Losavio 2014).

3.1.4. *The intersection of DevOps and digital twin for security*

In industry 4.0, exchange and connectivity of data are major factors. The transfer of environmental data from the physical system to the central server is done by IoT, which has a central role in this work. IoT does not always rely on traditional encryption methods like AES for data protection. In the context of Industry 4.0, digital twins emphasize the importance of securing data exchange between IoT devices and digital systems. Additionally, a new standardized lightweight encryption method named ASCON has been proposed. The outcome of SLR can be indicated by digital tools. According to the 5G network study, it is suggested that communication systems must be designed to ensure confidentiality.

3.2. Background information

3.2.1. *Evolution of smart cities and digital twins*

The digital twin in the urban environments has gained a lot of attention in recent years because of its potential to drive sustainable smart city development. By creating a virtual replica of the physical system and its surroundings, digital twins enable the transfer of data between the physical and virtual realms, enhancing our understanding and management of urban infrastructure. Urban Digital Twins (UDTs) play a critical role in large-scale modeling and analysis of urban physical systems, supporting environmental sustainability. Their integration with technologies like the Internet of Things (IoT) and artificial intelligence (AI) further amplifies their impact.

3.2.2. *Issues of smart cities*

Smart cities and the 6G are exciting new technologies that make people work quicker and smarter. However, despite being useful, they also have some issues. One serious issue is that all the computers and machines in a smart city must "speak" to one another, and sometimes they do not communicate with one another. This is an example of a communication issue.

Another major issue is the protection of personal data. Smart cities collect vast amounts of information, including individuals' movements and activities. Without proper safeguards, this data is vulnerable to breaches, posing serious privacy risks. Ensuring robust data security is therefore essential. Additionally, the high cost of implementing smart city technologies creates inequality. While some communities can afford and benefit from these advancements, others are left behind, exacerbating the digital divide.

Constructing smart cities also requires much time, effort and money. And 6G – which is an even faster internet – requires new towers and machines. Some areas do not have access to 6G yet, particularly small towns. It can be very costly, and not everybody can afford 6G internet. 6G also has to be safe for use. The individuals who make it have to obey rules, and governments and corporations have to cooperate in order to make it a reality. They also have to agree on how to distribute the internet throughout the entire world. That is difficult because each country wants something different.

Finally, 6G requires numerous towers and devices everywhere, even more than 5G. This means investing lots of money to ensure everyone can use it (Murroni et al. 2023).

3.2.3. *Relevance of DevOps in the fighting of security requirements*

DevOps is becoming more of a critical component in meeting security requirements by incorporating security management throughout the software development process. This method, commonly known as DevSecops, has the advantage of having development, operation and security. Using security processes early in the process identifies and prevents weaknesses, reducing significant risks to the organization. The static application security testing and dynamic application security testing are for the automated security testing which will help in improving the human error. Devops will also enable reinnovations and rapid reinnovations by providing access to teams to respond quickly without interruption. DevOps also encourages team collaboration to achieve a positive security culture. Continuous monitoring adds more security by real-time recognition and reacting to threats. By inclusion of security in DevOps methods, organizations can automate workflows and minimize costs associated with late stage (Hakiri et al. 2024) challenges, including availability of spectrum, expenses, security threats and regulatory compliance. In fact, 6G requires new technologies and infrastructure that are difficult to create and implement. In addition, 6G requires sufficient spectrum availability. Developing and implementing 6G are expensive, and we may have questions about the cost of using 6G services. Like other new technologies, 6G security issues can be met to ensure the security and privacy of users. Finally, 6G advancements and implementation include cooperation between the government and the private sector, and there may be regulatory issues that must be suspended. Global cooperation and orientation are also required to achieve global reporting through 6G

3.3. Relevance to the edited book's theme

3.3.1. *Convergence of AI, digital twin and DevOps*

With the convergence of AI and digital twin technology, DevOps is revolutionizing contemporary cyber-physical systems through increased automation, efficiency and predictive strengths. A physical asset allowing monitoring in real time and predictive analysis is the exact virtual replica of a digital twin. The addition of AI further strengthens digital twins by analyzing huge datasets, detecting patterns and optimizing operations based on machine learning (ML) algorithms. When paired with DevOps practices, this intersection makes continuous development, testing and deployment possible, minimizing errors and speeding up innovation. AI-based digital twins facilitate predictive maintenance, enabling organizations to predict failures and maximize resource allocation. At the same time, DevOps practices make iterative refinements more efficient by incorporating feedback loops from digital twin simulations into the software development lifecycle. This synergy-based strategy enables better decision-making, operational robustness and economical system management, and is thus most suitable for sectors such as manufacturing, aerospace and smart cities. As these technologies advance, their convergence is likely to be pivotal in driving automation, security and green digital transformation (Hugues et al. 2022).

3.3.2. *Contribution to sustainable ultra-smart cities*

The spatial planning aspects of smart cities – those that shape the physical structure and layout – have not been extensively studied. Many current smart city initiatives appear to be mismatched with their local environmental and socio-technical contexts. To address this issue, this chapter investigates various spatial planning models and categorizations using case studies of leading smart cities, such as Stockholm and several Indian metropolitan areas. The authors introduce two main topologies within the smart city framework. The first focuses on the functional use of space, district characteristics and the technical infrastructure targeted for enhancement. The second categorizes planning based on spatial scale, distinguishing among national, regional-metropolitan, municipal-local, and distributed or project-specific levels (Angelidou and Mora 2019).

3.4. Key questions or problems addressed

3.4.1. *Integration of digital twins for security applications*

According to Jeremiah (2024), over the past two decades, advancements in AI and big data analytics within cloud computing have significantly propelled technological progress. These developments have a direct positive impact on digital twins and their ability to replicate physical objects. Digital twins also enhance visualization capabilities. Despite their extensive use, DT systems are becoming increasingly susceptible to a variety of security threats and attacks. Though the studies of DT applications and their resultant security issues are growing in number, there has been no thorough, domain-level review embracing their architectural and functional layers. The results are structured under a common security framework, with the potential for mitigation. Additionally, Jeremiah (2024) investigates DT defenses against current cyber-attacks and provides current research challenges and future directions. A DT basically replicates a physical entity within a virtual space, allowing real-time simulation and examination. It uses APIs and specification-based technologies for asset definition and is normally executed through virtual machines, containers or special servers for the handling of digital content (Jeremiah et al. 2024).

3.4.2. *Role of DevOps in ensuring continuous security updates*

DevOps, which combines software development and operations, has changed how teams deliver high-quality software by fixing problems earlier in the process. In recent times, there has been an interest in combining DevOps with cybersecurity, forming what is known as Secure DevOps. As these practices grow, it is important for teams to view them through the field of risk management.

This approach encourages the integration of risk assessment tools, such as threat modeling (TM), at the initial stages of the software upgrade life cycle. Our work suggests a step-by-step plan for applying secure DevOps while aligning with risk management goals. It emphasizes improving TM techniques and building strong security practices in organizations that focus on developing software-based services and products.

We also compare reliable and proven strategies from the literature, discuss different tools and technologies, and present a case study from a real organization using this secure DevOps model. Implementing these new security measures requires significant training, investment and stakeholder involvement. However, understanding the benefits of automation in CI/CD (Continuous Integration/Delivery) environments is key to delivering safer and more reliable software to the market (Czekster 2024).

3.4.3. *Addressing security gaps in 6G-enabled environments*

The emergence of 6G wireless networks is ushering in unprecedented features such as ultra-low latency, enormous data rates and ubiquitous connectivity over smart environments. These developments pose significant security threats that need to be mitigated to provide safe and reliable communication. One such concern is preserving privacy in 3D fog computing, especially for use cases such as drones and unmanned aerial vehicles (UAVs), where strong mechanisms are needed to secure spatiotemporal data. Also, the adoption of software-defined networking (SDN) in the 6G infrastructure opens up networks to risks of cyber-attack because of the centralized control protocol, requiring security SDN schemes. A challenge also arises when designing efficient and secure routing algorithms to deal with the gigantic communication scenarios in 6G. Also, leveraging the terahertz (THz) frequency band, in addition to increasing data transfer rate, poses a risk at the physical layer and necessitates highly sophisticated security requirements. The advent of quantum computing also jeopardizes conventional cryptographic techniques, so quantum-resilient security protocols become a necessity in 6G networks. Ultimately, blockchain-based distributed security architectures are also good options in the form of decentralizing data integrity mechanisms, although scalability and privacy challenges still need to be addressed. Closing these security loopholes is essential for the successful deployment of 6G technologies, requiring ongoing research and the creation of dynamic security frameworks to combat changing cyber threats.

3.5. Objectives and scope

3.5.1. *Objectives of the chapter*

In this chapter, we will try to delve into the revolutionary potential of AI and virtual replica technology techniques and technologies in catalyzing innovation for 6G-fueled sustainable ultra-smart cities. The authors explore how AI-based analytics and real-time digital twin simulations can enhance urban infrastructure optimization, improve decision-making and enhance overall city governance. The chapter also looks into how 6G networks make a difference in terms of sustainability through energy-efficient communication, smart grid management and environmentally friendly urban solutions. The chapter also tackles major security and privacy issues related to AI, digital twins and 6G integration, suggesting solid solutions for maintaining the integrity of data and cybersecurity. In addition, it evaluates the ability of these technologies to streamline smart city functions, such as mobility, healthcare, public safety and environmental monitoring, to enhance resilience and flexibility. Lastly, it points out emerging research directions and technology developments that would further stimulate innovation in urban development, leading to next-generation ultra-smart green cities.

3.5.2. *Delimitation of scope*

According to Alibrandi (2022), a digital twin represents the digital counterpart of physical entities such as buildings, processes, structures, individuals and systems. It is continuously created and updated to reflect and respond to inquiries related to its physical counterpart. Smart buildings and infrastructure serve as examples of physical twins (PTs), and the synchronization between digital twins (DTs) and PTs enables continuous learning and adaptation. In this chapter, Alibrandi introduces a new concept called Risk-Informed Digital Twin (RDT), which emphasizes risk-aware modeling. In DT, the predictions and analyses are driven by integrated tools and algorithms. Through various sources of life cycle testing, the performance and adaptability of smart city systems can be assessed. This platform provides access to housing-related data and introduces a new information-theoretical framework.

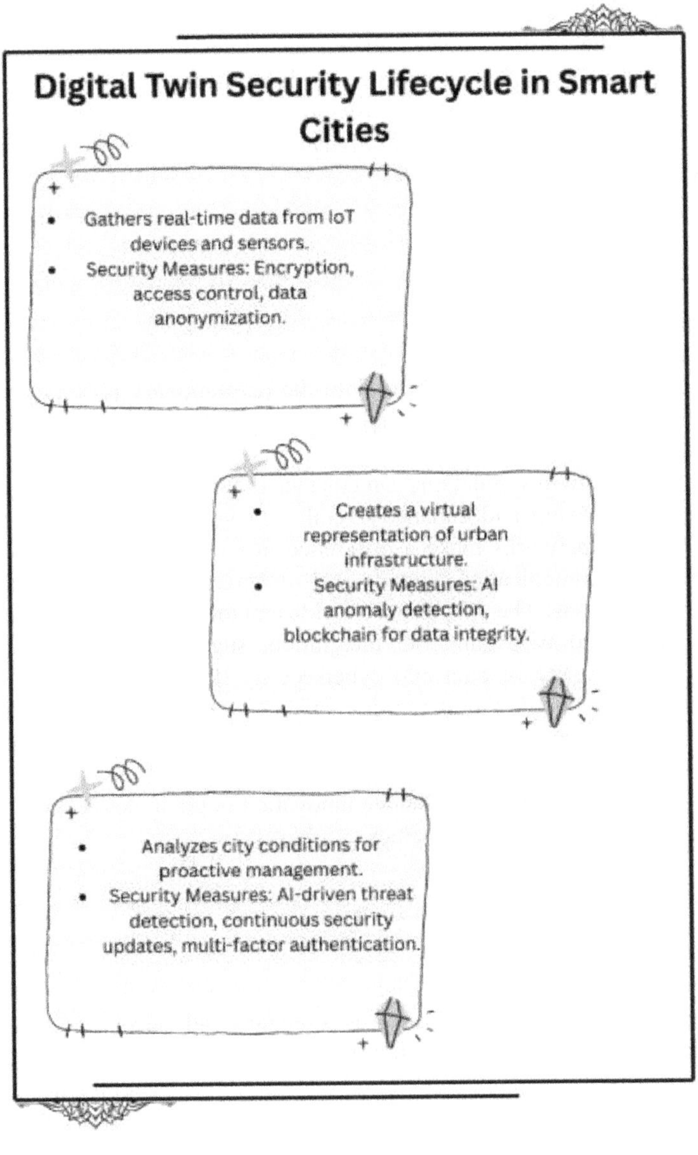

Figure 3.1. *Digital twin security lifecycle in a smart city*

3.6. Literature review

This research uses the PRISMA (Preferred Reporting Items for Systematic Reviews and Meta-Analyses) method approach in selecting the best research papers available in established databases. As structured literature review then followed in assessing and contrasting those studies chosen. Using the systematic searching methodology ensures a biased-free analysis, which is absolutely essential when a field of study is following rapid developments such as smart cities or future emerging technologies such as 6G. The literature search was mainly conducted on publications that were published between 2019 and April 2024. Besides database findings, relevant literature from other reliable sources was also taken into account. Upon gathering all the records from both primary and secondary sources, 1,830 articles were identified. These were then filtered through title and abstract screening, exclusion of duplicates, and strict inclusion and exclusion criteria. Finally, 287 articles fulfilled the criteria and were used in the final systematic review (Sharma et al. 2024).

3.6.1. *Summary of existing research*

The initial phases of pre-6G technology research investigated a case study focused on Helsinki, located in southern Finland. Helsinki intends to use these innovations in the future for healthcare – where 6G can be used to conduct remote surgery – and industrial automation – where improved machine-to-machine communication might become a reality. As these technologies further advance, the incorporation of RIS with 6G will be a large leap towards establishing totally connected smart cities, whereby digital connectivity enables everything that takes place in the city. Tests also provide critical performance measures, such as reduced latency, increased data rates and improved system reliability. These results show the technological breakthroughs achieved through implementation (Firoozi and Firoozi 2025).

3.6.2. *Identified gaps in literature*

In spite of the increasing interest in AI-based digital twins for sustainable ultra-smart cities enabled by 6G, there are some gaps in the existing literature. The current studies do not have an overarching framework that effectively embeds AI with digital twin technology to enhance real-time urban operations. Most of the studies address standalone use cases and not a generic architecture that supports interoperability, regulatory compliance and scalability. In addition, there is minimal investigation into AI-based sustainability metrics, and more importantly, to improve energy efficiency, resource use and carbon neutrality analyzing the use of AI. Privacy and security also pose a critical challenge since bringing 6G networks together with AI-based digital twins will translate into enormous exchanges of data which need strong security measures and moral governance. In addition, although pre-6G experiments in urban areas such as Helsinki prove technological feasibility, large-scale deployment in real-world scenarios is untested, and concerns regarding cost-effectiveness and operational complexity are being raised. Finally, the interactions among AI, digital twins and other novel technologies – blockchain, IoT and quantum computing – remain an underemphasized topic, even though it has the potential to propel innovation in urban infrastructure. Closure of these gaps will be most important in defining the destiny of genuinely intelligent, sustainable and networked smart cities.

3.6.3. *The contribution of this chapter*

An overview of the recent literature suggests that while certain studies report very narrow technical approaches to AI and adjacent technologies, others take the metaverse into view from more generalized viewpoints, in terms of digital, social and economic impacts. Yet, coverage is narrow, particularly where applications that involve sustainable smart cities within metaverse environments are concerned. This work is mainly concerned with the application of AI to facilitate metaverse technologies for urban planning. The research also examines key AI-fundamental methods and technologies such as LLMs, CV and large data platforms and demonstrates how they can improve decision-making capabilities and customize the user experience in the metaverse. The examples showcase how city-level data-driven planning and context-sensitive solutions in metaverse applications are facilitated by AI.

Apart from this, various burning issues concerning the usage of metaverse systems in smart cities are revealed in this review. These are scalability, security and privacy, ethics, system interoperability and performance measurement. Future studies are invited to overcome these limitations by proposing scalable designs, establishing benchmark measures of evaluation and enforcing ethical guidelines of AI use. A conceptual model grounded in the technology acceptance model (TAM) is also provided to further discuss metaverse adoption in cities (Lifelo et al. 2024).

3.7. Methodology

3.7.1. *Software development methodologies*

Different agile methodologies, their categorization and real-world applications are reviewed. Agile software development is described as a collection of methodologies that focus on flexibility, teamwork and customer satisfaction through iterative and incremental development. The research classifies agile methods into lightweight and hybrid methods, where lightweight methods such as Extreme Programming (XP) and Scrum concentrate on minimal documentation and flexibility, and hybrid methods combine traditional and agile principles. The chapter examines 10 agile methods on the basis of flexibility, customer participation and cyclical advancement, noting that XP prioritizes technical excellence with practices such as pair programming and continuous integration, whereas Scrum targets project management via formalized roles and sprint iterations. Feature-driven development (FDD) integrates model-driven and feature-based development to produce working software increments. In spite of their variations, all of these approaches have fundamental principles such as collaboration with the customer, iterative development and self-organizing teams. The study also points out the challenges in the future, such as making agile processes scalable for very large projects, having more appropriate measurement metrics and combining Agile with sequential development. This research is useful in understanding how to choose the most appropriate approach for different software development situations (Abrahamsson et al. 2017). By promoting continuous integration, deployment and delivery, agile and DevOps approaches have revolutionized software development and provided faster and more reliable product releases. DevOps builds upon the principles of Agile by uniting development and operation teams to automate processes and enhance deployment efficiency. Agile puts high importance on the iterative development, cross-functional teamwork and customer input. Through the decomposition of programs into small, loosely coupled services that can be individually developed, deployed and scaled, this further enhances these principles. Using this approach, teams can implement a modular development plan, which improves system resiliency, scalability and fault isolation.

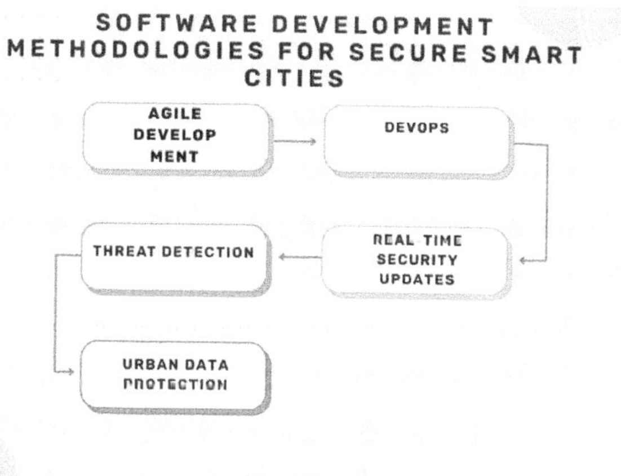

Figure 3.2. *Software development methodologies for secure smart cities. For a color version of this figure, see: www.iste.co.uk/taneja/6gurban.zip*

Software development and operations are being revolutionized concurrently by AI-driven predictive analytics, which uses ML algorithms to predict failures and improve resource allocation.

3.7.2. *Justification of methodology*

The implementation of Agile and DevOps techniques, microservices architecture and AI-driven predictive analytics is warranted because they can increase the efficiency, scalability and reliability of software development. Agile practices facilitate iterative development, instant feedback and ongoing improvement, which are most suitable for volatile and rapidly changing software projects. DevOps bridges Agile by automating and optimizing collaboration among development and operation teams to deploy cycles quickly through the adoption of Microservices Architecture, which is warranted because it fosters modularity whereby each component can be developed, tested, deployed and scaled in isolation. This architecture improves system resilience since failures are isolated from one another, decreasing downtime and enabling quick updates without compromising the entire system. Its decentralized design is in tune with the Agile and DevOps philosophy, enabling quick iterations and optimized resource use. AI-driven predictive analytics complements this methodology by providing proactive detection of issues, optimization of performance and automated decision-making. ML algorithms are able to assess historical incidents and real-time data to discover impending system failures that optimize deployment patterns and improve security. This predictive potential minimizes downtime, maximizes software reliability and offers best-in-class resource allocation (Anand and Miglani 2024).

3.8. Discussion of analysis and findings

The 6G network architecture is highly heterogeneous in nature. OFDMA and NOMA are technologies that offer flexible access schemes that enable the convergence of various types of networks – ranging from land and satellite systems to underwater communication – into a single, three-dimensional network structure (Kumar et al. 2023).

3.8.1. *Case studies on digital twin security in smart cities*

In this research, we investigate the transformative power of 6G technology and how it will create a new paradigm of human-centric connectivity. Our results highlight the need to develop core areas such as security, privacy and confidentiality as imperative factors that need to be developed to address the increasing need for secure wireless communication. Through realistic use cases, we illustrate the various possibilities brought about by 6G, including improved digital twin systems and immersive digital realms. We further venture into base enablers and design innovations predicted to transform wireless systems. Some of these encompass the addition of terahertz communication, intelligent reflective surfaces (IRS), as well as breakthroughs in quantum communication. Upon conclusion, we can clearly see that the shift towards 6G signifies not only an evolutionary step forward in technology but also a wholesale overhaul in terms of how connectivity is going to drive intelligent, secure and interlinked city environments. Our analysis suggests an initial framework to inform future studies, focusing on an overall approach that harmonizes technological progress with socio-economic, regulatory and environmental factors while deploying and evolving 6G systems (Siddiky et al. 2024).

3.8.2. *Analysis of DevOps in smart city infrastructure*

Implementation of DevOps in smart city infrastructure is essential in enhancing system efficiency, scalability and reliability. Smart cities rely on interconnected systems, including IoT networks, cloud computing and AI analytics, that require continuous monitoring, real-time updates and rapid deployment of software solutions. DevOps practices enable the integration and automaton of such items easily to make smart city apps run with minimal downtime. One of the most important advantages that DevOps has over smart cities is that CI/CD pipelines are possible and, with it, can enable instant software updating and security patching. This is important for critical infrastructure such as traffic flow networks, power grids and public safety networks, where system failure can be deadly. Infrastructure as Code (IaC) in DevOps also allows auto-scaling and automated provisioning of cloud resources to deliver optimal performance based on demand. The second essential domain is security and resiliency. Smart cities generate huge amounts of data through surveillance systems, citizen services and sensors and thus are prime candidates to be hacked with cyber-attacks. DevSecOps, an extension of the process, mitigates risk by introducing automated threat detection and security testing capabilities (Horvath et al. 2024).

3.9. Suggestions and recommendations

3.9.1. *Best practices for implementing security solutions*

An effective security solution should be deployed to protect digital infrastructure, especially in adaptive environments such as 6G networks and digital twins. Best practices for deploying security solutions include encryption, authentication mechanisms, threat intelligence and continuous monitoring. Zero-trust security architecture is one such root practice that entails the continuous verification of the device and user before providing access to systems or networks. End-to-end encryption ensures confidentiality of data in transit, while multi-factor authentication (MFA) ensures extra authentication of the identity of the user. AI and ML are also used to detect anomalies in order to enable the active detection and prevention of cyber-attacks. Periodic security audits and adherence to industry standards such as ISO/IEC 27001, NIST cybersecurity framework and GDPR for data protection are other best practices. Blockchain technology can be applied to improve security via tamper-proofed transactions and decentralized identity management (Ridhawi et al. 2023).

3.9.2. *Role of standardized protocols in 6G and digital twins*

Standards-based protocols are crucial for guaranteeing interoperability, security and efficiency in 6G networks and digital twin technologies. As technology keeps evolving in the 6th generation, new communication standards must be developed. IEEE, ITU and 3GPP are some of the organizations at the forefront of shaping the standards. In 6G networks, standardized protocols facilitate smooth integration of terahertz (THz) communication requirements. These standards establish data transmission processes, security structures and reliability levels to make connectivity high performance. Common data models and communication protocols in digital twins allow real-time synchronization of virtual and physical entities. OPC unified architecture (OPC UA), MQTT and 5G/6G-based IoT protocols provide secure data exchange in smart manufacturing, healthcare and autonomous transport (Khan et al. 2021).

3.10. Future scope for research

3.10.1. *Quantum computing for digital twin security*

In today's quantum computing world, there is lots of potential to influence several faces which need to be optimized efficiently and have testable solutions. A novel solution to improve processes can be inspired by quantum computing. Quantum computing is the best method for solving intricate problems; specifically, quantum computing can also solve problems which range from security to stock trading. Quantum computing can perform complex calculations and run advanced algorithms, enabling it to solve problems that classical computers cannot. In the context of smart cities, this technology holds the potential to support equitable living conditions by enabling efficient, sustainable, and intelligent solutions. As urban zones are analyzed, quantum computing is increasingly being explored as a transformative tool to address the challenges and optimize the performance of smart city systems.

3.10.2. *Digital twin ethical challenges for smart cities*

The application of digital twins in intelligent cities is very problematic and requires serious moral reflection to prevent reckless development. Helbing and Argota Sánchez-Vaquerizo (2022) engage in arguments about privacy infringement, security risks and even prejudice due to biased data. They propose the adoption of stringent ethical norms to mitigate these risks through urban planning and decision-making. A Reuters (2024) news report describes the legal and ethical problem with digital twins, emphasizing the requirements of data minimization, informed consent and secure security in order to neutralize cyber-attacks. All of these reports identify the imperative of having strong guidelines to the extent that technological advancements are still aligned with societal values and protecting the rights of the individual (Helbing and Argota Sánchez-Vaquerizo 2022).

3.11. Conclusion

3.11.1. *Summary of key contributions*

The application of digital twins in smart cities raises severe ethical issues, including privacy risks, data protection, potential biases and surveillance issues. Huge data gathering may lead to privacy infringement and security threats unless properly managed. Fairness is required at the time of decision-making in order to prevent biased outcomes. In addition, legal and moral problems must be addressed by minimizing data, consensual data and strong cybersecurity measures to preserve citizens' information and prevent unsolicited surveillance.

3.11.2. *Final thoughts on digital twin and DevOps integration*

An investigative literature review was conducted to analyze how digital twins are being implemented in the software industry, especially when existing infrastructures and organizations are being operated under the application lifecycle management framework. As a vital driver of digital innovation, DTs play a significant role in the advancement towards Industry 4.0 by facilitating system optimization, reducing inefficiencies, increasing productivity and minimizing operational costs. While DT adoption has grown considerably in industrial domains such as manufacturing, their integration into the software domain has been relatively modest. However, foundational research from manufacturing applications offers valuable insights for their potential use in software processes – particularly in the early stages of software development and, to some extent, within application lifecycle management. Traditional software development approaches and tools have evolved into more integrated and streamlined infrastructures that oversee the entire software lifecycle – from development and governance to quality assurance, security, operations and business alignment within the ALM context. Within this evolving structure, DTs offer powerful solutions for managing the complexity of software lifecycle processes. They even support the potential for full automation of these processes (Guinea-Cabrera and Holgado-Terriza 2024).

3.12. References

Abrahamsson, P., Salo, O., Ronkainen, J., Warsta, J. (2017). Agile software development methods: Review and analysis. *arXiv* [Online]. Available at: https://arxiv.org/abs/1709.08439.

Alibrandi, U. (2022). Risk-informed digital twin of buildings and infrastructures for sustainable and resilient urban communities. *ASCE-ASME Journal of Risk and Uncertainty in Engineering Systems*. doi: 10.1061/AJRUA6.0001238.

Anand, R. and Miglani, A. (2024). Real-time AI-driven predictive analytics for agile software development: Enhancing decision-making, resource optimization, and risk mitigation. [Online]. Available at: https://www.researchgate.net/publication/384112410.

Angelidou, M. and Mora, L. (2019). Exploring the relationship between smart cities and spatial planning: Star cases and typologies. In *Smart Cities in the Post-Algorithmic Era*, Komninos, N. and Kakderi, C. (eds). Edward Elgar, Cheltenham, 217–234. doi: 10.4337/9781789907056.00019.

Bhide, P., Shetty, D., Mikkili, S. (2025). Review on 6G communication and its architecture, technologies included, challenges, security challenges and requirements, applications, with respect to AI domain. *IET Quantum Communication*, 6(1), e12114.

Czekster, R.M. (2024). Continuous risk assessment in secure DevOps. *arXiv*. doi: 10.48550/arXiv.2409.03405.

Dangi, R., Choudhary, G., Dragoni, N., Lalwani, P., Khare, U., Kundu, S. (2023). 6G mobile networks: Key technologies, directions, and advances. *Telecom.*, 4(4), 836–876. doi: 10.3390/telecom4040037.

Elmaghraby, A.S. and Losavio, M.M. (2014). Cyber security challenges in Smart Cities: Safety, security and privacy. *Journal of Advanced Research*, 5(4), 491–497. doi: 10.1016/j.jare.2014.02.006.

Firoozi, A.A. and Firoozi, A.A. (eds) (2025). From fifth generation to sixth generation networks: Enhancing smart city communications through cutting-edge technologies. In *Integrating Artificial Intelligence and Reconfigurable Intelligent Surfaces in Urban Infrastructure: Enhancing Connectivity and Resilience*. Science Publishing, San Francisco, CA.

Guinea-Cabrera, M.A. and Holgado-Terriza, J.A. (2024). Digital twins in software engineering—A systematic literature review and vision. *Applied Sciences*. 14(3), 977. doi: 10.3390/app14030977.

Hakiri, A., Gokhale, A., Yahia, S.B., Mellouli, N. (2024). A comprehensive survey on digital twin for future networks and emerging Internet of Things industry. *Computer Networks*, 110350. doi: 10.1016/j.comnet.2024.110350.

Helbing, D. and Argota Sánchez-Vaquerizo, J. (2022). Digital twins: Potentials, ethical issues, and limitations. *arXiv*. doi: 10.48550/arXiv.2208.04289.

Horvath, K., Abid, M.R., Merino, T., Zimmerman, R., Peker, Y., Khan, S. (2024). Cloud-based infrastructure and DevOps for energy fault detection in smart buildings. *Computers*, 13(1), 23. doi: 10.3390/computers13010023.

Hugues, J., Hudak, J., Yankel, J., Hristozov, A. (2022). TwinOps: Digital twins meets DevOps. Software Engineering Institute Technical Report CMU/SEI-2022-TR-0010.

Jeremiah, S.R., El Azzaoui, A., Xiong, N.N., Park, J.H. (2024). A comprehensive survey of digital twins: Applications, technologies and security challenges. *Journal of Systems Architecture*, 151, 103120. doi: 10.1016/j.sysarc.2024.103120.

Khan, L.U., Saad, W., Han, Z., Hossain, E., Hong, C.S. (2021). Federated learning for internet of things: Recent advances, taxonomy, and open challenges. *IEEE Communications Surveys & Tutorials*, 23(3), 1759–1799.

Kumar, R., Gupta, S.K., Wang, H.-C., Kumari, C.S., Korlam, S.S.V.P. (2023). From efficiency to sustainability: Exploring the potential of 6G for a greener future. *Sustainability*, 15(23), 16387. doi: 10.3390/su152316387.

Lifelo, Z., Ding, J., Ning, H., Qurat-Ul-Ain, Dhelim, S. (2024). Artificial intelligence-enabled metaverse for sustainable smart cities: Technologies, applications, challenges, and future directions. *Electronics*, 13(24), 4874. doi: 10.3390/electronics13244874.

Murroni, M., Anedda, M., Fadda, M., Ruiu, P., Popescu, V., Zaharia, C., Giusto, D. (2023). 6G – Enabling the new smart city: A survey. *Sensors*, 23(17), 7528. doi: 10.3390/s23177528.

Reuters (2024). AI and digital twins raise ethical questions, experts say [Online]. Available at: https://www.reuters.com/technology/article1234.

Ridhawi, I.A., Otoum, S., Aloqaily, M. (2023). Decentralized zero trust framework for digital twin-based 6G. *arXiv*. doi: 10.48550/arXiv.2302.03107.

Sharma, S., Popli, R., Singh, S., Chhabra, G., Saini, G.S., Singh, M., Sandhu, A., Sharma, A., Kumar, R. (2024). The role of 6G technologies in advancing smart city applications: Opportunities and challenges. *Sustainability*, 16(16), 7039. doi: 10.3390/su16167039.

Siddiky, M.N.A., Rahman, M.E., Uzzal, M.S. (2024). Beyond 5G: A comprehensive exploration of 6G wireless communication technologies. doi: 10.20944/preprints202405.0715.v1.

4

Convergence of Twin Technology with AI for Secure 6G Communication

The 6G Twin Technology, integrated with Artificial Intelligence (AI), is set to transform secure communication in 6G by enhancing prediction. 6G networks are made more efficient and secure with the use of Twin Technology, which includes computational twins and similar models made up of AI. This technology focuses on the optimization, prediction and simulation of network settings. To reduce and decrease the risk of cyberthreats and cyberattacks and provide strong data security with integrated AI-driven and powered technologies such as machine learning and deep learning, it allows us to support predictive analysis, smart managing networks, and anomaly detection. Network operators can control resource allocation, approximate potential vulnerabilities and start implementing proactive security methods with the help of the AI-enhanced process of digitizing twins. This integration enables enhanced mobile broadband and ultra-reliable low latency communication. This chapter explains how to collaborate and integrate with Twin and AI technology.

4.1. Introduction

There has been rapid progress and growth toward the 6G Communication networking for wireless communication with the new connectivity high-ultra data speeds and extremely low latency and extensive persuasive interconnectivity (Giordani and Zorzi 2021; Tataria et al. 2021). In this new world, creating and establishing solid security while governing complexity of data transmission and constant changing of networks is a significant task (Saad et al. 2020). The combination of Digital Twin technology with Artificial Intelligence (AI) delivers a promising solution (Liu et al. 2021). Digital Twin technology provides real-time virtual reproductions and details mirroring the framework of actual networks,

---

Chapter written by Srinibas PATTANAIK, Jasneet KAUR, Sachin AHUJA, Sartajvir Singh DHILLON and Alessandro VINCIARELLI.

thereby enabling continuous oversight, game and predictive maintenance (Wu and Zhang 2020). When integrated with AI, these digital models may evolve to adjust to changing networking conditions, proactively recognizing and eliminating necessary potential risks to security while optimizing performance (Chen et al. 2019; Samad et al. 2020). This integrated strategy not only increases the security architecture of the 6G networks, but also fosters creativity, making networks more robust, efficient and adjusted to emerging difficulties encountered in an increasingly connected world (Dang et al. 2020). An AI-driven future, powered by advanced AI technologies, enables effective analysis and prediction of network traffic while identifying security threats in communication systems (Huang et al. 2019; Chen et al. 2020). The rapid advancement of wireless communication technologies has significantly enhanced the performance of 6G networks, enabling ultra-fast data rates, reduced latency, and massive device interconnectivity through higher network frequencies and AI integration. Twin technology (digital twin and quantum twin) has developed recognition as a new solution to solve these difficulties by enabling immediate formatting of the modeling, optimization and security advances in networked platforms (Letaief et al. 2019; Di Renzo et al. 2020).

4.1.1. *Significance and relevance of privacy and security in 6G networks*

The integration of digital twin technology with 6G networks, enhanced by AI, marks a major step toward the next generation of ultra-fast, intelligent connectivity. As 6G evolves alongside AI advancements, it promises high-speed communication with automated intelligence and real-time responsiveness; primarily, the development of 6G technology integrated with AI aims to enable ultra-fast and automated connectivity. In contrast, these major developments represent serious security issues including cyberthreats, data privacy, risks and vulnerabilities in networks. The security of 6G technologies is crucial and integrates with the availability and confidentiality of integrating with data using AI and the Internet of Things (Jiang et al. 2017; Bennis et al. 2018).

– The real-time cyberthreats are using AI and machine learning techniques, making them harder to detect. However, 6G networks use AI/ML defensively for anomaly detection in real-time, ensuring uninterrupted network functioning (Elsayed and Erol-Kantarci 2019; Noman et al. 2023).

– With the help of networks, distributed ledger technology can improve data processing–pre-processing with the connected network database and improve the resilience of networks. Contracts with sensors lower the danger of cyber fraud by enabling automatic and impenetrable security enforcement. Furthermore, user authentication is kept strong and unchangeable through the usage of decentralized identification and authorization systems for confidential confirmation of identity (Al Ridhawi et al. 2023; Yigit et al. 2023).

– 6G networks are being designed with a strong emphasis on security, which guarantees ultra-fast and intelligent connectivity to remain secure, reliable, and compliant with privacy laws. With the intention to secure vast IoT networks and reduce the dangers associated with it, it will be crucial to integrate AI, blockchain technologies, quantum data encryption and zero-trust model frameworks. 6G can offer a robust, intelligent and impenetrable communication network for sectors such as financial services, medical care self-navigating devices, and smart towns and cities by implementing proactive precautions against attack. According to what the 6G technology develops further, having a strong security framework will safeguard user information in order to gain network integrity, while also enabling the following generation of wireless communication to reach the limits of its capabilities (Masaracchia et al. 2022).

4.2. Comprehension of twins' technology

Understanding digital twins involves recognizing their role in replicating, assessing, and optimizing.

Digital twin technology involves a virtual model of a physical entity, an object or a process, which is continuously monitored using real-time data from the physical counterpart. It enables better decision-making by optimizing operations and anticipating failures based on real-time feedback. In the process of replicating network elements, including base stations and directional antennas, alongside the other network processes, DTs are vital for communication systems. Data collecting technologies, intelligent analyzing data, an ongoing simulation model and maintenance predictions tools are crucial aspects of a DT in wireless communication networks. The elements enable continuous surveillance while participating, enhancing the efficiency of network performance. DTs assist the network development and management by offering real-time insights on network activity, detecting faults before they occur, and dynamically modifying resources to increase efficiency. By integrating machine learning with AI, DTs boost network automation, reduce latency, and optimize energy usage, ensuring efficient communication for next generation applications such as self-driving cars, smart cities and automated industrial processes.

The primary materials of a DT in messaging systems include data gathering techniques, based on artificial intel data science, simulation with real-time computations and forecasting maintenance tools. These features enable continuous supervision thus optimizing the network performance. DTs help in the management of network optimization by offering real-time insights on network activity, detecting faults before they break down and dynamically modifying commodities to increase efficiency. By integrating machine learning and AI, DTs boost network automation, minimize process latency and optimize energy usage, ensuring efficient communication for the next generation of applications such as self-driving vehicles, smart cities and manufacturing automation.

– The physical twin refers to the tangible physical components that includes network routers, switches, fiber optic cables and communication towers. The physical twin represents tangible components like routers, switches, and towers, and AI-powered digital twins, enabling perceptive network administration and secure 6G communication.

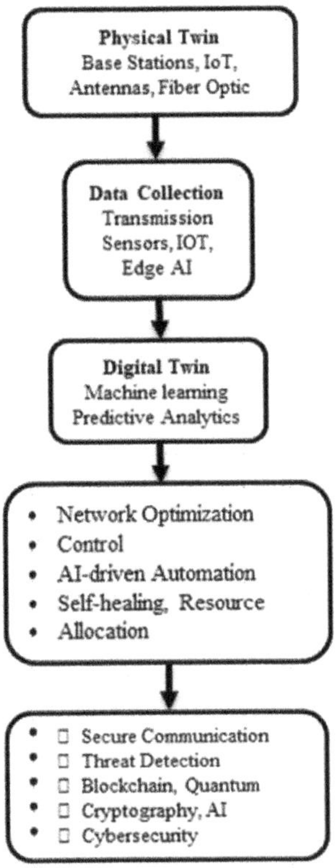

Figure 4.1. *Flowchart of overview and integrating with twins, physical and digital*

4.3. Application of twin technology with AI network security

AI, which is part of machine learning and deep learning, is the most essential part of twin technology as well as network security; these future technologies are advancing to detect and find all of the network threats and are integrated with cybersecurity. The machine learning and deep learning algorithms enable predictive analytics to detect network failure and to identify complex malware attack patterns using neural networks. These AI-driven technologies reduce the need for human intervention and enhance cybersecurity defenses and response measures.

4.4. Network analysis and intelligence of prediction

For the network security, the prediction analysis is carried out using AI technologies to analyze the data related to wireless communication and network security threats. The predictive analysis help identify the future trends and improve threat detection. Models created via machine learning are a significant component of intelligent decision-making systems, which use them to evaluate risks, optimize processes and provide optimal recommendations. Industries such as financial services and medical care in addition to providing chain management benefit considerably from AI, which is the technique of predictive analytics, as it promotes performance improvements, reduced uncertainties and improves planning for strategic success. By continuously learning from fresh and primary data, these systems grow over time, giving increasingly precise comprehension and automating processes of decision-making. AI, integrated with secure 6G communication, is controlled by humans, and provides the best options to create new AI models that are integrated with the new upgraded connection and communication.

4.5. AI 6G communication infrastructure and security constraints

The integration of AI with 6G communication and digital twins, aim to enhance the analysis of security threats. The deployment of 6G will rely on modern network designs such as software-defined networking (SDN), network function virtualization (NFV), and potentially quantum communication, which guarantees efficient usage of network resources and performance optimization. Additionally, 6G is expected to support large scale IoT connectivity and transform emerging sectors including healthcare, intelligent transportation, and smart cities by delivering ultra-reliable, high-capacity wireless communication support. However, the proliferation of interconnected devices and increased data exchange also raise significant concerns related to eavesdropping, audio surveillance, and signal interference. Moreover, the shift toward collaborative construction and computing at the edge increases targets, making it easier for hackers to launch sophisticated online attacks, such as AI viruses and malware, persistent and sophisticated viruses (artificially intelligent devices), and quantum-based hacking. Securing 6G networks will involve proactive threat detection, better encryption technologies and comprehensive cybersecurity frameworks.

As cyberthreats increase, networking networks with 6G connection become more vulnerable to emerging attacks. AI technologies may introduce device-level vulnerabilities that pose threats to network security. The rise of autonomous attacks, where malware adapts and spreads via botnets, presents significant threats to 6G network security. The integration of supply chain systems with distributed networks has increased the security concerns, rendering the traditional safety methods inadequate. To combat these evolving threats, robust measures are required such as the use of connected Ethernet systems, wireless communication frameworks, continuous threat monitoring, automated security mechanisms, and AI-driven anomaly detection. The advanced authentication protocols and optimized user registration processes are needed for a secure future 6G communication.

4.6. Development and implement for AI-twin connectivity

The implementation and integration of AI digital twins into next-generation networks will be driven by advancements in AI, edge computing, and cloud computing technologies. This integration will rely on seamless interface with edge data environments to enhance data security against cyber threats.

The perception layer is the core of the foundation of network transmission. This layer is mainly used for gathering data from sensors and IOT-based devices to collect and receive data using wireless transmission. The edge processing layer functions by analyzing local data through AI-powered models. This minimizes latency and enhances responsiveness. This guarantees that we can make critical decisions in real time without depending solely on cloud infrastructure. The cloud and core AI layer operate like a central engine, delivering significant processing power for comprehensive learning analytics and handling of large-scale data. This layer is tasked with overseeing detailed analysis and facilitating integrated and intelligent decisions; this is alongside the two digital layers, which replicate the elements, devices and infrastructures of the physical network within a virtual setting. By modeling various scenarios, it aids in forecasting outcomes and improving performance. Ultimately, the application layer acts as a bridge between the system and end users, offering real-time monitoring, support for decision-making, and machine and automation capabilities. Collectively, these layers form an efficient intellectual system for managing and analyzing data across multiple disciplines and are mentioned for performance evaluation.

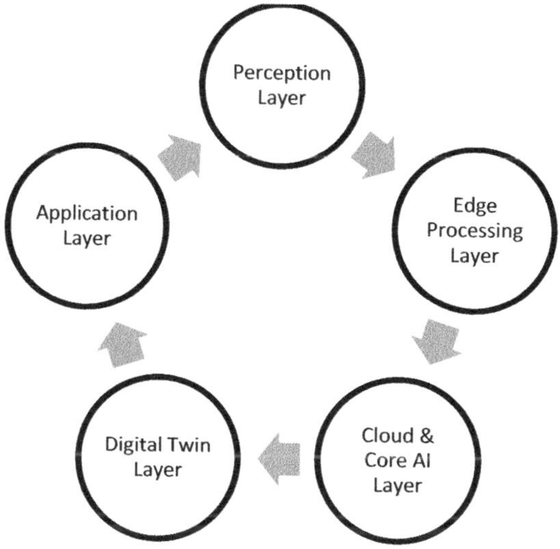

Figure 4.2. *AI integrated and enabled with 6G multi-layered architecture*

The cloud layer is a critical component in the integrated AI architecture, combining cloud computing capabilities with the convergence of AI at the computational layer. It serves as a foundational element for industry stakeholders involved in core AI development, enabling the deployment of virtual replicas of physical network components. Functionally, it aligns with the digital twin layer and operates in coordination with other architectural layers.

Component	Description	Role in AI-twin connectivity
IOT sensors	Collect real-time data from the physical system	Data acquisition
Edge computing	Pre-processes and filters data before cloud upload	Local processing
Cloud platform	Stores, processes and manages AI models	Centralized AI processing
AI twin	Virtual representation of physical entities	Simulation and prediction
User interface	Dashboard, API and control panel for interaction	Visualization and control
Actuators	Respond to AI decisions and execute actions	Feedback and optimization

Table 4.1. *AI integrated with twin technology and connectivity for deployment*

The cloud layer is a critical component in the integrated AI architecture, combining cloud computing capabilities with the convergence of AI at the computational layer. It serves as a foundational element for industry stakeholders involved in core AI development, enabling the deployment of virtual replicas of physical network components. Functionally, it aligns with the digital twin layer and operates in coordination with other architectural layers.

4.7. Security and privacy in the AI 6G technology

Security and privacy are the main concerns in 6G technology, owing to the large volumes of sensitive data it handles. When integrated with AI, it supports numerous real-time applications. Any security lapse or data delay could lead to serious failures, thus making security and privacy a top priority in 6G AI research. One of the key issues is the susceptibility of standard cryptography approaches to quantum computing attacks.

Quantum-safe cryptography is vital to counteract this threat, adopting post-quantum algorithms that defy quantum decryption approaches. Additionally, with the rise of IoT and edge computing in 6G, AI-based anomaly detection becomes a critical protection mechanism.

AI-integrated technologies can continuously monitor network traffic, detect unexpected trends and neutralize cyberattacks in real time, and also cancel all of the network attack ratings, assuring proactive protection. Moreover, blockchain integration plays a critical role in protecting communication over decentralized 6G networks.

The O-GAN controller controls the AI and blockchain's immutable ledger and consensus procedures. 6G provides end-to-end encryption, secure identity management, secure connectivity and tamper-proof data sharing through encrypted transactions.

The combination of these technologies such as quantum-safe cryptography, AI-driven anomaly detection and blockchain security create a solid framework for addressing the growing cyber risks in 6G networks.

In 6G technology, the most important aspect is the post-quantum cryptography to secure and enhance the 6G communication. The emergence of technologies like deepfake and AI-generated malware pose significant security threats to newly upgraded technologies. Data confidentiality and privacy are other security challenges.

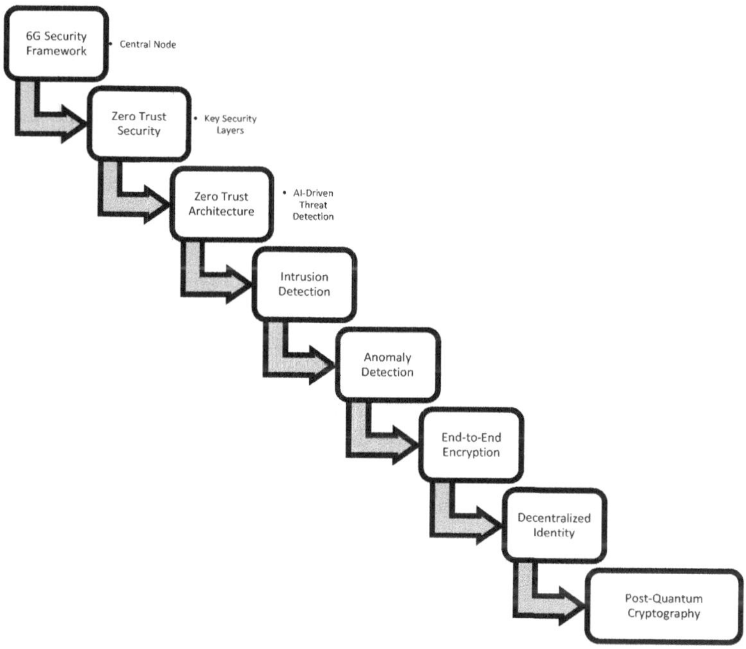

Figure 4.3. *6G network secure architecture*

Figure 4.3 shows the 6G security architecture and framework to secure connection. For the security of next-generation communication systems, the graphic depicts a 6G security architecture. It takes a multi-layered approach. Future-oriented privacy protection is built on top of the 6G cybersecurity. This framework is responsible for guaranteeing secure connections across government and industry sectors. It supports a zero trust security paradigm, which minimizes potential risks by eliminating implicit trust and enforcing rigorous verification of all users, devices, and applications prior to granting access. To further improve security, the architectural profession adds stringent identification confirmation, access controls and ongoing monitoring. AI-driven attack identification uses anomaly identification, which detects unexpected variations from typical behavior to stop cyberattacks, and intrusion detection, which detects unauthorized access attempts, to detect risk factors in continually.

Information security relies on techniques such as encryption particularly end-to-end encryption which ensures data integrity and protects against interception throughout its transmission. Decentralized identity frameworks further strengthen authentication by enabling secure and tamper-resistant identity verification without reliance on a central authority. Post-quantum cryptography which uses digital currencies are designed to be resistant to quantum-based attacks and are becoming essential. These quantum-resistant algorithms are being integrated into modern security frameworks in response to the potential threats posed by advances in quantum computing, which could undermine traditional encryption schemes. In conclusion, by using blockchain, AI and data encryption innovations, this phased security strategy guarantees that the implementation of 6G networks is protected against changing cyberthreats. The architecture creates a strong, future-ready safety apparatus that can resist new threats in the digital world by fusing a zero-trust model based on artificial intel detection, centrally controlled identification and password authentication, while participating in quantum-resistant encryption to protect it.

4.8. Conclusion

A revolutionary method for protecting 6G communication channels is presented by a combination of twin technological innovation and AI. The integration of machine learning-based digital twins enhances security, safety, reliability, and efficiency by enabling real-time network monitoring and predictive analytics. This approach also strengthens the automated detection of potential threats and system anomalies. In addition to improving network performance, this combination makes proactive cyberthreat mitigation possible, guaranteeing robust and flexible 6G systems. With a safety-conscious, intelligent, additionally future-ready wireless connection, an environment will be shaped by the collaboration of AI and twin industries technological advancements as 6G communication advances. Additionally, suited safety processes are made possible based on artificial intel, the automation of tasks, which minimizes people taking part and speeds up response times to possible intrusions. 6G communication becomes more reliable and effective when AI and digital twins are combined to enable deft control of traffic, moving resource allocation and developing our own network's capacity.

4.9. References

Al Ridhawi, I., Otoum, S., Aloqaily, M. (2023). Decentralized zero-trust framework for digital twin-based 6G. *arXiv*. doi: 10.48550/arXiv.2302.03107.

Bennis, M., Debbah, M., Poor, H.V. (2018). Ultra-reliable and low-latency wireless communication: Tail, risk, and scale. *Proceedings of the IEEE*, 106(10), 1834–1853.

Chen, M., Challita, U., Saad, W., Yin, C., Debbah, M. (2019). Artificial neural networks-based machine learning for wireless networks: A tutorial. *IEEE Communications Surveys & Tutorials*, 21(4), 3039–3071.

Chen, S., Liang, Y.-C., Sun, S., Kang, S., Cheng, W., Peng, M. (2020). Vision, requirements, and technology trend of 6G: How to tackle the challenges of system coverage, capacity, user data-rate, and movement speed. *IEEE Wireless Communications*, 27(2), 218–228.

Dang, S., Amin, O., Shihada, B., Alouini, M.-S. (2020). What should 6G be? *Nature Electronics*, 3(1), 20–29.

Di Renzo, M., Zappone, A., Debbah, M., Alouini, M.-S., Yuen, C., de Rosny, J. (2020). Smart radio environments empowered by reconfigurable intelligent surfaces: How it works, state of research, and road ahead. *IEEE Journal on Selected Areas in Communications*, 38(11), 2450–2525.

Elsayed, M. and Erol-Kantarci, M. (2019). AI-enabled future wireless networks: Challenges, opportunities, and open issues. *IEEE Vehicular Technology Magazine*, 14(3), 70–77.

Giordani, M. and Zorzi, M. (2021). Non-terrestrial networks in the 6G era: Challenges and opportunities. *IEEE Network*, 35(2), 244–251.

Huang, C., Zappone, A., Alexandropoulos, G.C., Debbah, M., Yuen, C. (2019). Reconfigurable intelligent surfaces for energy efficiency in wireless communication. *IEEE Transactions on Wireless Communications*, 18(8), 4157–4170.

Jiang, C., Zhang, H., Ren, Y., Han, Z., Chen, K.-C., Hanzo, L. (2017). Machine learning paradigms for next-generation wireless networks. *IEEE Wireless Communications*, 24(2), 98–105.

Letaief, K.B., Chen, W., Shi, Y., Zhang, J., Zhang, Y.-A. (2019). The roadmap to 6G: AI empowered wireless networks. *IEEE Communications Magazine*, 57(8), 84–90.

Liu, Y., Liu, X., Mu, X., Hou, T., Xu, J., Hanzo, L. (2021). Reconfigurable intelligent surfaces: Principles and opportunities. *IEEE Communications Surveys & Tutorials*, 23(3), 1546–1577.

Masaracchia, A., Sharma, V., Canberk, B., Dobre, O.A., Duong, T.Q. (2022). Digital twin for 6G: Taxonomy, research challenges, and the road ahead. *IEEE Open Journal of the Communications Society*, 3, 840–859.

Noman, H.M.F., Hanafi, E., Noordin, K.A., Dimyati, K., Hindia, M.N., Abdrabou, A., Qamar, F. (2023). Machine learning empowered emerging wireless networks in 6G: Recent advancements, challenges and future trends. *IEEE Access*, 11, 83017–83051.

Saad, W., Bennis, M., Chen, M. (2020). A vision of 6G wireless systems: Applications, trends, technologies, and open research problems. *IEEE Network*, 34(3), 134–142.

Samad, A., Saad, W., Nandana, R., Kapseok, C., Steinbach, D., Sliwa, B., Wietfeld, C., Mei, K., Hamid, S., Zepernick, H.J. et al. (2020). White paper on machine learning in 6G wireless communication networks. *6G Research Visions*, 7.

Tataria, H., Shafi, M., Molisch, A.F., Dohler, M., Sjöland, H., Tufvesson, F. (2021). 6G wireless systems: Vision, requirements, challenges, insights, and opportunities. *Proceedings of the IEEE*, 109(7), 1166–1199.

Wu, Q. and Zhang, R. (2020). Towards smart and reconfigurable environment: Intelligent reflecting surface aided wireless network. *IEEE Communications Magazine*, 58(1), 106–112.

Yigit, Y., Chrysoulas, C., Yurdakul, G., Maglaras, L., Canberk, B. (2023). Digital twin-empowered smart attack detection system for 6G edge of things networks. *arXiv*. doi: 10.48550/arXiv.2310.03554.

You, X., Wang, C.X., Huang, J., Gao, X., Zhang, Z., Wang, M., Huang, Y., Zhang, C., Jiang, Y., Wang, J. et al. (2021). Towards 6G wireless communication networks: Vision, enabling technologies, and new paradigm shifts. *Science China Information Sciences*, 64, 1–74.

5

AI-driven Digital Twin Framework for Securing 6G Networks: Overarching Challenges and the Way Forward

The unique combination of digital twin technology and artificial intelligence promises higher reliability and predictive capability through real-time optimization in secure 6G communications. This is a domain that demands ultra-low latency, high-speed data transfer and security. AI digital twin technologies can create virtual replicas of network environments that will include functions such as active threat detection, dynamic resource allocation and anomaly prediction. This integration empowers intelligent decision-making for secure and seamless communication. In turn, blockchain-based digital twin frameworks and AI-fueled intrusion detection systems strengthen cybersecurity in 6G. Critical challenges such as computational complexity, scalability and data privacy can be tackled using federated learning and quantum-safe encryption. This chapter discusses the role of AI and DT in securing 6G networks, while key challenges, possible applications and future research prospects are also being discussed.

5.1. Introduction

Along with speeds beyond imagination, near-to-zero latency and artificial intelligence (AI)-driven automation, 6G networks have already opened the doors for upcoming applications, such as autonomous systems and the Internet of Everything (IoE). On the contrary, this development presents a number of complex security challenges, i.e. on the one hand, cyber threats multiply, and, on the other hand, privacy risks appear for data due to the various decentralized architecture vulnerabilities. Adding to this, the vast possible security measures of existing defenses fail to accommodate the inscrutable and intelligent nature of 6G networks. To put things right, much emphasis is accounted for AI-driven digital twins as

Chapter written by Pasham SOWMYA, T. Monika SINGH and C. Kishor Kumar REDDY.

powerful security solutions. A digital twin is a real-time virtual copy of physical network elements, which means it is capable of performing continuous monitoring, anomaly detection and predictive threat mitigation. Therefore, coupling AI with digital twins gives 6G networks the possibility of cyber threat detection, simulation of attacks and self-enhancement of security mechanisms. Furthermore, this approach achieves proactive cybersecurity through the prediction of vulnerabilities and adaption of real-time threats (Saad et al. 2020). Harnessing machine learning (ML), a blockchain and quantum-resistant encryption, AI-driven digital twins construct an adaptive and resilient defense framework for 6G security. This chapter discusses the potentials, challenges, applications and future trajectories of AI-powdered digital twins towards securing the 6G networks, assuring a communication ecosystem that is trusted and intelligent (Wu et al. 2024).

5.1.1. *Understanding digital twin technology*

In a digital twin, real-time simulation, monitoring and analysis of any physical entity, system or process is complemented with a virtual representation. Such a technique allows companies to replicate physical identities in a digital platform that enhances the ability to make decisions and take actions that fine-tune performance. The digital twin that is now understood has evolved tremendously from being named and first used in manufacturing in 2002 by Dr. Michael Grieves, who later had it popularized in 2010 by NASA's John Vickers (Grieves and Vickers 2017). Improvements in AI, the Internet of Things (IoT) and cloud computing have bolstered the capacities of digital twins over the years. Digital twins are now created in a range of industries, from manufacturing to health, from smart cities to other sectors, for increasing operation efficiency and innovation by delivering predictive information and optimizing performance while seamlessly tying physical and digital assets (Zayed et al. 2023). Considered as a key element in the evolution of cyber-physical systems, digital twinning is becoming popular for the creation of real-time virtual representations of production lines, machines and indeed the entire factory. This is found to be a valuable tool for identifying inefficiencies, failures that might occur and for conducting what-if simulations for performance optimization. The predictive maintenance aided by the digital twin is geared towards that early detection of failure from equipment, which can, in turn, contribute to reduced downtime and higher overall equipment effectiveness (OEE) (Soori et al. 2023). Digital twins would also contribute towards making operations cost-effective, yet robust against disruption, by simulating various logistics scenarios. With the help of AI-driven analytics, digital twin structures further enable autonomous decision-making to diversify productivity and operations agility in Industry 4.0 environments (Tao et al. 2019). In the health sector, such digital twins construct a specific model of a patient's organs and physiological systems and these models will be used to simulate disease progression, treatment response and the optimum surgical procedures for a patient with high precision. For example, mathematical frameworks are developed for liver digital twins that construct replicas of liver function in order to fine-tune disease management strategies in hepatology (Laamarti et al. 2020). They would also relate digital twins to the discovery of new drugs, synthetically producing behavior that would have occurred in human metabolism without relying on animal testing, thus accelerating clinical trial processes. Digital twins are used in medical device engineering to help with design and verification processes for prosthetics, implants and wearable health technologies by modeling real-world performance under variable conditions (Corral-Acero et al. 2020).

5.1.2. *Role of AI in digital twin technology*

AI employs the "digital twin" framework, which captures actual-system real-time data and updates it through predicting such features and intelligent decision-making. Technology uses predictive modeling and intelligence to develop a system called AI digital twins, which use machine-learning (ML)-based systems, "deep-learning" (DL)-based systems and "reinforcement-learning"-based systems to deal with massive amounts of sensor data, analyzing patterns and optimizing the operations within (Boschert and Rosen 2016). While self-adapting, forecasting of failures and improving system performance, AI-powered digital twins significantly improve performance across various industries such as manufacturing, healthcare and smart cities (Bruynseels et al. 2018). Predictive maintenance is one of the most important areas of contribution made by AI into digital twin, where ML models analyze previous data to determine the likely occurrence of failures before they happen, so that there is less downtime and maintenance costs (Glaessgen and Stargel 2012).

Also, AI-based optimizations in industrial systems operate through real-time insights and dynamically change processes (Grieves and Vickers 2017). AI digital twins mimic patient conditions and then allow a doctor to devise more tailored and effective treatment habits around them (Jones et al. 2020). AI digital twins automate decision-making based on simulations, testing what-if scenarios and learning from actual real-time data behavior (Kapteyn et al. 2020). In this case, this becomes very useful in smart cities, revealing how AI-based digital twins use resources in optimizing energy efficiency, traffic throughput and management within the infrastructure of the city (Khajavi et al. 2019). AI has made digital twins not only digital models but intelligent, self-learning systems which lead to efficiencies, savings and innovations across various domains, defining a turning point for industries. AI and digital twin frameworks are transforming the rules of the game by bringing dependency and adaptability and predicting concrete realities to across-the-field applications (Uhlemann et al. 2017).

5.1.3. *Importance of security in 6G networks*

While it is predicted that the 6G networks would revolutionize connectivity, AI integrations and ultra-low-latency communications, new security challenges demand efficient security solutions. Increased levels of data rates, network density and even the infusion of AI and edge computing have made the 6G networks so susceptible to cyber threat, privacy breach and even quantum attacks (Dang et al. 2019). Security on the 6G front is a quintessential technological necessity and the sine qua non trust, reliability and resilience of the next generation of wireless communications. One of the most important issues in 6G security is the threat posed by quantum computing. Quantum computers can break existing algorithms under which traditional methods of encryption cannot, and therefore it is necessary to develop post-quantum cryptography (PQC) to secure our communications (Siriwardhana et al. 2021). As AI will evolve, alongside AI-led cyber threats, the need for AI-trained security solutions, which have the capability of real-time detections for attacks, would also be essential (Nguyen et al. 2021). Another issue is privacy protection in 6G-based smart environments. With billions of connected devices in IoT ecosystems, it becomes imperative that end-to-end encryption, user authentication and sharing of secured data are all put in place (Alhammadi et al. 2024). Technologies such as blockchain-based security frameworks and zero trust architectures are expected to make important contributions in strengthening the mechanisms for identity verification and decentralized security (Hasan et al. 2024). Above all, the applications supported by 6G will be mission-critical such as autonomous vehicles, remote surgeries, industrial automation and many others. Hence, these networks become attractive targets for cyber housebreakers (Pirandola et al. 2020). Such an attack could bring disastrous conditions, making proactive threat detection, security in network slices and AI-based anomaly detection worthwhile (Wang et al. 2020). In this regard, future security becomes important for 6G networks, as they secure data and privacy and keep intact next-generation communication systems. Future security measures will consider the significance of AI, blockchain, post-quantum encryption and zero trust models towards emerging challenges in the cybersecurity domain to create a secure, resilient and trusted 6G ecosystem (Liu et al. 2020).

5.2. Evolution of digital twin technology in telecommunications

5.2.1. *From 4G to 5G: the transition to digital twins*

From 4G to 5G, digital twins underwent a transition from a basic communication enhancement to carrying out ultra-reliable low-latency communication (URLLC), massive machine-type communication (mMTC) and enhanced mobile broadband (eMBB). 4G had barely managed real-time synchronization due to limited bandwidth, but speed coupled with edge computing enables instantaneous data transfer between physical and virtual entities by 5G (Jiang et al. 2021). Such changes are transforming smart manufacturing, self-governing systems and precision healthcare; the possibilities of real-time monitoring and predictive maintenance are now possible (Ismail and Buyya 2022). Furthermore, 5G network slicing guarantees efficient resource provisioning for DT applications, thereby improving system performance as well as reliability. These advancements can be regarded as the consideration for 6G, which, as anticipated, will merge AI-powered automation, communication in the terahertz (THz) band and quantum security in the design of hyper-realistic and intelligent digital twins (Alsabah et al. 2021).

5.2.2. *Key advancements leading to 6G*

As many energy-efficient features are demanding advances in wireless communication, AI and edge computing, all these will lead to a 6G evolution as mentioned in Table 5.1. Furthermore, terahertz frequencies are one of the main innovations, promising broader bandwidth and ultra-low latency, making real-time digital twin simulations and immersive extended reality (XR) applications possible (Yao and Teng 2024). A 6th generation network architecture that is AI native will enable self-optimizing capacities and autonomous decision-making for achieving energy efficiencies and security (Haque et al. 2024). Also, new dimensions of security will be offered by blockchain-based security frameworks, enabling further integrity and privacy in data protection and resolving cyberspace security issues in hyper-connectivity (Hasan et al. 2024). By revolutionary mechanisms of quantum communication and computing, encryption will significantly change towards making 6G networks more resilient to cyberattacks. These advances will, therefore, support the independent integration of AI, IoT and digital twins, creating intelligent, ultra-reliable and sustainable networks.

Feature	4G	5G	6G
Network speed	Mbps	Gbps	Tbps
Digital twin integration	Limited	Emerging	Fully integrated
AI utilization	Basic	Moderate	Advanced (autonomous)
Security approach	Perimeter-based	Hybrid	AI-driven zero trust
Real time monitoring	No	Partial	Full real time simulation

Table 5.1. *A comparative study of digital twin evolution in telecommunications*

Table 5.1 presents the various milestones in the journey from 4G to 6G, portraying AI, IoT and digital twins as the fulcrum of modern-day telecommunication.

5.2.3. *Convergence of AI, IoT and digital twins*

The convergence of AI, the IoT and digital twins is causing a major revolution in smart industries, healthcare and autonomous systems. IoT devices generate large amounts of real-time data from physical assets that AI-driven digital twins can analyze to provide predictive insights, automated decision capabilities and operational enhancements (Awouda et al. 2024). AI also brings in adoption by means of self-learning, anomaly detection and an increase in performance forecasting using digital twin models (Syed et al. 2024). Most significant are the techniques that relate to edge computing in such a merger, bringing low-latency data management by maximizing data independence from the cloud infrastructures involved (Huang et al. 2021). This unique interaction sets the stage for autonomous industrial systems, precision healthcare and smart city optimizations, developing ecosystems that are resilient, adaptive and intelligent. Enabled with further advancements in the 6G networks, AI-powered digital twins will therefore deliver real-time decision-making and automation at an unprecedented level across the multiple domains.

5.3. Architectural foundations of AI-driven digital twins

5.3.1. *Components of a digital twin framework*

Three main segments characterizing a digital twin framework include a physical entity, a virtual model and a data communication system (Qi and Tao 2018). The first physical entity comprises the actual object that is being monitored, exemplified in this case by an industrial machine, an urban infrastructure or a human body for healthcare applications. The virtual model is the digital representation that correlates the form, behavior and performance of the physical entity. This digital doppelganger is fueled by advanced AI, machine-learning and IoT technologies and props predictive analytics and decision-making (Mylonas et al. 2021). The data communication system ensures that both physical and digital twins can simultaneously monitor and control for performance behavior representations. 5G and edge computing, together with cloud-based architectures, propels seamless real-time data exchange between these segments (Rasheed et al. 2020). Real-time, predictive maintenance, and intelligent automation stand to enhance performance optimization across industries, including but not limited to manufacturing, smart cities and healthcare (Jones et al. 2020).

5.3.2. *Integration of AI, ML and big data analytics*

The AI, ML and big data analytics empower digital twin frameworks to become even more intelligent (see Figure 5.1). AI and ML provide for self-learning mechanisms that are continuously being improved through large query runs with real-time data, enhancing predictive accuracy and improving the general decision-making processes (Hu et al. 2024), whereas operational data pattern identification – anomaly detection – and trend recognition relying on ML algorithms allow industries such as manufacturing, healthcare and smart cities to prepare for maintenance, optimize three resources and enhance performance (Lu et al. 2019). Big data analytics ensures that data processing, storage and retrieval happens in real time, which is a vital aspect for large-scale digital twin operations. The coexistence of AI-based analytics and edge computing enables an improved response time with low latencies and a sufficient level of trust to support autonomous decision-making (Javaid et al. 2023). Hence, a successful implementation of this integration parameter is most relevant for the emerging era of industrial automation, where predictive insights are key to efficiency, sustainability and resilience in ever-more-complex systems.

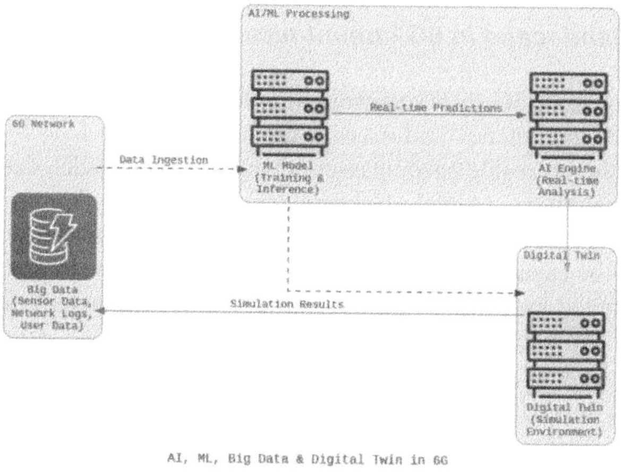

Figure 5.1. *AI, big data and digital twin in 6G*

5.3.3. *Real-time data processing and predictive modeling*

Essential for digital twins, real-time data processing endows analysis to vast data streams being acquired from IoT devices, sensors and industrial systems instantaneously. Digital twins analyze incoming data using advanced computing architectures such as edge computing and cloud integration, thus reducing latencies and guaranteeing sufficiently quick decisions in return (Rasheed et al. 2020). This applies to fields such as manufacturing, healthcare and smart cities, where real-time insights facilitate efficiency and safety. ML and AI systems use predictive models for various digital twin applications as early indications of changes in performance and system failures before they occur. The models are trained to recognize patterns by using both historical and real-time data to trigger timely maintenance and optimize performance for the systems concerned (Tao et al. 2018). So, for example, predictive analytics can predict failure in industrial equipment, which can help limit downtime and maintenance costs. Digital twins also create further possibilities for "what-if" scenario analyses through real-time simulation capabilities, providing industries with the opportunity to assess multiple approaches and responses to potential disruptions. Such interfaces are quite useful in supply chain management by considerable degrees in mitigating risks towards operational resilience (Song et al. 2023). Notwithstanding, to realize higher efficacy in real-time processing and predictive analytics, the challenges of computational resources, data security threats and model accuracy need to be addressed.

5.4. Security challenges in 6G networks

5.4.1. *Threat landscape in 6G communication systems*

Transitioning from 5G to 6G networks implies enhanced reliance on AI-driven automation, ultra-low latency and massive connectivity with IoT. In 6G, the entire arena in which threats reside encompasses advanced cyberattacks, data breaches and network vulnerabilities (Abdel Hakeem et al. 2022). As a result of the implementation of the decentralized frameworks and edge computing into 6G, attackers would be capable of deploying APTs and DOS attacks by exploiting weak points in distributed systems. It has become a victim of attack surface expansions because of the growing number of IoT devices and sensors; everywhere in the passage for an easy attack by cybercriminals, IoT devices lacking strong security mechanisms are there just to infiltrate the network and compromise sensitive data (Kazmi et al. 2023). All these pronounced threats include an AI-driven cyberattacking capacity by adversarial ML, whereby the network models are manipulated by injected malicious data leading to misclassification, thus resulting in system failures. Another varying threat that mainly arises is that of quantum computing, whose advent will render traditional encryption obsolete; consequently, this will make the present cryptographic techniques vulnerable (Abura 2024). There is an urgent need for the upcoming quantum-safe cryptographic algorithms complemented by AI-induced threat detection mechanisms, and versatile security solutions that could adapt towards evolved threats. Their rectification mandates worldwide cooperation and regulatory advancement alongside a never-ending upgrading of security technologies under the 6G ecosystem.

5.4.2. *Cybersecurity risks and vulnerabilities*

The evolution towards 6G networking technology essentially has ultra-low latency, massive machine-type communications and AI-driven automation for its advanced capabilities. Yet, this techno-advancement brings in cybersecurity threats and vulnerabilities that greatly affect networks. 6G threats include an attack surface enhanced due to an upsurge of IoT devices, edge computing and a decentralized network architecture as discussed in Table 5.2 (Abdel Hakeem et al. 2022) (see Figure 5.2 for an overview of the 6G security threat model). 6G relies not as traditional networks on centralized intelligence but rather on distributed intelligence to make itself possible to a different mode of cyber threat, typically including but not limited to adversarial AI attacks, distributed denial-of-service (DDoS) attacks and deepfake-based identity fraud. One of the key subjects regarding the security of 6G involves the susceptibility of AI-driven network management. The AI and ML models used in real-time threat detection as well as traffic optimization can also be misled by adversarial ML techniques that can inject false data into the learned behavior of a model (Kazmi et al. 2023). Furthermore, quantum computing poses a real threat because it can break through existing encryption standards and make all traditional security protocols ineffective (Haque et al. 2024). Supply chain vulnerabilities in the hardware and software components in 6G can create backdoors, potential malware injections and espionage threats. Thus, advanced persistent threats (APTs) could be trapped and turn critical infrastructure into target areas. Solutions will need to implement post-quantum cryptographic algorithms, AI-powered anomaly detection and multi-layered security frameworks that dynamically adapt to new threats.

Threat type	Description	Potential impact
Cyberattacks	Unauthorized network intrusion	Data breaches, service disruption
AI exploitation	Adversarial attacks on AI models	Model manipulation, biased decisions
Data privacy risks	Insecure data handling	Identity theft, regulatory non-compliance
Quantum computing threats	Breaking cryptographic security	Need for post-quantum cryptography

Table 5.2. *Security threats in 6G networks and their impacts*

Table 5.2 provides a summary of important cybersecurity threats: data breaches, AI-driven attacks, and privacy-related concerns, as well as their impact on digital twin security.

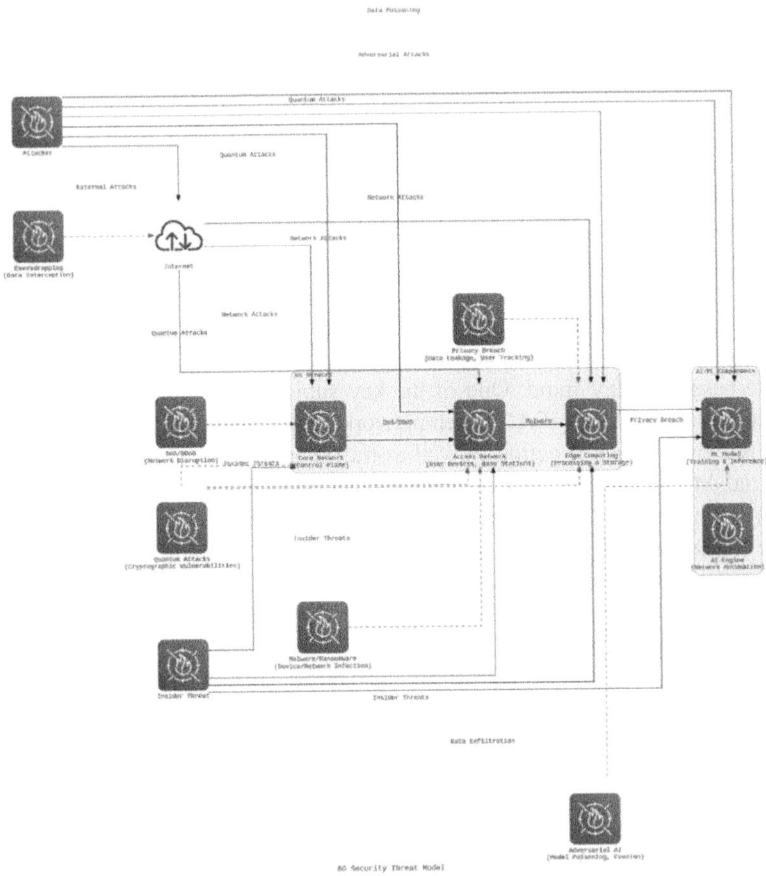

Figure 5.2. *6G security threat model*

5.4.3. *Privacy and data protection concerns*

Hailed to be the one setting up new dimensions for connectivity, speed and AI automation, the prospects of 6G accommodate some serious privacy and data protection concerns. 6G will involve billions of IoT devices, control systems and AI-enhanced edge computing, which potentially means real-time processing of sensitive personal and corporate data in huge volumes. Such massive data collection, with high potentiality of privacy violations, poses a tremendous opportunity for unauthorized access and data manipulation (Shahriar et al. 2023). With data processing capabilities residing on the edge, a decentralized scheme of 6G raises another main concern: latency results favoring easier interception for illicit cyberactivity. Enforcing strict access control and encryption mechanisms is, therefore, a contentious issue (Jin et al. 2022). Furthermore, the rise of AI-based decision-making was thought to promote ethical concerns regarding 6G with respect to data ownership, consent management and algorithmic bias, as automated systems are capable of processing data with user consent being clearly bypassed. Another pressing subject is compliance with the local and international data protection laws that are currently being set up, such as the general data protection regulation (GDPR) and emergent new laws on AI governance. Most importantly, by embracing such laws, 6G networks will find themselves working in trans-border fashions with different national or regional frameworks for data security, making it a major headache to standardize with functional security from an international framework. In this context, integrating privacy-enhancing technologies (PETs) such as homomorphic encryption, differential privacy and federated learning into the security architecture within the 6G system will adequately address the highlighted challenges (Gill et al. 2022). These suggested technologies permit secure data processing under minimal exposure to probable breaches.

5.5. Role of AI in securing 6G networks

5.5.1. *AI-based threat detection and mitigation*

Integrating AI in frameworks created to secure 6G networks becomes an instrument of real-time deterrence and combating cyberthreats. AI-driven security frameworks can look at tons of network data for anomaly detection and respond proactively to possible attacks. While rule-based security models are concerned with definition-based detection, AI models rely on adaptive learning methodologies to ascertain new cyberthreats, hence fewer false positives and better detection (Salem et al. 2024). AI-enabled security solutions are intrusion detection systems (IDS), AI-boosted firewalls and autonomous response mechanisms reacting to threats before they can cause considerable damage. AI systems, apart from these types, also change and upgrade the security scheme in real time by threat intelligence, keeping users safe from sophisticated cyberattacks (Alhammadi et al. 2024)

5.5.2. *Anomaly detection using machine learning*

In terms of anomaly detection in 6G networks, ML constitutes the key building block. ML models are trained on large datasets in order to detect normal and abnormal network behaviors for the identification of threats in real time (see Figure 5.3 for an illustration of ML-based anomaly detection in 6G). Zero-day attacks, insider threats and distributed denial-of-service (DDoS) attack detection involve supervised, unsupervised and reinforcement learning techniques (see Table 5.3

for an overview of ML techniques used in anomaly detection for 6G networks) (Schummer et al. 2024). High-level ML techniques such as deep learning and ensemble models improve detection accuracy and offer adaptive learning based on network traffic patterns. Thus, 6G networks can adopt AI-enabled anomaly detection to improve security without being hampered by static and pre-defined rules, thus further adapting and reinforcing defense systems against any possible attack (Bhavsar et al. 2023).

AI technique	Application in security	Example use case
Machine learning	Anomaly detection	Identifying unusual traffic patterns
Deep learning	Intrusion detection	Recognizing sophisticated attacks
Federated learning	Decentralized security model	Training security models across nodes
Reinforcement learning	Adaptive security policies	Automated threat response

Table 5.3. *AI techniques to secure 6G networks*

Table 5.3 names AI-based security methods that include anomaly detection, predictive threat modeling and blockchain for security in digital twin environments.

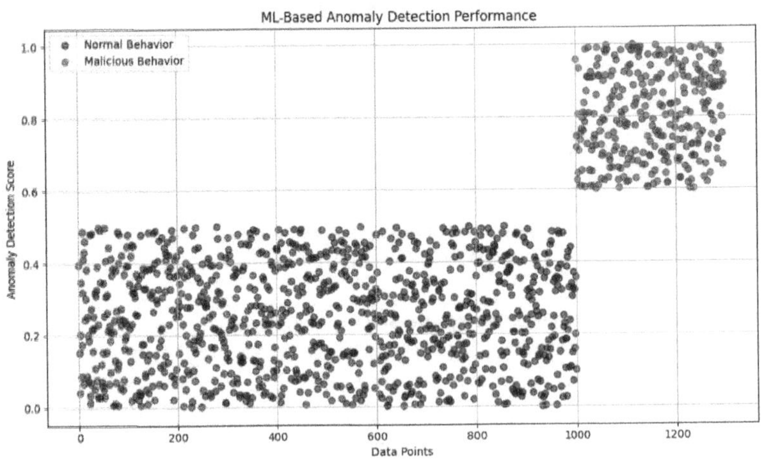

Figure 5.3. *ML-based anomaly detection framework in 6G networks*

5.5.3. *Predictive security models for proactive defense*

Predictive security models in 6G networks use AI and ML in predicting possible threats due to probable cyber incidents. This estimation uses patterns of historical attack events, behavioral states of users and vulnerabilities of the system to assess the potential risks, thereby allowing for the anticipatory mitigation of threats (Kaur et al. 2023). In security, prediction abilities will enable defense to move from being reactive to anticipating threats, with automated threat modeling and vulnerability assessments and dynamically adjusting security policies. Further, AI-facilitated analysis of risk metrics will increase network resilience by prioritizing high-risk areas for the optimum allocation of security resources. This proactive strategy will not only diminish the probability of successful cyberattack occurrences but also guarantee continued mitigation of threats within the highly intricate 6G environment (Homaei et al. 2024).

5.6. Digital twin framework for 6G security

5.6.1. *Real-time network monitoring and simulation*

This is real-time monitoring and simulation in a 6G network that uses AI for analytics to reveal any possible aberrations concerning the network status optimization and prevention of cyberthreats. The synergetic efficacy that is displayed by these innovations in terms of performance has a new need as 6G communication systems get more complicated. Traditional monitoring tools are not sufficient to handle large-scale, high-speed data traffic. Intelligent traffic analysis via AI and ML models captures irregularities and possible security threats in real time (Collins et al. 2021). These digital twins simulate the different attack scenarios and, subsequently, predict the state of the network under different conditions (Al-Shareeda et al. 2024). Therefore, these simulations allow the operators to anticipate-associated vulnerabilities and their exploitation. On top of that, real-time monitoring solutions make networks resilient through automatic alerts, optimization of incident response mechanisms and adaptive policy enforcement to mitigate security risks (Mao et al. 2023).

5.6.2. *AI-powered attack prevention and response*

AI systems aimed at preventing attacks are designed to improve cybersecurity by recognizing, predicting and either preventing or mitigating threats before they ever impact network service (see Figure 5.4). The AI models analyzing network traffic, devices' behaviors and past attack-patterns define the ever-emerging landscape of threats (Cremer et al. 2022). The systems could, for example, identify deep learning campaigns advanced cyberattacks such as zero-day attacks/APTs. Response could include automated options such as AI-based IPS (intrusion prevention systems) which instead would mitigate real-time threats without human intervention (Uysal et al. 2022). Additionally, AI-powered cybersecurity frameworks intervene immediately in the incident response efforts to provide their rapid containment and restoration strategies in order to limit damage and maintain network operation during mitigation of any disruptive occurrence (Muneer et al. 2024).

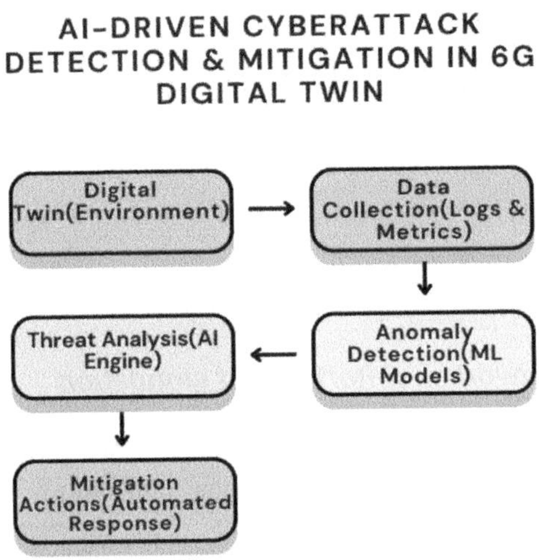

Figure 5.4. *AI-driven cyberattack prevention and response framework*

5.6.3. *Adaptive security policies and autonomous decision-making*

The continuous evolution of 6G networks and their demand for adaptive security policies are such that they have to vary in real time because of changing attack scenarios. Security through AI helps achieve this autonomous decision-making by always monitoring the controllable and relevant risk parameters so that every modification of security policies happens automatically (Sandeepa et al. 2025). Attached to these adaptive policies are AI algorithms that manage access control, policy violation detection and encryption protocol reconfiguration to guarantee secure communications. Additionally, AI decision-making systems make cybersecurity defense even stronger with judicious prioritization of high-level threats while they maximize the potential efficient deployment of resources for defense of the network (Luo et al. 2021). Autonomy in security management significantly reduces human intervention, redundancies in security operations and thus results in a substantial increment in robustness of the 6G systems against cyber threats.

5.7. Ethical and privacy considerations

5.7.1. *Ethical use of AI in 6G security*

AI must be used ethically and responsibly for generating 6G security because it plays an essential role in any system. Privacy, surveillance and decision-making transparency are among the concerns and other issues raised by AI participation in cybersecurity. The ethical use of AI emphasizes explainability as an important issue for security because it helps audit and justify the AI-driven decisions related to security (Jobin et al. 2019). Fairness in AI models is also important to prevent discriminatory security policies that would adversely affect some user categories (Chen et al. 2023). Researchers recommend that the ethical aspects of AI inclusion should feature security policies – in which ways, AI would fall under regulatory requirements as well as the protection of user trust and data (González et al. 2024).

5.7.2. *Addressing bias, transparency and accountability*

AI-based security models can unintentionally carry forward some of the biases in training data or classification rules into unfair or inaccurate threat detection. Thus, bias in AI could result in misclassification of what really happens on the network, leading to varied false positives and negatives by cybersecurity systems (Malatji and Tolah 2024). Making transparent AI-driven security models is a prerequisite for their reliability and effectiveness (see Table 5.4 for key challenges and solutions in AI bias and explainability for 6G security). Explainable artificial intelligence (XAI) techniques help interpret the decisions made by AI so that we can understand how different threats to security are classified and tackled (Ali et al. 2023). This needs to be complemented by accountability measures for AI systems and their developers in case there are security breaches or improper evaluation of threats. Regulatory frameworks such as compliance policies and AI ethics guidelines are critical for ensuring that responsible use of AI technology occurs in 6G (Goodman and Trehu 2023).

Ethical concern	Challenge	Proposed solution
AI bias	Unfair decision-making	Regular bias audits, diverse datasets
Transparency	Black-box AI models	Explainable AI frameworks
Data privacy	Unauthorized access to personal data	Privacy-preserving AI, homomorphic encryption
Accountability	Who is responsible for AI decisions?	Policy enforcement, human oversight

Table 5.4. *Ethical and privacy implications of AI in 6G security*

Table 5.4 discusses issues such as AI ethics, data privacy, bias and transparency, coupled with measures to ensure responsible deployment of AI in 6G security.

5.7.3. *Privacy-preserving AI models*

However, in moving towards AI-enabled cybersecurity solutions, the detection of malicious attacks in user privacy needs to be handled. Similar marriage-preserving AI models such as federated learning and homomorphic encryption enhance the ability to examine data covertly and cross without opening secure collection of user-sensitive data (Sébert et al. 2023). With both techniques, it typically becomes possible for an AI model to learn from decentralized datasets without breaching specific data protection rules, such as those from GDPR (Aziz et al. 2023). The methods add further security features of differential privacy into noisy datasets, disallowing the identification of individual users while preserving analytical accuracy (Ye et al. 2023). With 6G networks encompassing volumes of personal data-trading, these privacy-centric AI solutions remain necessary for the future within stronger walls of cybersecurity but keeping user secrets.

5.8. Potential benefits of AI-driven digital twins in 6G

5.8.1. *Enhanced network performance and reliability*

6G is all about providing ultra-high reliability and high data rate connectivity with extremely low latency to applications that will spring up in the future, such as autonomous systems, smart cities and extended reality systems. Complex AI automates resource-allocation operations, where the resources – such as bandwidth and power – are dynamically adjusted in near real time, driven purely by demand (Zhang and Zhu 2020). “Continuous predictive maintenance through digital twins will monitor the network health and prevent incipient failures that affect performance” (Lin et al. 2023). Self-optimizing features of 6G networks improve reliability through the detection of anomalies and reconfiguration in such a way as to maintain quality of service – such enhancements will enable reliable services to critical applications even in cases of disturbance affecting the 6G network (Chataut et al. 2024).

5.8.2. *Proactive threat prevention and mitigation*

Parting with the traditional security model, which tends to react to intrusion after its occurrence, 6G goes beyond to adopt a proactive security posture. The algorithms of AI and ML analyze large datasets in real time to deter potential attack patterns and vulnerabilities even before actual intrusion (Siriwardhana et al. 2021). With respect to security threat assessment and anomalous behavior detection, the networks are able to change their posture under decentralized control to meet the ever-changing requirements of cyber threats. Automated security orchestration reinforces this posture through the application of security patches, firewall rule changes and access-control updates (Porambage et al. 2023). In effect, this proactive approach immensely diminishes the likelihood of any major data breach and service interruption, thus allowing for a secure and resilient networking environment.

5.8.3. *Cost reduction and operational efficiency*

AI automation in 6G networks simplifies operations and reduces the costs involved in the management of the network, as well as the execution of actions for network cybersecurity. Predictive analytics allow power usage to be dynamically adjusted and therefore optimize the energy consumed, thus resulting in a lowered cost of operation (Mahmoud et al. 2021). Other than this, the self-healing networks further reduce costs by maintenance because they can automatically detect performance problems and resolve them without human intervention. Besides the savings from automated security systems, there will be reduced human resource interventions and so a reduction in the costs of hiring and training such professionals (Rajoria and Mishra 2022). Essentially, 6G networks will be substantially efficient as we could expect them to be economically viable and scalable approaches for continuous growth towards next-generation digital ecosystems.

5.9. Challenges and risks in implementing AI-driven digital twins

5.9.1. *Computational and resource constraints*

The emergence of 6G networks has brought forth an opportunity to develop unprecedented computation and resource demand on the backbone of their AI automation, real-time analytics and big data processing requirements (You et al. 2025). The integration of AI, IoT and digital twins needs powerful computing infrastructures able to operate at scale within the limits of minimal latency. They also come with considerable challenges unique to their deployment, especially in an edge computing environment with limited processing power. While cloud computing can eliminate some workload, the weight of remote storage in the form of remote servers that incur delays is contrary to the concept of ultra-low latency of 6G. Energy consumption is another key issue. AI and ML models for predictive analytics and automation of 6G become very computation-intensive, leading to greater power usage (Zhang et al. 2021). Thus, they build sustainability challenges as increased energy consumption may affect the environment and increase operational costs. Balancing performance with sustainability calls for optimizing energy-efficient hardware and software solutions such as neuromorphic computing and AI-based resource management. Hardware limitations are also critical for restricting computation capabilities. More advanced processors, high-speed memory and specialized AI accelerators have yet to pose the problem. These limitations can be overcome by developing new solutions and incorporating quantum computing, edge AI and intelligent workload distribution into future architectures of the continents' 6G rollout. With the help of these solutions, it will be possible to advance an intelligent architectured approach to the global management of the computational load, energy efficiency and seamless operations of the entire network.

5.9.2. *Data integrity and reliability issues*

Protecting data integrity and reliability becomes a serious business for 6G networks to support mission-critical applications such as autonomy systems, remote surgery and smart infrastructure (Shahen Shah et al. 2023). In contrast to traditional networks, 6G will be a massive real-time carriage – a highly dynamic distributed environment – all of which are onboard a domain, thus leading to disastrous consequences from any corruption, loss or unauthorized alteration of data information, especially during AI-driven decision-making processes. Real-time data verification stands out among the various challenges. The emerging 6G networks will rely extensively on AI and big data analytics; therefore, the integrity and accuracy of data for training and decision-making should not be compromised. Blockchain-based secure ledgers are suggested to guarantee data integrity by creating decentralized tamper-proof records (Liu et al. 2024).

However, such solutions have several hurdles of their own, including computational overheads and storage limitations for large-scale implementation of blockchains. Another level of inconsistency would be triggered by what could be defined as multi-source data fusion. The 6G data aggregation comes from diverse IoT sources, combined with digital twins, simulation and AI models, which may eventually lead to inconsistencies in decision-making. Inputting inaccurate or unreliable data can degrade the performance of networks, resulting in vulnerabilities to security breaches. These issues will then fall under the response of developing a robust end-to-end encryption protocol with advanced error detection systems and redundant data storage frameworks. AI anomaly detection systems would also point out and correct the discrepancies in real time so that reliable data would continuously flow through the entire network (Maalem et al. 2024).

5.9.3. *Regulatory and compliance barriers*

This global 6G rollout imposes enormous regulatory and compliance challenges, particularly with respect to safety, privacy and ethical AI use. For the earlier generations, the law might be taken in a generalized way. However, 6G will essentially operate in an interconnected AI-driven digital ecosystem; hence, the broad-spectrum establishment of a regulatory framework ensuring data protection and transparency of systems is imperative (Navaie 2024). Data sovereignty stands tall as one of the foremost challenges. Since each country has its own data protection laws, driving a uniform standard for compliance becomes a real challenge. The EU's GDPR lays stringent data privacy requirements, while other areas may be more lenient, to complicate matters for multinational companies navigating different jurisdictions with the 6G (Rifa-Pous et al. 2024). Who holds accountability and transparency in the case of AI-driven decision-making? AI algorithms will be useful in network optimization, security and management of user data. Algorithmic bias and unintended consequences are crucial considerations. The regulatory framework must pinpoint who takes the blame and that AI-based decision-making be understandable, auditable and just. Legal liability is invoked in the event of security breaches or cyberattacks against 6G networks. Given the presence of AI in cybersecurity and real-time network responses, this opens ambiguity on who is to carry the can during a failure. Organizations must apply innovation in privacy protection while addressing timely challenges of ever-changing compliance requirements (Cheong 2024). To keep technology evolution on course, international cooperation among states, companies and researchers is a condition for reaching security standards to solve those problems.

5.10. Future directions and innovations

5.10.1. *Emerging trends in digital twin security for 6G*

Digital twins (DTs) have become an essential piece in the 6G networks' realities, providing capabilities for real-time simulations, predictive analytics and guided decisions. However, as these virtual representatives mirror physical counterparts, they usher in a new array of security challenges, which need to be addressed to deter the threats of cyberspace infiltration, unauthorized access and data manipulation (Ridhawi et al. 2023). In relation to the 6G digital twin security trends, blockchain-based trust management is among the predominant ones, which helps in ensuring data integrity and preventing tampering by keeping an immutable record of the transactions. The other emerging trend is the implementation of zero-trust security models in digital twin environments (see Table 5.5 for an overview of key security trends in 6G digital twins). This model radically differs from any traditional security architecture that assumes trust within its perimeter, by continuously enforcing authentication and verification of any and all entities that interact with the digital twin construct, thereby greatly minimizing any risk of unauthorized access (Sedjelmaci and Ansari 2024). Besides, AI-based anomaly detection tools are integrated for real-time DT monitoring and detection of deviation from normal behavior, enabling response to threats before they escalate. Additionally, there is research into enabling homomorphic encryption to keep digitally twin-secure data exchanges private. With this method, computations are possible on the cipher-text objects that have never been decrypted, making sure that all sensitive information is secure even in a cloud-based environment (Ye et al. 2023). Thus, ensuring that security for digital twins will be at the center stage as the 6G networks mature.

Trend	Description	Expected benefits
AI-driven autonomous defense	Self-adaptive security models	Faster threat response, reduced manual intervention
Blockchain for security	Tamper-proof records of transactions	Improved trust and integrity
Quantum-resistant encryption	Protection against quantum attacks	Long-term security assurance
Edge AI security	AI processing closer to devices	Reduced latency, real-time anomaly detection

Table 5.5. *Future trends in AI-driven 6G digital twin security*

Table 5.5 foresees major advancements, such as AI-based autonomous response, homomorphic encryption and global policy frameworks for 6G security.

5.10.2. *AI-enhanced autonomous network defense mechanisms*

The increasing complexity of cyber threats in 6G networks has brought an evolution of strategies for cybersecurity, thus enhancing AI-powered autonomous defense mechanisms (see Figure 5.5) (Sandeepa et al. 2025). Autonomous security AI systems serve as anti-cyber threat mechanisms that proactively monitor and mitigate cyber threats in real time, as opposed to the traditional reactive security models. The deep learning and ML capabilities have been used to process all kinds of network data in the scales of many terabytes and to develop a pattern of attack signatures on them without human interference (Siriwardhana et al. 2021). The self-healing networks are probably the most prominent innovation in AI-improved defense, in which AI security paradigms learn with the attack continuously and change security policies to prevent equivalent intrusions in the future. This involves the ability to initiate an automatic threat response mechanism, capable of isolating affected parts of the network, rerouting traffic and applying security patches instantaneously. With federated learning, we are moving towards training excellent AI security models without having to centralize sensitive data. Through the federated learning, several devices and nodes on a network can jointly learn threat patterns while keeping their data private, increasing security across decentralized 6G infrastructures (Kaur et al. 2024). The other major area is predictive cyber threat intelligence; AI learns from previous incidents and, based on the evolution of the threat landscape, predicts future likely attacks before they occur. This ensures that the proactive approach provides better resilience to 6G networks against high-sharing cyberattacks, with a reduced period of downtime and collateral damage. As cyber threats continue to evolve, AI-enhanced autonomous network defense will underpin the resilient and adaptive security postures in 6G ecosystems.

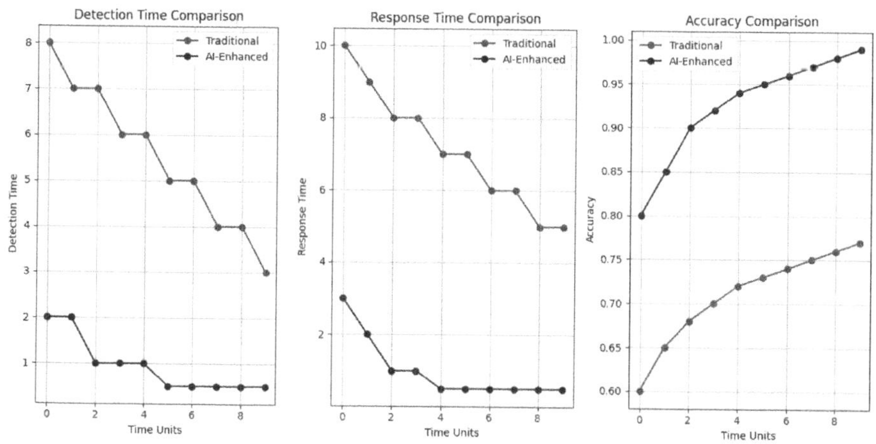

Figure 5.5. *AI-enhanced autonomous network defense in 6G ecosystems*

5.10.3. *Policy recommendations and global collaboration*

Such a communication is always accompanied by the regulation and the missing policy issue that goes along with the development of 6G networks. In this context, international cooperation will be required to create a framework for security standards, policy for privacy and AI deployment that is ethical. The 6G communication system is global, so there should be a cooperation approach of different countries to devise unified cybersecurity standards, policies on data protection and governance frameworks for AI. Therefore, harmonizing the data privacy regulations across diverse jurisdictions is a significant policy proposition.

There are several data privacy laws present across various topographies, for example, the CCPA law in California and the GDPR in Europe. The standardization of such laws is an important guarantee for compliance among the different branches of an international organization deploying 6G technologies while guaranteeing user data against misuse. Another equally important recommendation is to create transparency and accountability in AI use in 6G networks. This is because AI is implicated in security, automation and network intelligence functionalities. Therefore, policymakers must ensure clear AI processes that are free from bias and subject to audits. Research and development for ethical AI must be set up together with public–private collaboration in innovation given the many security segments involved. Governments, academia and the technology industry must also work together to fund research in 6G security, cybersecurity best practices and development of a globally recognized compliance framework. Their pooling of resources and harmonization of activities will therefore lead towards global collaborative strategies, building a secure, efficient and inclusive environment for 6G.

5.11. References

Abdel Hakeem, S.A., Hussein, H.H., Kim, H. (2022). Security requirements and challenges of 6G technologies and applications. *Sensors*, 22(5), 1969. doi: 10.3390/s22051969.

Abura, S. (2024). Quantum computing and wireless networks security: A survey. *GSC Advanced Research and Reviews*, 20, 199–230. doi: 10.30574/gscarr.2024.20.2.0308.

Al-Shareeda, S., Huseynov, K., Cakir, L.V., Thomson, C., Ozdem, M., Canberk, B. (2024). AI-based traffic analysis in digital twin networks. In *Digital Twins for 6G*. Ahmadi, H., Duong, T.Q., Nag, A., Sharma, V., Canberk, B., Dobre, O.A. (eds). The Institution of Engineering and Technology, London. doi: 10.1049/PBTE109E_ch4.

Alhammadi, A., Shayea, I., El-Saleh, A.A., Azmi, M.H., Ismail, Z.H., Kouhalvandi, L., Saad, S.A. (2024). Artificial intelligence in 6G wireless networks: Opportunities, applications, and challenges. *International Journal of Intelligent Systems*, 8845070. doi: 10.1155/2024/8845070.

Ali, S., Abuhmed, T., El-Sappagh, S., Muhammad, K., Alonso-Moral, J.M., Confalonieri, R., Guidotti, R., Del Ser, J., Díaz-Rodríguez, N., Herrera, F. (2023). Explainable artificial intelligence (XAI): What we know and what is left to attain Trustworthy Artificial Intelligence. *Information Fusion*, 99, C. doi: 10.1016/j.inffus.2023.101805.

Alsabah, M., Naser, M., Mahmmod, B., Abdulhussain, S.H., Eissa, M., Al-Baidhani, A., Noordin, N., Sait, S., Alutaibi, K., Hashim, F. (2021). 6G wireless communications networks: A comprehensive survey. *IEEE Access*, 9. doi: 10.1109/ACCESS.2021.3124812.

Annas, A.H., Zainuddin, A.A., Ramlee, A.W., Ya Omar, A.S., Md Saifuddin, M.H.F., Sidik, N.F.I., Sapuan, M.S., Amerolazuam, A.Q., Nizam, M.H.Z.H., Mazlan, F. et al. (2024). Analysis of 6G-network and blockchain-network application security: Future research prospect. *International Journal on Perceptive and Cognitive Computing*, 10(2), 31–50. doi: 10.31436/ijpcc.v10i2.478.

Awouda, A., Traini, E., Bruno, G., Chiabert, P. (2024). IoT-based framework for digital twins in the industry 5.0 era. *Sensors*, 24(2), 594. doi: 10.3390/s24020594.

Aziz, R., Banerjee, S., Bouzefrane, S., Le Vinh, T. (2023). Exploring homomorphic encryption and differential privacy techniques towards secure federated learning paradigm. *Future Internet*, 15(9), 310. doi: 10.3390/fi15090310.

Bhavsar, M., Roy, K., Kelly, J., Odeyomi, O. (2023). Anomaly-based intrusion detection system for IoT application. *Discover Internet of Things*, 3. doi: 10.1007/s43926-023-00034-5.

Boschert, S. and Rosen, R. (2016). Digital twin – The simulation aspect. In *Mechatronic Futures: Challenges and Solutions for Mechatronic Systems and their Designers*, Hehenberger, P and Bradley, D. (eds). Springer, Cham.

Brik, B., Chergui, H., Zanzi, L., Devoti, F., Ksentini, A., Siddiqui, M.S., Costa-Pérez, X., Verikoukis, C. (2024). Explainable AI in 6G O-RAN: A tutorial and survey on architecture, use cases, challenges, and future research. *arXiv* [Online]. Available at: http://arxiv.org/abs/2307.00319.

Bruynseels, K., Santoni de Sio, F., van den Hoven, J. (2018). Digital twins in health care: Ethical implications of an emerging engineering paradigm. *Frontiers in Genetics*, 9. doi: 10.3389/fgene.2018.00031

Camilleri, M.A. (2023). Artificial intelligence governance: Ethical considerations and implications for social responsibility. *Expert Systems*, 41. doi: 10.1111/exsy.13406.

Chataut, R., Nankya, M., Akl, R. (2024). 6G networks and the AI revolution – Exploring technologies, applications, and emerging challenges. *Sensors*, 24(6), 1888. doi: 10.3390/s24061888.

Chen, P., Wu, L., Wang, L. (2023). AI fairness in data management and analytics: A review on challenges, methodologies and applications. *Applied Sciences*, 13(18), 10258. doi: 10.3390/app131810258.

Cheong, B.C. (2024). Transparency and accountability in AI systems: Safeguarding wellbeing in the age of algorithmic decision-making. *Frontiers in Human Dynamics*, 6. doi: 10.3389/fhumd.2024.1421273.

Collins, C., Dennehy, D., Conboy, K., Mikalef, P. (2021). Artificial intelligence in information systems research: A systematic literature review and research agenda. *International Journal of Information Management*, 60, 102383. doi: 10.1016/j.ijinfomgt.2021.102383.

Corral-Acero, J., Margara, F. et al. (2020). The "Digital Twin" to enable the vision of precision cardiology. *European Heart Journal*, 41(48), 4556–4564. doi: 10.1093/eurheartj/ehaa159.

Cremer, F., Sheehan, B., Fortmann, M., Kia, A.N., Mullins, M., Murphy, F., Materne, S. (2022). Cyber risk and cybersecurity: A systematic review of data availability. *The Geneva Papers on Risk and Insurance. Issues and Practice*, 47(3), 698–736. doi: 10.1057/s41288-022-00266-6.

Dang, S., Amin, O., Shihada, B., Alouini, M.-S. (2019). What should 6G be? *Nature Electronics*, 3(1), 20–29. doi: 10.36227/techrxiv.10247726.

Gill, S.S., Xu, M., Ottaviani, C., Patros, P., Bahsoon, R., Shaghaghi, A., Golec, M., Stankovski, V., Wu, H., Abraham, A. (2022). AI for next generation computing: Emerging trends and future directions. *Internet of Things*. 19, 100514. doi: 10.1016/j.iot.2022.100514.

Glaessgen, E. and Stargel, D. (2012). The digital twin paradigm for future NASA and U.S. air force vehicles. In *53rd Structures, Structural Dynamics, and Materials Conference: Special Session on the Digital Twin*. doi: 10.2514/6.2012-1818.

González, A., Moreno Espino, M., Moreno Román, A.C., Pérez, N. (2024). Ethics in artificial intelligence: An approach to cybersecurity. *Inteligencia Artificial*, 27, 38–54. doi: 10.4114/intartif.vol27iss73pp38-54.

Goodman, E.P. and Trehu, J. (2023). Algorithmic auditing: Chasing AI accountability. *Santa Clara High Technology Law Journal*, 39(3) [Online]. Available at: https://digitalcommons.law.scu.edu/chtlj/vol39/iss3/1.

Grieves, M. and Vickers, J. (2017). Digital twin: Mitigating unpredictable, undesirable emergent behavior in complex systems. In *Transdisciplinary Perspectives on Complex Systems*, F.-J. Kahlen, S. Flumerfelt, A. Alves (eds). Springer, Cham. doi: 10.1007/978-3-319-38756-7_4.

Haque, M., Ahmad, S., Abboud, A., Hossain, Md.A., Kumar, K., Haque, S., Sonal, D., Rahman, M. (2024). 6G Wireless communication networks: Challenges and potential solution. *International Journal of Business Data Communications and Networking*, 19(1), 1–27. doi: 10.4018/IJBDCN.339889.

Hasan, K.M., Sajid, M., Lapina, M., Shahid, M., Kotecha, K. (2024). Blockchain technology meets 6G wireless networks: A systematic survey. *Alexandria Engineering Journal*, 92, 199–220. doi: 10.1016/j.aej.2024.02.031.

Homaei, M., Mogollón-Gutiérrez, Ó., Sancho, J., Ávila, M., Caro, A. (2024). A review of digital twins and their application in cybersecurity based on artificial intelligence. *Artificial Intelligence Review*, 57, 201. doi: 10.1007/s10462-024-10805-3.

Hu, S., Li, C., Li, B., Yang, M., Wang, X., Gao, T., Xu, W., Dambatta, Y.S., Zhou, Z., Xu, P. (2024). Digital twins enabling intelligent manufacturing: From methodology to application. *Intelligent and Sustainable Manufacturing*, 1(1), 10007. doi: 10.35534/ism.2024.10007.

Huang, Z., Shen, Y., Li, J., Fey, M., Brecher, C. (2021). A survey on AI-driven digital twins in industry 4.0: Smart manufacturing and advanced robotics. *Sensors*, 21(19), 6340. doi: 10.3390/s21196340.

Ismail, L. and Buyya, R. (2022). Artificial Intelligence applications and self-learning 6G networks for smart cities digital ecosystems: Taxonomy, challenges, and future directions. *Sensors*, 22(15), 5750. doi: 10.3390/s22155750.

Javaid, M., Haleem, A., Suman, R. (2023). Digital twin applications toward Industry 4.0: A review. *Cognitive Robotics*, 3. doi: 10.1016/j.cogr.2023.04.003.

Jiang, Y., Yin, S., Li, K., Luo, H., Kaynak, O. (2021). Industrial applications of digital twins. *Philosophical Transactions of the Royal Society A: Mathematical, Physical and Engineering Sciences*, 379, 20200360. doi: 10.1098/rsta.2020.0360.

Jin, X., Katsis, C., Sang, F., Sun, J., Kundu, A., Kompella, R. (2022). Edge security: challenges and issues. *arXiv*. doi: 10.48550/arXiv.2206.07164.

Jobin, A., Ienca, M., Vayena, E. (2019). The global landscape of AI ethics guidelines. *Nature Machine Intelligence*, 1. doi: 10.1038/s42256-019-0088-2.

Jones, D., Snider, C., Nassehi, A., Yon, J., Hicks, B. (2020). Characterising the digital twin: A systematic literature review. *CIRP Journal of Manufacturing Science and Technology*, 29. doi: 10.1016/j.cirpj.2020.02.002.

Kapteyn, M., Willcox, K., Knezevic, D. (2020). Toward predictive digital twins via component-based reduced-order models and interpretable machine learning. *AIAA Scitech 2020 Forum*. doi: 10.2514/6.2020-0418.

Kaur, R., Gabrijelčič, D., Klobučar, T. (2023). Artificial intelligence for cybersecurity: Literature review and future research directions. *Information Fusion*, 97, 101804. doi: 10.1016/j.inffus.2023.101804.

Kaur, N., Kshetri, N., Pandey, P.S. (2024). 6AInets: Harnessing artificial intelligence for the 6G network security: Impacts and challenges. *arXiv* [Online]. Available at: http://arxiv.org/abs/2404.08643.

Kazmi, S.H.A., Hassan, R., Qamar, F., Nisar, K., Ibrahim, A.A.A. (2023). Security concepts in emerging 6G communication: Threats, countermeasures, authentication techniques and research directions. *Symmetry*, 15(6), 1147. doi: 10.3390/sym15061147.

Khajavi, S., Hossein Motlagh, N., Jaribion, A., Werner, L., Holmström, J. (2019). Digital twin: Vision, benefits, boundaries, and creation for buildings. *IEEE Access*, 7, 147406–147419. doi: 10.1109/ACCESS.2019.2946515.

Laamarti, F., Badawi, H., Ding, Y., Arafsha, F., Hafidh, B., El Saddik, A. (2020). An ISO/IEEE 11073 standardized digital twin framework for health and well-being in smart cities. *IEEE Access*, PP(99), 1-1. doi: 10.1109/ACCESS.2020.2999871

Lin, X., Kundu, L., Dick, C., Obiodu, E., Mostak, T., Flaxman, M. (2023). 6G digital twin networks: From theory to practice. *IEEE Communications Magazine*, 61(11), 72–78. doi: 10.1109/MCOM.001.2200830.

Liu, M., Shuiliang, F., Dong, H., Xu, C. (2020). Review of digital twin about concepts, technologies, and industrial applications. *Journal of Manufacturing Systems*, 58. doi: 10.1016/j.jmsy.2020.06.017.

Liu, Y., Peng, S., Zhang, M., Shi, S., Fu, J. (2024). Towards secure and efficient integration of blockchain and 6G networks. *PLOS ONE*, 19(4), e0302052. doi: 10.1371/journal.pone.0302052.

Lu, Y., Liu, C., Wang, K., Huang, H., Xu, X. (2019). Digital twin-driven smart manufacturing: Connotation, reference model, applications and research issues. *Robotics and Computer-Integrated Manufacturing*, 61. doi: 10.1016/j.rcim.2019.101837.

Luo, G., Yuan, Q., Li, J., Wang, S., Yang, F. (2021). Artificial intelligence powered mobile networks: From cognition to decision. *arXiv* [Online]. Available at: http://arxiv.org/abs/2112.04263.

Maalem, S., Derdour, M., Bennour, A., Abdelatif, S. (2024). A multi-level blockchain-based architecture for securing and controlling data flow in 6G networks. *SN Computer Science*, 5, 1165. doi: 10.1007/s42979-024-03548-z.

Mahmoud, H., Amer, A., Ismail, T. (2021). 6G: A comprehensive survey on technologies, applications, challenges, and research problems. *Transactions on Emerging Telecommunications Technologies*, 1–14. doi: 10.1002/ett.4233.

Malatji, M. and Tolah, A. (2024). Artificial intelligence (AI) cybersecurity dimensions: A comprehensive framework for understanding adversarial and offensive AI. *AI Ethics*. doi: 10.1007/s43681-024-00427-4.

Mao, B., Liu, J., Wu, Y., Kato, N. (2023). Security and privacy on 6G network edge: A survey. *IEEE Communications Surveys and Tutorials*, 25(2), 1095–1127. doi: 10.1109/COMST.2023.3244674.

Muneer, S., Farooq, U., Athar, A., Raza, M.A., Ghazal, T.M., Sakib, S. (2024). A critical review of artificial intelligence based approaches in intrusion detection: A comprehensive analysis. *Journal of Engineering*, 3909173. doi: 10.1155/2024/3909173.

Mylonas, G., Kalogeras, A.P., Kalogeras, G., Anagnostopoulos, C., Alexakos, C., Munoz, L. (2021). Digital twins from smart manufacturing to smart cities: A survey. *IEEE Access*, 1-1. doi: 10.1109/ACCESS.2021.3120843.

Navaie, K. (2024). Personal data protection in AI-native 6G systems. *arXiv* [Online]. Available at: http://arxiv.org/abs/2411.03368.

Nguyen, V.-L., Lin, P.-C., Cheng, B.-C., Hwang, R.-H., Lin, Y.R. (2021). Security and privacy for 6G: A survey on prospective technologies and challenges. *IEEE Communications Surveys & Tutorials*. doi: 10.1109/COMST.2021.3108618.

Pirandola, S., Andersen, U.L., Banchi, L., Berta, M., Bunandar, D., Colbeck, R., Englund, D., Gehring, T., Lupo, C., Ottaviani, C. et al. (2020). Advances in quantum cryptography. *Advances in Optics and Photonics*, 12(4), 1012–1236.

Porambage, P., Liyanage, M., Siriwardhana, Y. (2023). AI/ML for 6G Security. In *Security and Privacy Vision in 6G: A Comprehensive Guide*, Porambage, P. and Liyanage, M. (eds). John Wiley & Sons, Hoboken, NJ, 257–265. doi: 10.1002/9781119875437.ch17.

Qi, Q. and Tao, F. (2018). Digital twin and big data towards smart manufacturing and industry 4.0: 360 degree comparison. *IEEE Access*, 6, 3585–3593. doi: 10.1109/ACCESS.2018.2793265.

Rajoria, S. and Mishra, K. (2022). A brief survey on 6G communications. *Wireless Networks*, 28. doi: 10.1007/s11276-022-03007-8.

Rasheed, A., San, O., Kvamsdal, T. (2020). Digital twin: Values, challenges and enablers from a modeling perspective. *IEEE Access*, 8, 21980–22012. doi: 10.1109/ACCESS.2020.2970143.

Ridhawi, I.A., Otoum, S., Aloqaily, M. (2023). Decentralized zero-trust framework for digital twin-based 6G. *arXiv* [Online]. Available at: http://arxiv.org/abs/2302.03107.

Rifa-Pous, H., Garcia-Font, V., Nunez-Gomez, C., Salas, J. (2024). Security, trust and privacy challenges in AI-driven 6G networks. *Computer Science, Engineering and Information Technology*, 95–113. doi: 10.5121/csit.2024.141408.

Saad, W., Bennis, M., Chen, M. (2020). A vision of 6G wireless systems: Applications, trends, technologies, and open research problems. *IEEE Network*, 34(3), 134–142.

Salem, A.H., Azzam, S.M., Emam, O.E., Abohany, A.A. (2024). Advancing cybersecurity: A comprehensive review of AI-driven detection techniques. *Journal of Big Data*, 11, 105. doi: 10.1186/s40537-024-00957-y.

Sandeepa, C., Zeydan, E., Samarasinghe, T., Liyanage, M. (2025). Federated learning for 6G networks: Navigating privacy benefits and challenges. *IEEE Open Journal of the Communications Society*, 6, 90–129. doi: 10.1109/OJCOMS.2024.3513832.

Schummer, P., del Rio, A., Serrano, J., Jimenez, D., Sánchez, G., Llorente, Á. (2024). Machine learning-based network anomaly detection: Design, implementation, and evaluation. *AI*, 5(4), 2967–2983. doi: 10.3390/ai5040143.

Sébert, A., Checri, M., Stan, O., Sirdey, R., Gouy-Pailler, C. (2023). Combining homomorphic encryption and differential privacy in federated learning. In *2023 20th Annual International Conference on Privacy, Security and Trust* (PST), August, Copenhagen. doi: 10.1109/PST58708.2023.10320195.

Sedjelmaci, H. and Ansari, N. (2024). Zero trust architecture empowered attack detection framework to secure 6G edge computing. *IEEE Network*, 38(1), 196–202. doi: 10.1109/MNET.131.2200513.

Shahen Shah, A.F.M., Ali Karabulut, M., Rable, K. (2023). Mission-critical Internet of Things on the 6G network: Services and apps with networking architecture. In *2023 IEEE 98th Vehicular Technology Conference (VTC2023-Fall)*, Hong Kong, 1–5. doi: 10.1109/VTC2023-Fall60731.2023.10333821.

Shahriar, S., Allana, S., Hazrati Fard, S.M., Dara, R. (2023). A survey of privacy risks and mitigation strategies in the artificial intelligence life cycle. *IEEE Access*, 1-1. doi: 10.1109/ACCESS.2023.3287195.

Siriwardhana, Y., Porambage, P., Liyanage, M., Ylianttila, M. (2021). AI and 6G security: Opportunities and challenges. In *2021 Joint European Conference on Networks and Communications & 6G Summit (EuCNC/6G Summit)*, Porto, 616–621. doi: 10.1109/EuCNC/6GSummit51104.2021.9482503.

Song, Z., Hackl, C.M., Anand, A., Thommessen, A., Petzschmann, J., Kamel, O., Braunbehrens, R., Kaifel, A., Roos, C., Hauptmann, S. (2023). Digital twins for the future power system: An overview and a future perspective. *Sustainability*, 15(6), 5259. doi: 10.3390/su15065259.

Soori, M., Arezoo, B., Dastres, R. (2023). Digital twin for smart manufacturing. A review. *Sustainable Manufacturing and Service Economics*, 2, 100017. doi: 10.1016/j.smse.2023.100017.

Syed, T.A., Khan, M.Y., Jan, S., Albouq, S., Alqahtany, S.S., Naqash, M.T. (2024). Integrating digital twins and artificial intelligence multi-modal transformers into water resource management: Overview and advanced predictive framework. *AI*, 5(4), 1977–2017. doi: 10.3390/ai5040098.

Tao, F., Qi, Q., Liu, A. (2018). Data-driven smart manufacturing. *Journal of Manufacturing Systems*, 48, 157–169. doi: 10.1016/j.jmsy.2018.01.006.

Tao, F., Zhang, M., Liu, A., Nee, A.Y.C. (2019). Digital twin in industry: State-of-the-art. *IEEE Transactions on Industrial Informatics*, 15(4), 2405–2415.

Uhlemann, T., Lehmann, C., Steinhilper, R. (2017). The digital twin: Realizing the cyber-physical production system for industry 4.0. *Procedia CIRP*, 61, 335–340. doi: 10.1016/j.procir.2016.11.152.

Uysal, D., Yoo, P., Taha, K. (2022). Data-driven malware detection for 6G networks: A survey from the perspective of continuous learning and explainability via visualisation. *IEEE Open Journal of Vehicular Technology*, PP(99), 1–11. doi: 10.1109/OJVT.2022.3219898.

Wang, M., Zhu, T., Zhang, T., Zhang, J., Yu, S., Zhou, W. (2020). Security and privacy in 6G networks: New areas and new challenges. *Digital Communications and Networks*, 6. doi: 10.1016/j.dcan.2020.07.003.

Wu, W., Huang, X., Luan, T.H. (2024). AI-native network digital twin for intelligent network management in 6G. *arXiv* [Online]. Available at: http://arxiv.org/abs/2410.01584.

Yang, M., Qu, Y., Ranbaduge, T., Thapa, C., Sultan, N., Ding, M., Suzuki, H., Ni, W., Abuadbba, S., Smith, D. et al. (2024). From 5G to 6G: A survey on security, privacy, and standardization pathways. *arXiv* [Online]. Available at: http://arxiv.org/abs/2410.21986.

Yao, S. and Teng, J. (2024). Terahertz communication for 6G networks: Opportunities and challenges. *Applied and Computational Engineering*, 46, 232–241. doi: 10.54254/2755-2721/46/20241431.

Ye, W., Qian, C., An, X., Yan, X., Carle, G. (2023). Advancing federated learning in 6G: A trusted architecture with graph-based analysis. *arXiv* [Online]. Available at: http://arxiv.org/abs/2309.05525.

You, X., Huang, Y., Zhang, C., Wang, J., Yin, H., Wu, H. (2025). When AI meets sustainable 6G. *Science China Information Sciences*, 68, 110301. doi: 10.1007/s11432-024-4257-6.

Zayed, S., Attiya, G., El-Sayed, A., Hemdan, E.E.-D. (2023). A review study on digital twins with artificial intelligence and internet of things: Concepts, opportunities, challenges, tools and future scope. *Multimedia Tools and Applications*, 82. doi: 10.1007/s11042-023-15611-7.

Zhang, S. and Zhu, D. (2020). Towards artificial intelligence enabled 6G: State of the art, challenges, and opportunities. *Computer Networks*, 183, 107556. doi: 10.1016/j.comnet.2020.107556.

Zhang, V., Erol-Kantarci, M., Sun, W., Dai, Y., Hoydis, J., Gursoy, M.C. (2021). Guest editorial: AI and 6G convergence: An energy efficiency perspective. *IEEE Network*, 35(6), 10–11. doi: 10.1109/MNET.2021.9687499.

6

Harnessing Artificial Intelligence and Digital Twin Technologies for Sustainable Agripreneurship: A Path Toward Smart Agriculture

Artificial intelligence (AI) and digital twin, the two technologies applied in the agriculture sector, seek to increase sustainability by means of efficiency and profitability of operations. This chapter will present creative agri-technologies that enable agripreneurs to properly run their company by gathering data in real time and providing insights using virtual modeling and predictive analytics. AI-based models enhance detection, pest and yield forecasting, crop monitoring and identification. Digital twins model farming in virtual environments to improve planning and resource management, therefore strengthening general performance. Together, all of these technologies allow scalable agribusiness models, lower environmental impact and precision agriculture. This chapter will also cover case studies showing the socioeconomic effects of implementing these technologies, the socioeconomic drivers engaged and issues including cost, accessibility and the degree of digital presence. Lastly, it illustrates how agripreneurs can improve their operations using AI and digital twin technologies in agripreneurship, enabling smart agriculture, sustainable development, food security, small farms and rural development.

6.1. Introduction

The lack of population growth, resource and climate change is creating crucial challenges in the world agricultural economy. Food production requires 70% growth to fulfill future demand, as the world population will reach more than 10 billion by the year 2050 (United Nations 2019). However, the traditional farming practices, which for decades have been based on extensive resource and chemical use, are

Chapter written by A. IYAPPAN, G. ILANKUMARAN and Tripuraneni JAGGAIAH.

becoming increasingly immune to it. Such practices include soil erosion, water scarcity, loss of biological diversity and greenhouse gas emissions – the effects of climate change (FAO 2017; IPCC 2021). Entrepreneurial innovation has been integrated with regulatory frameworks to address the major challenges in sustainable agriculture. This marks a transformative approach in agriculture. Sustainable Agri principles announce a paradigm shift in agriculture, emphasizing the need for economically viable, environmentally sustainable, and socially acceptable practices. Sustainable development goal 2 (Zero Hunger) and sustainable development goal 12 (sustainable consumption and production) are highly convergent. The aim of sustainable agripreneurship is to combine productivity and longevity to fulfill today's agriculture needs without harming future generations' needs. This balance requires massive impediments, including technology-constrained access, poor structural infrastructure and the unwanted effects of climate change (FAO 2017; IPCC 2021). Artificial intelligence (AI) is defined as simulating human intelligence in computers so that they can learn, reason and make decisions (Kamilaris et al. 2019). AI applications in agriculture include predictive analytics, image recognition, robotics and automation.

Digital twins (DT) refers to a virtual model of a present object, system or process. It uses real-time data, AI algorithms and simulation models to track, analyze and optimize farm operations. By providing a dynamic and interactive visualization of a farm or farm process, DT facilitates real-time decision-making.

Recent advances in AI and DT technologies have helped propose solutions to help mitigate these obstacles. AI is helping to revolutionize agriculture by allowing precision farming, predictive analysis and automation of agricultural activities, because it is the process of evaluating large amounts of data and producing new information for better decision-making. AI-based programs can determine optimal irrigation schedules, identify crop diseases early and provide the predictive analysis of supply and demand to help farmers increase productivity and reduce wastage of resources (Liakos et al. 2018). In a similar vision, DT technologies, with their ability to optimize, model and monitor in real time virtual models of physical systems, have opened up opportunities for experimentation, testing, modeling of farms, crops and supply chains in many scenarios, identifying opportunity cost from inefficiencies in current practices and informing better decision-making (Tao et al. 2019).

The possibilities for synergy between DT and AI technologies for sustainable agripreneurship are unlimited. These technologies can be used to better manage resource use, mitigate harmful environmental effects and improve resilience to climate change. Precision agriculture with AI can improve efficiency through the decreased use of water, fertilizers and herbicides, and DT can assist farmers in modeling the effects of climate change on their agricultural systems and help growers adapt quickly. The use of pre-emptive responses to climate change can be key to farmer resiliency (Zhang et al. 2020). The technologies have the potential to enhance well-being opportunities by giving smallholder farmers and vulnerable groups access to real-time data and market information, which improves inclusive and resilient agricultural livelihoods (Tao et al. 2019).

However, despite the potential of digital technologies, there are barriers to the use of AI and DT in agriculture. The high cost in the implementation of such technologies, an absence of technical capability and limited access to digital networks are often considerable barriers to deployment, particularly in developing nations (World Bank 2017). Data security and privacy along with ethical issues also need to be properly managed to facilitate the most beneficial use of AI and DT (Kamilaris et al. 2019). Closing these gaps requires coordinated action by governments, industry and research organizations to form policy frameworks that promote uses of technologies that address adoption and technology transfer (NITI Aayog 2019).

6.1.1. *The call for sustainable agripreneurship in India*

Sustainable agripreneurship provides a holistic and integrated view of using entrepreneurship, innovation and sustainability to create resilient, environmentally conscious and economically sustainable agricultural systems. As India has many agricultural producers, especially smallholder farmers, sustainable agripreneurship can play an effective role in addressing critical issues such as:

– Scarcity of resources: overconsumption of water, soil health degradation, unsustainable use of fertilizers and pesticides, among other issues, are driving down agricultural productivity (NITI Aayog 2019).

– Climate change: erratic weather patterns, floods, droughts, etc., increase uncertainty which increases in crop yields or risk to world food security (ICAR 2021).

– Economic viability: low and even negative profits, no market and rising input costs are driving farmers into debt and therefore agrarian distress (National Crime Records Bureau 2022).

Sustainable agripreneurship offers potential solutions to these problems using models and practices such as precision agriculture, organic farming and agroecology, which optimize inputs, minimize costs, maximize use of resources, care for the environment and improve farmer's livelihoods. Innovative solutions and especially new technologies will play a role as necessary conditions for sustainable agripreneurship.

Figure 6.1. *Digital twins – seeing double with a predictive eye. For a color version of this figure, see: www.iste.co.uk/taneja/6gurban.zip*

6.2. Role of AI and digital twin in sustainable agripreneurship

Agripreneurship, the incorporation of entrepreneurial thinking into the agricultural industry, is undergoing rapid development as industry participants pursue means to meet new challenges associated with world food security (Kamilaris et al. 2019). New technology, specifically AI and DT, has the potential to transform the agricultural industry through increased productivity, sustainability and profitability (Bechar and Vigneault 2016; Kamilaris et al. 2019).

6.2.1. *Precision farming and resource management*

Precision farming harnesses technology to give crops and soil what they need for optimum health and yield. Liakos et al. (2018) and Tao et al. (2019) believe agripreneurs can make farm operations more efficient and sustainable, using AI algorithms and DT:

– Soil and crop monitoring: AI soil-based sensors monitor pH, nutrient levels, moisture and soil temperature. DT predict crop responses to different inputs to support agripreneurs with data-based decision-making.

– Variable rate application (VRA): by means of AI analysis, farmers can apply pesticides, fertilizer and water as required for excess application, so are aware of different areas in the field. Using drones and autonomous tractors, space-time VRA lets farmers minimize the chemicals or resources they apply that are wasted.

– Yield forecasting: DT will combine all weather data, soil health data, crop disease data, etc. This will let growers more precisely forecast yield based more on fact. Knowing yield levels helps with inventory control and better planning; it also helps to secure any resources required for operations.

– Decision-making with real-time data: AI software is able to detect incoming data that may determine irrigation, fertilization or pest management decisions in real time. The access to real-time data enables agripreneurs to make swifter adjustments regarding changing circumstances.

– Environmental impact: farmers reduce their environmental impact by only applying what they need. Less water, less chemistry and a better way of farming will achieve sustainability in the long run.

– Cost and resource efficiency: precision farming reduces costs to the farm by improving resource efficiency, higher yields per hectare and not misapplying any additional inputs.

– Climate adaptive capacity: AI and DT are exploring the impacts of climate variability on farming; what farmers can reasonably expect in relation to mitigation actions such as changing planting date, or planting drought-tolerant variety or watering according to their irrigation system management practice only when necessary.

– Smart equipment management: AI software tracks equipment performance and predicts maintenance needs, thus preventing unexpected breakdowns and reducing downtime.

DT can simulate machine behavior under different conditions, recommending efficient usage patterns.

6.2.2. *Enhanced crop monitoring and predictive analytics*

Both DT and AI technologies greatly enhance crop monitoring, predictive analytics capabilities and useful actionable sciences for agripreneurs:

– Research satellite and drone images: AI-enabled drones and satellites take high-resolution images of agripreneurs' fields. Agri-tech uses machine learning algorithms to review and analyze the images to spot crop health issues, mainly diseases, nutrient deficit, pest infections and water stress, which are harmful to the yield of the crops.

– Computer vision and image-based hyperspectral sensors: advanced image recognition software detects plant stress early (Gonzalez-Hilario et al. 2021). Agripreneurs use DT to leverage both data on crop growth (root structure and the establishment of certain characteristics) and environmental factors from harvested crop data to predict growth under specific conditions and enact preventive measures.

– Predictive pests and diseases: AI and data technologies review past pest and disease trends by modeling with weather data (temperature, humidity, precipitation) and soil types, and present agripreneurs with probabilities of pest and disease incursion, enabling, as appropriate, prophylactic treatments in a timely fashion that would save large portions of their crops.

– Monitoring crop growth and prediction: DT model crop growth by integrating real-time information on weather, soil and agricultural practices. Agripreneurs apply AI-generated predictive algorithms that provide crop yield predictions and use them to maximize their input and market with realistic yield expectations.

– Soil health management: AI-based soil sensors ("smart sensors") measure the amount of nutrients, pH and water that is in the soil. The predictive conductivity analysis gives suggestions for soil amendments, cover crops and crop rotation types to mitigate soil health problems.

– Climate resilience support: AI algorithms process huge sets of climate observations to predict extreme weather; DT simulate how crops will behave in those conditions and allow agripreneurs the opportunity to adopt the appropriate management practice.

– Farm-level decision support: AI systems recommend practical suggestions for agripreneurs, including sowing time, pest management and optimization of inputs. AI systems can incorporate real-time analysis, allowing agricultural land owners to make informed decisions that minimize uncertainty.

6.2.3. *Smart irrigation and water management*

AI- and DT-based intelligent irrigation systems are vastly changing the way water is managed. Water management can ensure all forms of sustainability, especially if there is a lack of water:

– Real-time soil monitoring: AI fed soil sensors which continuously monitor soil moisture content, temperature, soil health, etc. Sensor data is delivered to DT which simulates different irrigation scenarios and provides recommendations on how best to use water.

– Automated irrigation system: AI software analyzes weather data, Evapotranspiration rates and soil water levels before automatically scheduling irrigation. Automated irrigation systems are efficient as they provide plants with just enough water, without additional water waste.

– Precision irrigation: DT technologies create a holistic representation of how the water moves through soil and into plant roots, allowing farmers to deliver water in smaller quantities, where required, and avoid over-irrigating.

– Weather forecast integration: AI is able to use rainfall and other weather forecasts to gear itself around the other scheduled irrigation patterns. Also, if rain is forecast, scheduled irrigation can be reduced, thereby saving both water and cost.

– Water source management: AI models are developed to focus on water availability from all sources, i.e. wells, rivers, reservoirs, etc. Water consumption and usage behaviors are modeled using DT. Recommendations can be given based upon sustainability regarding rates of water withdrawal.

– Leak detection and prevention: sensors in irrigation systems can detect leaks and warn about potential leakages. The early warning means that water loss can be avoided. AI algorithms analyze data to identify anomalies, reducing downtime and maintenance costs.

– Energy efficiency: smart irrigation solutions offer energy efficiency since pumps and valves only run when necessary. This leads to greater sustainability and lower operational costs.

– Crop-specific irrigation: AI solutions investigate the water usage necessary for numerous crops and all of their stages. DT simulates plant growth under different irrigation patterns, suggesting optimal water usage.

6.2.4. *Supply chain optimization*

AI and DT technologies are evolving the area of agricultural supply-chain management. The technologies can provide visibility throughout the complete supply chain, reduce redundancy and waste, and expose opportunities for sustainability, leading to improvements in costs and reduction in resource utilization:

– Real-time visibility and monitoring: AI-enabled systems can follow the real-time movement of farm products and provide as a monitoring system. DT provide a virtual twin of the supply chain and then allow tracking and monitoring of certain aspects of the supply chain, for example, temperature, humidity and time-sensitive in-transit food products that require expiry management.

– Predictive demand planning: machine learning technologies take historical sales information, weather trends and past trends in the market, apply their analysis and then yield recommendation and predictions on demand possible.

– Agripreneurs can use data analytics to assist with production planning and inventory management, thus minimizing waste and preventing overproduction in the first place.

– Inventory management: DT can use simulations of different storage conditions to determine the best method for storing perishables. Moreover, AI can help ensure that the amount of perishables in an inventory is not excessive so that waste is minimized and operational costs are reduced.

– Route optimization and logistics management: AI algorithms analyze modes of transport to determine routes for transport based on the goal of lowering both carbon and time spent in transport. Additionally, these algorithms factor in road quality, fuel consumption and traffic patterns.

– Quality control and traceability of services: AI and sensor systems are used to manage the quality of food during the entire journey. With DT and blockchain traceability, the opportunity for end-to-end traceability provides a higher level of visibility, demonstrating that suppliers comply with conditions/criteria relating to food safety, sustainability and environmental compliance.

– Risk management: DT can predict when interruptions in the supply chain are imminent based on climate events, geopolitical parameters or uncertainty in international markets. They can also model scenarios and provide solutions to minimize losses.

– Sustainability management: AI can collect, manage and track environmental impacts, including carbon footprints across the supply chain. Agripreneurs can use this data to make decisions about sustainability, including whether they should use electric vehicles for transport in place of diesel vehicles, and decisions regarding plastic packaging.

– Collaboration and partnership management: DT can allow suppliers, retailers and distributors to communicate and collaborate. AI-enabled contract management systems can help with contracts, including fairness pricing, ensuring timely payments and that negotiations relate to fair and reasonable actions during the course of the contract.

– Market access and fair trade: agripreneurs can also take advantage of AI-enabled platforms to connect the owner of the farm directly to buyers, eliminating the middlemen in the supply chain. Connecting farmers directly to buyers opens up opportunities for farmers not only to get a better price for their products, but also the opportunity for fair trade.

By leveraging AI with DT technology, agripreneurs have opportunities to build strong, transparent and efficient supply chains that align with sustainability goals.

6.2.5. *Risk management and climate adaptation*

Characteristics of DT and AI solutions present valuable opportunities for agripreneurs in terms of risk management and climate change adaptation:

– Climate change models and scenarios: AI systems analyze historical climate data, historical to current weather data and environmental data to provide climate model forecasting and prediction information. DT can test climate scenarios to understand the effects of different potential scenarios on yield and soil health and combine experiments to observe their interactivity.

– Incident warning and preparedness: AI models can provide warnings for extreme conditions happening outside of normal seasonal ranges such as extreme drought, floods or storms. If a warning occurs, agripreneurs can modify their plans and practices, for example, by changing their historical sowing date, adjusting an irrigation plan or applying more resilient crop varieties.

– Identification of soil and crop stress: IoT devices and drones provide soil moisture, temperature and crop health reporting in real time. AI-enabled apps provide useful data to the user indicating stress type, such as drought or nutrient stress. DT can provide simulated stress relieving strategies enabling useful insights and actions.

– Pest and disease forecasting and management: AI-enabled risk forecasting allows agripreneurs to be alerted about the risk of pest and disease outbreaks based on past data and weather data. Risk management can involve implementing preventative steps such as biopesticide applications or natural enemy releases to prevent yield loss.

– Water resource management: AI-enabled decision support systems are used to analyze and forecast water resources, rain and soil moisture levels.

– Carbon footprint monitoring: emissions of greenhouse gases stemming from farm activities are continually monitored by AI systems. DT will simulate a range of possible emission reduction strategies. Agripreneurs can integrate sustainable farming techniques such as no-till, cover cropping and agroforestry into their business model.

– Supply chain risk management: AI technology is capable of constantly monitoring market price fluctuations, transport disruptions and geopolitical activity. DT can evaluate the potentially negative ramifications on supply chains and offer alternatives for alternative routes and suppliers to mitigate loss.

– Financial risk management: the AI system is capable of estimating farm level financial risks with yield predictions, input prices and market prices as surrogate indicators. Agripreneurs can use these estimates to gauge insurance coverage adequacy, support financing through a loan and manage and optimize financial budgets.

– Climate change planning: DT are capable of simulating how the farm landscapes will change under different climate scenarios. Agripreneurs can start their planning and long-term adaptations, such as changing to climate-resilient plants, improving soil health and transitioning to regenerative agriculture, before the climate change-induced shifts occur.

By using AI and DT technologies for risk management and climate change planning strategies, agripreneurs can build resilience, manage risk and create a sustainable farm business.

6.3. Challenges in implementing AI and digital twins for sustainability

6.3.1. *Data availability and quality*

AI and DT commonly require a significant amount of accurate and real-time data to generate meaningful conclusions. Obtaining such data is not easy. Many industries do not own the necessary infrastructure to adequately collect, store and analyze data. Data may not only be outdated, inconsistent or absent in some cases, but all of these factors may skew the correct representation of DT simulations and AI predictions where there may be a minor change or alteration on purpose, which varies depending on, at times excessively, the data. The merging of several services is also challenged due to differing data formats and data standards. The result of standards is to drive toward integrable systems which make the implementation of AI and DT technologies more manageable. Overcoming these issues will require robust data management strategies that have defined preliminary data governance structures and robust data cleansing and validation mechanisms.

6.3.2. *Scalability*

Despite the potential for DT and AI to perform incredible tasks at a smaller scale, they encounter substantial challenges in scaling these technologies for large operations. The utilization of AI systems in urban infrastructures, energy networks or global supply chains requires the use of substantial computing power and connectivity.

As scale increases, their potential for real-time data processing and analytics has more disruptive implications. Large-scale AI and DT use relies on high-performance computing infrastructure and robust cloud-based systems. Building and maintaining scalable solutions pose both financial and technical challenges for organizations as well.

6.3.3. *Cybersecurity risks*

As DT and AI are closely associated, their cybersecurity implications are related. Cybercriminals can target the DT and AI systems and obtain private information, disrupt actions and inflict financial damage by accessing them. DT are especially vulnerable since they process real-world systems, making attractive targets for bad actors.

The cybersecurity of AI and DT systems involves constant monitoring, highly developed threat detection persona and security protocols. The deployment of DT and AI systems, as well as their overall cybersecurity, will significantly depend on an implementation of an extensive cybersecurity system, and regular vulnerability assessments.

6.3.4. *High implementation costs*

DT and AI require substantial capital investments in hardware, software and related costs, storage and computing resources. Customization of algorithms is only one part of the overall cost equation and the integration of technology and ensuring that even the real-time data has utility contributes to the overall cost.

SMEs are limited in capacity and thus limited in sustainable innovations. However, governments and firms can help ease some of this burden through incentives, supportive technologies or supporting co-op innovation hubs.

6.3.5. *Skill gaps*

The successful implementation of AI and DT requires proficiency in data science, machine learning, software engineering and domain-specific knowledge. Unfortunately, there is a dearth of skilled people who have these capabilities.

Closing the skill gaps will require mutual collaboration across disciplines, ensuring training courses are tailored to individual needs, and supporting STEM education. Businesses can also pay for upskilling their employees through their ongoing learning projects and partnerships with universities.

6.3.6. *Regulatory and ethical concerns*

The emergence of DT and AI raises ethical and legal issues of data privacy, algorithmic bias and transparency of decision-making processes. In many instances, the data collected by AI systems and its sensors include aspects of personal data, which raises issues about data ownership and consent.

The second issue, that AI systems may unconsciously perpetuate biases found in the training set and deliver biased and/or discriminatory outputs, regrettably means regulatory authorities must develop strict standards that incorporate openness, accountability and fairness in decision-making if there is to be any assurance of ethical application of AI.

6.3.7. *Environmental impact of technology*

The environmental impact of AI and DT can be adverse, despite AI and DT having sustainability benefits. Training large AI models and maintaining DT in real time are consuming energy-intensive processes that are commonly powered by non-renewable energy sources.

Businesses can mitigate this emission impact through deploying renewable energy for data centers, adopting energy-efficient computing usage strategies and prioritizing low-carbon AI model development. Researching strategic green data management approaches and sustainable computing solutions will further reduce the carbon footprint of AI and DT applications.

6.4. Overcoming the challenges

– Establishing data governance structures and applying AI algorithms to efficiently clean and control data will help to improve data management.

– Encouragement of cooperation among governments, businesses and academics to exchange resources and knowledge helps to build alliances.

– Funding programs for AI and DT education and upskill development in skills and training.

– Creating sustainable infrastructure: supporting AI activities by means of renewable energy sources and energy-efficient data centers.

– Establishing rules guaranteeing responsible AI development and application helps to support regulation.

6.5. Practical applications of harnessing artificial intelligence and digital twin technologies for sustainable agripreneurship

6.5.1. *A path toward smart agriculture*

Case study 1: precision farming in the Netherlands

Leading sustainable agriculture nation, the Netherlands uses DT- and AI-enabled sensors to maximize agricultural operations. Integrating data from sensors gauging humidity, temperature and CO_2 levels, Wageningen University & Research (WUR) created a DT model of a greenhouse. Examining the data, AI systems revealed information about plant health and growth rates.

Farmers cut pesticide use and water consumption by 30% using this system. The AI also recommended ideal times for harvesting, so raising 20% of yields. By balancing environmental responsibility with output, this application of AI and DT has set a model for sustainable agripreneurship.

Case study 2: AI-driven pest management in India

To prevent crop losses, agribusiness owners in India are implementing AI-powered pest detection systems. Agro AI, a startup, takes real-time photos of crops using drones fitted with multispectral cameras. The AI assesses the images to discern signs of early pest infestations. DT in a farm allows model variations of pest outbreaks, predicts how they expand and recommends targeted treatment using the farm's DT. This limits chemical pesticide applications and preserves productivity and the environment. Farmers who applied this solution reported a 25% yield increase and a 40% less pesticide cost.

Case study 3: smart irrigation in Israel

Israel is known for its scarcity of water, and there is a great deal of innovation in using DT and AI to optimize irrigation systems. One of the leading precision irrigation companies, Netafim, has built an AI-driven algorithm to measure crop needs for water, moisture in the soil and weather information.

The DT of the irrigation system runs several scenarios and provides a real-time recommendation to the farmer. As a result, yields increased by 25%, and the farmer used 40% less water. Today, many arid areas are putting in place this technology, in order to use water sustainably.

6.6. Conclusion

DT and AI have great promise for sustainable agripreneurship. Through specific decisions, effectively using resources and minimizing environmental impacts, these technologies can lead to a more sustainable food system. Cases from the Netherlands, India and Israel describe opportunities for AI and DT solutions with issues such as water scarcity, pest management and sub-optimal agricultural practices.

Embracing these technologies will provide additional benefits, such as more efficient production with resource savings, greater resilience to climate change, etc. Beyond the supporting environmental sustainability, data-driven insights will allow farmers to better use regenerative practices, minimize waste and prolong chemical reach.

Widespread acceptance calls for addressing issues including data accessibility, high implementation costs and skill gaps. Training depends on cooperative efforts among governments, technology companies, research institutes and infrastructure support.

Moving forward, the expected pace of innovation and rate of knowledge sharing will build on the enhancements created by AI and DT in agriculture. The integration of both technologies into agripreneurship will increase the momentum of global food security, climate resilience and sustainability.

6.7. References

Afia, O.E. (2024). Gender participation in agricultural digitalization: Prospects and challenges. In *e-Proceedings of the Faculty of Agriculture International Conference*, 153–162.

Agrawal, R.C. and Jaggi, S. (2024). Transforming agricultural education for a sustainable future. In *Transformation of Agri-Food Systems*, Bansal, K.C., Lakra, W.S., Pathak, H. (eds). Springer, Singapore, 357–369.

Bechar, A. and Vigneault, C. (2016). Agricultural robots for field operations: Concepts and components. *Biosystems Engineering*, 149, 94–111. doi: 10.1016/j.biosystemseng. 2016.06.012.

CropIn (2023). AI-powered farm management solutions [Online]. Available at: https://www.cropin.com.

FAO (2014). *The State of Food and Agriculture: Innovation in Family Farming*. Food and Agriculture Organization, Rome.

FAO (2017). *The Future of Food and Agriculture: Trends and Challenges*. Food and Agriculture Organization, Rome.

Gonzalez-Hilario, A., Martinez-Guanter, J., Ribeiro, Á., Miranda-Apodaca, J., Escola A., Sanz-Cortiella, R. (2021). Hyperspectral and thermal imagery from UAVs for early detection of disease and stress in crops: A review. *Remote Sensing*, 13(6), 1182. doi: 10.3390/rs13061182.

Grieves, M. and Vickers, J. (2017). Digital twin: Mitigating unpredictable, undesirable emergent behavior in complex systems. In *Transdisciplinary Perspectives on Complex Systems*, Kahlen, F.-J., Flumerfelt, S., Alves, A. (eds). Springer, Berlin, 85–113. doi: 10.1007/978-3-319-38756-7_4.

ICAR (Indian Council of Agricultural Research) (2021). Annual report 2020–21. Report, ICAR [Online]. Available at: https://icar.org.in/annual-reports.

IIT Madras (2022). Digital twin platform for precision agriculture [Online]. Available at: https://www.iitm.ac.in.

IPCC (2021). Climate change 2021: The physical science basis. Report, Cambridge University Press, Cambridge.

Kamilaris, A., Fonts, A., Prenafeta-Boldú, F.X. (2019). The rise of blockchain technology in agriculture and food supply chains. *Trends in Food Science & Technology*, 91, 640–652. doi: 10.1016/j.tifs.2019.07.034.

Kritzinger, W., Karner, M., Traar, G., Henjes, J., Sihn, W. (2018). Digital twin in manufacturing: A categorical literature review and classification. *IFAC-PapersOnLine*, 51(11), 1016–1022. doi: 10.1016/j.ifacol.2018.08.474.

Liakos, K.G., Busato, P., Moshou, D., Pearson, S., Bochtis, D. (2018). Machine learning in agriculture: A review. *Sensors*, 18(8), 2674. doi: 10.3390/s18082674.

Madaswamy, M. (2020). Digitalization of agriculture in India: Application of IoT, robotics and informatics to establish farm extension 4.0. *Journal of Informatics and Innovative Technologies*, 4(2), 23–32.

Madaswamy, M. (2023). Spices informatics network and value chain for open innovation and value creation network. In *Handbook of Spices in India: 75 Years of Research and Development*, Ravindran, P.N., Sivaraman, K., Devasahayam, S., Babu, K.N. (eds). Springer, Singapore, 1147–1191.

Ministry of Agriculture, India (2023). Annual report 2022-2023 [Online]. Available at: https://agricoop.nic.in.

National Crime Records Bureau (2022). Accidental deaths & suicides in India 2021. Ministry of Home Affairs, Government of India [Online]. Available at: https://ncrb.gov.in/en/accidental-deaths-suicides-india.

NITI Aayog (2019). National strategy for artificial intelligence. Government of India [Online]. Available at: https://niti.gov.in.

Nuthalapati, C.S. and Nuthalapati, C. (2021). Has open innovation taken root in India? Evidence from startups working in food value chains. *Circular Economy and Sustainability*, 1(4), 1207–1230.

Pretty, J. (2008). Agricultural sustainability: Concepts, principles, and evidence. *Philosophical Transactions of the Royal Society B: Biological Sciences*, 363(1491), 447–465. doi: 10.1098/rstb.2007.2163.

Schaltegger, S. and Wagner, M. (2011). Sustainable entrepreneurship and sustainability innovation: Categories and interactions. *Business Strategy and the Environment*, 20(4), 222–237. doi: 10.1002/bse.682.

Sood, K., Seth, N., Jindal, M., Sadawarti, H. (2021). Big data: A boon for food and servicepreneurship. In *Entrepreneurship and Big Data*, Chhabra, M., Hassan, R., Shamim, A. (eds). CRC Press, Boca Raton, 55–69.

Tao, F., Zhang, M., Liu, Y., Nee, A.Y.C. (2019). Digital twin driven prognostics and health management for complex equipment. *CIRP Annals*, 68(1), 169–172. doi: 10.1016/j.cirp.2019.04.055.

United Nations (2019). *World Population Prospects 2019: Highlights*. Department of Economic and Social Affairs, Population Division.

World Bank (2017). ICT in agriculture: Connecting smallholders to knowledge, networks, and institutions. World Bank Group. doi: 10.1596/978-1-4648-1002-2.

World Economic Forum (2020). Digital transformation initiative: Agriculture and food [Online]. Available at: https://www.weforum.org.

Zhang, C., Kovacs, J.M., Liu, Y. (2020). The application of small unmanned aerial systems for precision agriculture: A review. *Precision Agriculture*, 21(3), 605–621. doi: 10.1007/s11119-020-09725-3.

7

Role of AI and Digital Twin for Smart Transportation

Artificial intelligence (AI) and digital twin technology used together in smart transport systems is a new way to make towns safer, better for the environment and easier to get around in. AI makes it easy to look at the huge amounts of data that transport networks produce. This lets us learn from the past and make decisions right away. This feature predicts when cars and other equipment will need to be fixed, which makes traffic flow more smoothly. It also makes things safer by identifying and lowering potential threats. When AI is used with digital twin technology, virtual copies of real travel systems are made. Real-life events can be simulated by these moving models, which can then be used to test new transport ideas and theories without affecting real traffic. When city planners and transportation officials use AI and digital twin together, they can see how changes to traffic patterns, infrastructure and rules will affect people before they happen. This proactive and adaptable approach saves money, helps the environment and improves transportation. The digital copies of actual assets are always up-to-date with real-time data. This lets systems learn and get better all of the time based on new data and changes in the environment. This mix not only makes city transport systems more adaptable to new issues, but it also makes room for self-driving cars and other high-tech ways to get around. Actually, AI and digital twin technology are very important to the growth of smart transport systems because they can be used on a large scale to meet the needs of more people traveling around the world and growing cities.

7.1. Introduction

Transportation has always been an important part of society's growth because it makes it easier for people, goods and services to move around. However, as cities' populations grow quickly and people want more efficient and environmentally friendly ways to get around, standard transport systems are facing problems that

Chapter written by Ritesh Gangasingh BAIS, Vipan KUMAR, Manjushri JOSHI, Jainender SHARMA, Pradnya BORKAR and Mohammad Alamgir HOSSAIN.

have never been seen before (Deng et al. 2021). One promising approach to address these issues is by using cutting-edge technology such as digital twin (DT) and artificial intelligence (AI). These instruments might make transportation safer, more efficient and less detrimental to the environment, therefore altering its dynamics. Transport networks must adapt to suit smart cities as towns expand (Dang et al. 2022) Smart transport makes going around towns simpler, more efficient and more ecologically friendly by using new technology included in smart cities. AI and DT technologies are at the core of this shift, as they will provide fresh approaches to operating real-time transportation systems (Futai et al. 2022), including modeling and planning. This introduction talks about the problems that cities are facing with transport right now as well as the basic ideas behind AI and DT technologies. This makes it easier to understand how these two technologies will work together to shape the future of smart transport.

7.1.1. *Background and current challenges in urban transportation*

Transportation systems in cities are facing many problems, such as traffic jams, rising carbon pollution and worries about safety. More than half of the world's people now live in cities, which put a lot of stress on infrastructure. Sticky traffic not only loses time and gas, but it also makes air pollution and greenhouse gas emissions worse (Mohammadi and Taylor 2017). Studies show that traffic jams in cities cost businesses billions of dollars every year in missed productivity. This shows how important it is to find new ways to solve the problem. The safety of travel methods is still very important.

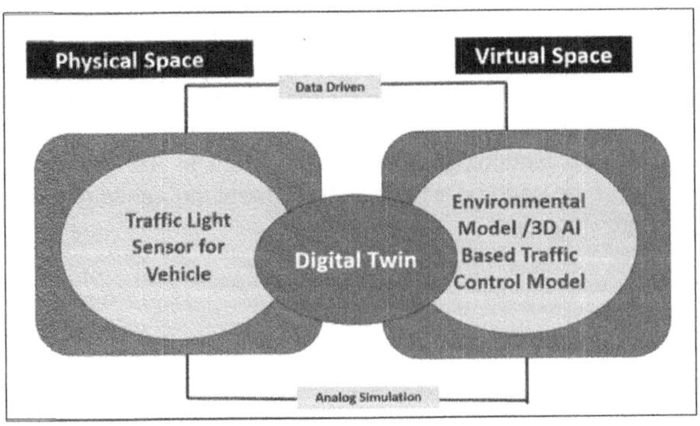

Figure 7.1. *Detailed digital twin architecture for transportation systems. For a color version of this figure, see: www.iste.co.uk/taneja/6gurban.zip*

Every year, millions of people die in car accidents around the world. Many of these accidents are caused by mistakes made by people. More people owning their own cars makes road safety risks even worse, so we need systems that can watch for, predict and reduce possible dangers. More and more people want transportation systems that work well with multiple types of transportation such as buses, trains, bikes and ride-sharing services (Alam and El Saddik 2017). Figure 7.1 shows that when these systems cannot share real-time information or talk to each other, it can cause errors and delays. Another important issue is keeping the infrastructure in good shape. When tracking systems are not up to par and equipment is getting old, things break down often and cost a lot to fix. It is becoming clearer that predictive and preventive repair plans are needed, which is pushing the development of technologies that can check on the health of infrastructure in real time.

7.1.2. *Overview of AI and DT technologies*

The fields of AI and DTs are changing the way smart transport works. AI is a branch of computer science that focuses on making smart systems that can learn, reason and make choices. Transportation has a lot of uses for AI. From managing traffic to making cars drive themselves, AI programs look at huge amounts of data to find the best ways to do things and make the user experience better (Bhatti et al. 2021). AI includes machine learning (ML), which lets systems learn from past data and get better over time. Deep learning and natural language processing (NLP) add to the power of AI-based solutions. DT technology, on the contrary, turns real systems or processes into virtual copies. These digital models are in sync with their real-world versions thanks to data streams. This lets tracking, simulating and optimizing happen in real time. DT technology was first used in industry and flight. It is now being used in transportation, where it lets people model traffic situations, check how well infrastructure is working and guess what will happen in different situations (Rathore et al. 2021). When AI and DT technology are combined, their potential is increased, making it possible for transport systems to be smart and changeable. AI-driven analytics give DTs predictive insights that help them make better decisions. At the same time, real-time data from DTs feeds AI models so they can keep getting better.

7.2. Related work

From smart cities to transportation to construction to industry, DTs have evolved into a game-changing instrument in many spheres. From building information modeling (BIM) to DTs, intelligent building representations have evolved greatly in the domains of architecture, engineering and construction (AEC) and facility management (FM). These models are becoming ever more data-driven and intelligent (Lv et al. 2021). Tracking structural stability has proven to benefit from deep learning and cloud-based DTs. This is so they may detect and stop issues before they start by combining cutting-edge ML techniques with real-time data. In the same line, the use of DT technologies in bridge inspection and maintenance has shown the difficulty in tying them to present infrastructure. To get around these problems, some ideas have been presented (Kumar et al. 2018). DTs have the potential to make cities more dynamic and responsive, especially when it comes to managing resources and disasters. This has been emphasized in the smart city field, and they can also be used to improve the performance of electric vehicles and make the best use of energy (Dasgupta et al. 2021). Cloud-based DTs are an important part of cyber-physical systems because they let industrial and urban systems make decisions and sync data in real time. When we combine DTs with AI, ML and Big Data, we can improve their uses. DTs are used in clever transportation systems to better control traffic, guess what drivers will do, and avoid traffic jams. Real-time data analysis makes it much easier to move around in cities (Aslani et al. 2017). Using DTs for adaptive traffic light control improves traffic flow during delays. In manufacturing, DTs combine AI-driven models with real-time tracking to make production processes better. DTs are very helpful for managing disasters and running cities because they give real-time data that helps people make better decisions and encourages participation from citizens (Fuller et al. 2020). The use of DTs in smart production and robots, especially in the context of Industry 4.0, shows how these technologies are coming together more and more to create smart, flexible industrial systems. The difference between DTs and digital ghosts has also been investigated, showing how digital images in built settings are changing and how this affects sustainability (Ford and Wolf 2020). Overall, DTs will change businesses in the future by making them more efficient, safe and environmentally friendly. As AI, Big Data and ML are added to them, they will become even more useful.

Area	Methodology	Key findings	Challenges	Pros	Cons	Application
Construction and AEC	Review of BIM to digital twin evolution	Digital twins represent a significant evolution from BIM, with more integrated data models in AEC and FM industries	Integration of new technologies with existing systems	Improves building management and maintenance	High implementation cost and complexity	Building information modeling (BIM), facility management and AEC
Structural health monitoring	Cloud-based digital twin integration with deep learning	Digital twins with AI and deep learning improve structural health monitoring and predictive maintenance	Need for real-time data processing and model updates	Enhances predictive capabilities and maintenance efficiency	Data privacy and security concerns	Structural integrity monitoring and predictive maintenance for bridges and buildings
Bridge inspection and maintenance	Digital transformation in bridge inspection and maintenance	Challenges exist in applying digital twin technologies to bridge maintenance; strategies for overcoming integration issues were discussed	Existing infrastructure compatibility and high costs of upgrading systems	Provides proactive maintenance solutions	High upfront costs, infrastructure compatibility issues	Bridge monitoring and infrastructure management

Smart cities	Application of digital twins for disaster management and urban planning	Digital twins in smart cities enable better disaster response, real-time resource management and urban planning	Ensuring data accuracy and synchronization across systems	Real-time data for improved decision-making and disaster management	Complexity in integration with existing city infrastructure	Urban planning, disaster management and resource management
Electric vehicles	Digital twin integration in vehicle performance optimization	Digital twins optimize electric vehicle performance and energy consumption	Real-time data collection and processing limitations	Enhances vehicle performance and energy efficiency	Data privacy concerns and high setup costs	Electric vehicle performance monitoring and energy optimization

Table 7.1. *Summarizes the literature review of various authors*

Table 7.1 shows a wide range of uses for DT in different fields, including the methods used, important discoveries, difficulties, pros and cons, and specific examples of their application. It includes construction, tracking the health of buildings, smart towns, electric cars, transportation and industry, among other things. Problems with using DT technologies are talked about, such as how to sync data, how much it costs to set up and how hard it is to connect different systems.

7.3. Foundational concepts

7.3.1. *Defining AI in the context of smart transportation*

AI is the process by which robots acquire human-like knowledge so they may learn, reason, solve problems and make choices. AI is what is enabling sophisticated systems in smart transportation, which can examine vast volumes of data, identify optimal solutions and improve user experience by means of their application.

7.3.2. *Introduction to DTs: concept and components*

DT technology creates a computerized copy of a real thing, system or process that is always being updated with new information. DTs let people in the transport industry make virtual versions of cars, equipment and whole transport networks. This gives everyone a full picture of how things are right now and how well they are working.

A DT is made up of several parts:

1) *Physical asset*: the thing in real life that is being modeled such as a car, a road or a bridge. Second, the virtual model is the computer copy of the real object.

2) *Data connection*: Internet of Things (IoT) sensors and data streams connect the real object to its virtual model, letting them be in sync in real time.

7.3.3. *Integration of AI and DT in transportation systems*

Combining the DT era with AI creates a mighty synergy that increases the fee of smart transport structures. AI's sophisticated statistics analytics, sample reputation and prediction technologies, and virtual twin's rigid models become smart, dynamic structures. A few of the maximum crucial programs of this dating are predictive renovation. Actual-time information from virtual twins permits synthetic intelligence systems to decide which vehicle or piece of infrastructure is the most likely to fail. This reduces downtime by enabling maintenance to be performed proactively, before issues occur. AI used with a virtual twin of a bus fleet, for instance, can monitor overall engine performance, detect wear and tear, and optimize maintenance scheduling. Another significant application is traffic management. Real-time traffic analysis and simulations, powered by DTs of metropolitan street networks, are further enhanced through AI. To perceive the optimum answers, the virtual twin simulates alternative moves such as rerouting automobiles or adjusting site visitors' lighting, as AI-powered systems forecast site visitors' congestion and the usage of digital and sensor data.

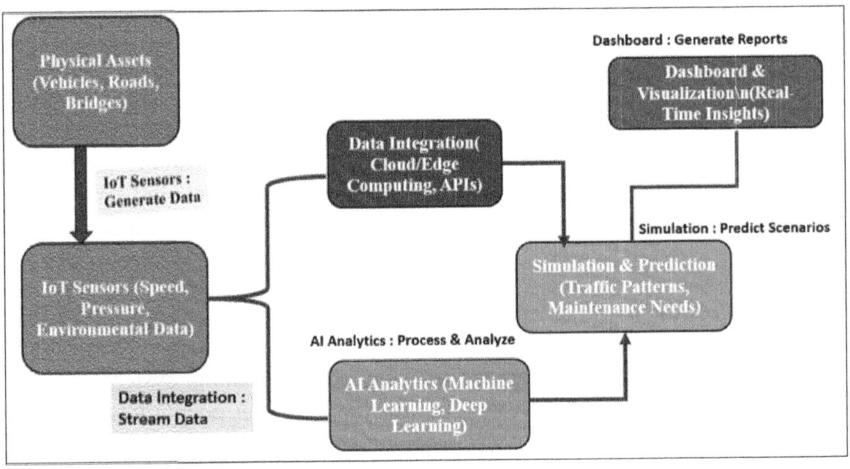

Figure 7.2. *Synergy of AI and DTs in urban mobility. For a color version of this figure, see: www.iste.co.uk/taneja/6gurban.zip*

Moreover, facilitating the development of journey structures capable of using themselves is the link. Powered by way of AI, DTs may mirror complicated places such as roadways and pedestrian crossings in order that self-driving automobiles may be tested and taught. This method guarantees that self-driving systems are secure and efficient, even as it hastens their deployment. Figure 7.2 shows how combined utilization of virtual twins and synthetic intelligence facilitates sustainable transportation-making plans. Those gadgets allow individuals to build green infrastructure, collect cars that use much less strength and make routes more efficient by searching for facts on pollutants and strength usage. Combining AI with virtual dual technologies creates a robust foundation for handling problems arising in contemporary transportation networks. Their mixed skills allow speedy decisions, unique forecasts and clever use of sources, consequently building the route toward better, safer and more longer-lasting mobility in the future.

7.4. AI-driven technologies in transportation

7.4.1. *ML models for traffic prediction and management*

Techniques of unsupervised learning, such as grouping, enable the identification of heavily traffic-congested regions and classifies them according to the degree of crowding. Traffic signal timing has been enhanced by use of reinforcement learning. By continuously learning from real-time traffic data, these systems may alter light phases on demand to lower delays and increase traffic flow. These kinds of flexible traffic management systems are already used in smart cities to reduce travel times and pollution by means of adaptation.

It becomes much more valuable when IoT devices and Global Positioning System (GPS) data are included into ML. ML models can therefore manage traffic and adjust paths on demand by being fed real-time data from linked automobiles and road infrastructure. Along with increasing the efficiency of urban transit, these technologies are making travel generally more fun.

7.4.2. *AI in vehicle autonomy and route optimization*

Making vehicles automated depends on AI, so self-driving automobiles and other autonomous transportation systems are feasible. Computer vision, NLP and sensor fusion among AI-powered technologies let self-driving vehicles sense their surroundings, make decisions on how to drive and view collected data. Using information from radar and cameras, computer vision systems locate and classify objects including people, vehicles and traffic signals.

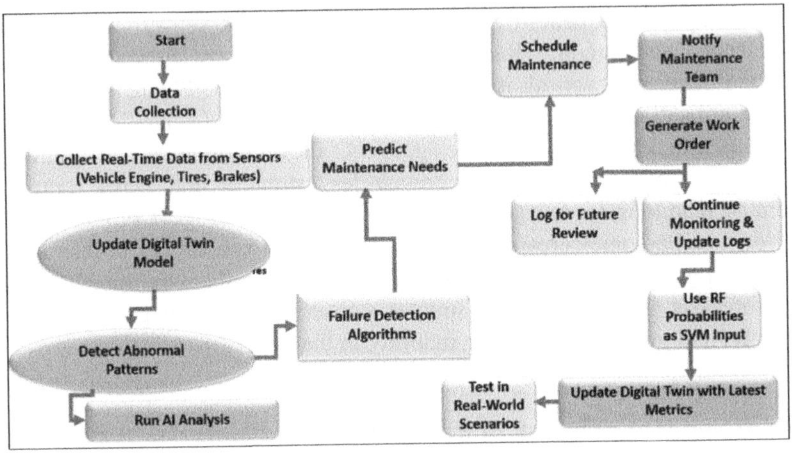

Figure 7.3. *Predictive maintenance workflow using digital twins. For a color version of this figure, see: www.iste.co.uk/taneja/6gurban.zip*

Using deep learning models, especially convolutional neural networks, these systems are excellent at identifying and recognizing things. NLP makes voice commands and seamless communication feasible, therefore enhancing the link between automated systems and human users even further. Route optimization is yet another significant use of AI in transportation. AI-powered guiding systems, as shown in Figure 7.3, search real-time traffic, road restrictions and weather data for the optimum driving paths. ML algorithms are used by these systems to guess how traffic will flow and change directions on the fly to save time and gas. AI-driven route optimization tools are helping transport companies cut costs and improve delivery speed in fleet management. These tools make sure that the best routes are planned for big teams by taking things such as car load, transport goals and road conditions into account.

7.4.3. *Real-time data processing and decision support systems*

One thing that makes AI-driven travel systems unique is their ability to handle data in real time. A huge amount of data is being created every second by IoT devices and equipment that is linked to the Internet. AI-powered decision support systems look at this data to give us useful information that we can use right away and help us make a quick decision. Public transport systems benefit from real-time data processing, as it enables exact arrival times, effective planning and vehicle tracking, therefore improving the plans. Data from GPS trackers, booking systems and traffic flow sensors is used in AI algorithms to ensure that operations go without a hitch and consumers are content. Real-time decision support systems search connected autos, traffic cameras and road monitor data for things such as roadblocks or accident causes. These devices enable traffic authorities to get instantaneous alerts, therefore enabling faster response and fewer disturbances. Through real-time monitoring of driver conduct and vehicle conditions, AI also makes transportation safer. AI-driven systems, for example, may identify indicators of a driver's tiredness or distraction using data from cameras and sensors inside the automobile. These sorts of technology reduce the possibility of collisions by allowing drivers to know when anything is wrong. Even more rapidly processing real-time data is made possible by using AI in tandem with cloud computing and edge computing. Edge computing allows localized processing, hence ensuring reduced latency for important applications such as traffic signal management and self-driving automobiles. For sophisticated analytics, cloud platforms provide the computing capability. By allowing us to manage traffic effectively, move about on our own and make choices in real time, AI-powered technologies are transforming our journey by method. These developments not only help to provide more ecologically friendly, safer and more user-friendly transportation systems but also to operate things more smoothly.

7.5. DT implementation in transportation

By allowing items to be tracked in real time, analytics-based forecasts and simulation-based choices are made, and DT technology has transformed the travel industry. Virtual duplicates of genuine assets and procedures are created by this revolutionary technology. This provides everyone engaged in transport systems with pertinent information about their performance as well as their areas of improvement. From monitoring a single automobile to controlling mass movement in cities, it could be used for anything. This section discusses DT design and models, examines some successful case studies and addresses issues arising from trying to use DT technology in transportation networks.

7.5.1. *Architectures and models of DTs for urban mobility*

Usually consisting of layers connected to one another, a DT in transportation facilitates data collecting, combining and application by means of various data sources. A DT is developed on real-time data from objects such as vehicles, road equipment and IoT. This data constantly matches the virtual model to provide an accurate representation of the actual system. Usually using cloud or edge computing to ensure that it can be scaled up or down and maintained in sync in real time, the interaction layer handles this data. Advanced analytics with AI and ML helps us get valuable insights from the data. DTs are able to operate at many sizes and are used at the level of the automobile to monitor performance and maintenance requirements such as engine wear or optimal fuel efficiency. Also, DTs create duplicates of certain infrastructure-related assets, such as bridges or crossings, to examine their structural integrity and determine their required maintenance. DTs represent complete transport ecosystems at the network level. This enables planners to examine traffic patterns, develop public transportation systems and see how infrastructure changes things. These models enable us to test possibilities and implement adjustments without influencing the actual state of affairs.

7.5.2. Challenges and solutions in digital twinning of transport infrastructure

DT technology is not straightforward to use in transportation even though it offers several advantages. Getting all of the information to cooperate and be the same is one of the primary challenges. Among other areas, transport systems from IoT devices, vehicles and outdated infrastructure provide a lot of data. Establishing open standards and methods is essential to ensure that these many data sources are fit and can interact. One further major issue is the high expense of implementing. Creating and deploying DTs spend a lot of money, time and resources on technology, talent and infrastructure. Public–private cooperation and test projects demonstrating the value of DTs will help to tackle this issue. This will provide funds for larger editions. Another rather crucial problem is data security and protection. Real-time private data sharing increases the likelihood that someone may access it without authorization or start an attack. DT systems' security has to be safeguarded by robust security measures. Among them include obeying data security policies, access restrictions and encryption. Two further issues needing resolution are scalability and real-time speed. Managing large DTs with continuous data synchronization calls for advanced computational capability. By allowing complex systems to manage high-volume processes with little delay, using cloud and edge computing may assist with these challenges. Not least of all, insufficient qualified personnel exist to create and oversee DT systems. Money must be invested in workforce development via partnerships between companies and colleges to let students learn how to use AI, data analytics and modeling technologies, thereby closing this disparity.

Although these issues are significant, more and more individuals are using DT technology, which is made possible by advancements in IoT and AI. This is creating new chances for better and more efficient transportation systems. Getting past these problems will allow everyone to fully realize how DTs can change how cities move people and how they handle infrastructure.

Aspect	Description	Challenges	Solutions	Examples
Architecture and models	Digital twin architecture involves layers for data collection, integration and real-time synchronization. Includes vehicle, infrastructure and network levels	Data integration from diverse sources, ensuring interoperability	Use of open standards and platforms to enable seamless integration	Vehicle-level monitoring (e.g. performance and maintenance), infrastructure-level models (e.g. bridges) and network-level simulations (e.g. traffic optimization)
Successful case studies	Demonstrates real-world implementations of digital twin technology across cities and sectors	High implementation costs for large-scale deployments	Public–private partnerships, pilot projects to demonstrate value and attract funding	Singapore's city-wide digital twin, London's Transport for London, Port of Hamburg and autonomous vehicle testing in the US
Data privacy and security	Real-time sharing of sensitive data raises risks of unauthorized access and cyberattacks	Ensuring data privacy and protection from cyber threats	Implementation of encryption, access controls and compliance with data protection regulations	Real-time monitoring of city infrastructure, logistics systems and autonomous vehicles

Table 7.2. *Overview of digital twin implementation in transportation*

Table 7.2 shows an organized list of the most important parts of DT technology used in transportation. It talks about the design and models of DTs, shows examples of successful application, talks about problems that come up and suggests possible answers. Concerns about data protection and security, scale and the need to grow the workforce are also covered in the table. As an example of how DT technology can be used and improved in the real world, each part is accompanied by cases from transport systems.

7.6. Data analysis and results

It is very important to analyze data in order for AI and DT technologies to work well in smart transportation. It is the basis for getting useful information, guessing what might happen in the future and making transport systems work better.

In this part, we will talk about how the data was collected, how it was analyzed and how the results were shown through case studies and model outputs.

7.6.1. *Data collection methods and sources*

Getting good data from trustworthy sources is the first step to performing good data analysis. In smart transportation, information is taken from many places, such as cars, infrastructure and how people interact with it. IoT monitors on roads, bridges and vehicles collect real-time information about how traffic flows, how fast vehicles are going, the weather and the health of infrastructure. GPS tracks, tracking systems and devices that count passengers on public transport add to the data that is collected. Logistics companies, ride-sharing platforms and companies that are developing self-driving cars can also give us useful information, such as route trends, changes in demand and measures for how well the vehicles are performing.

Metric	Before AI implementation	After AI implementation	Improvement (%)
Average travel time (min)	35	25	28.57
Traffic flow efficiency (vehicles/hour)	450	600	33.33
CO_2 emissions (kg/day)	2,000	1,500	25
Congestion incidents (per week)	15	5	66.67

Table 7.3. *Traffic management system performance before and after AI implementation*

Table 7.3 shows how the performance of a traffic control system was different before and after AI-powered prediction analytics were added. It displays the usual trip time, the effectiveness of traffic movement, CO_2 emissions and instances of traffic jams. When AI is used, travel time drops by 28.57% and CO_2 emissions drop by 25%. This shows that the system works better and is better for the Earth. The fact that traffic flow efficiency went up by 33.33% and congestion events went down by 66.67% shows that AI-driven dynamic traffic management can make traffic move more smoothly, cut down on delays and have less of an effect on the environment.

Real-time data from transport management systems is paired with historical data to give a full picture of long-term trends. Putting together data from different sources can be hard when it comes to standardization and sharing. To deal with this, transport systems often use open data platforms and standard files, which make it easy to combine and analyze data (see Figure 7.2). Advanced analytical methods are built on top of this thorough a process for gathering data.

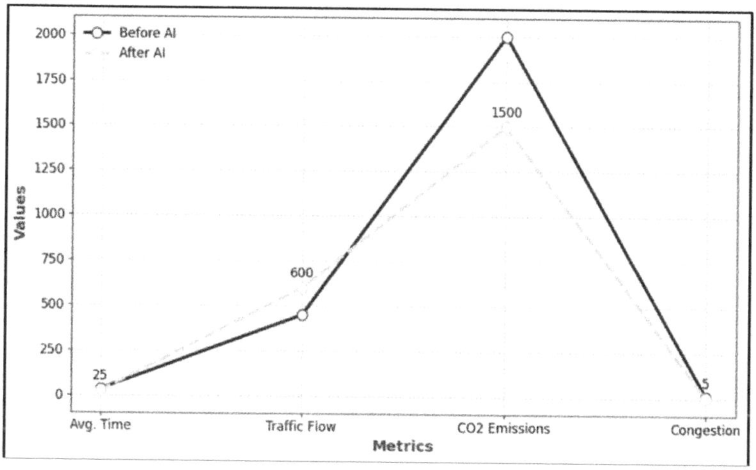

Figure 7.4. *Diagrammatic representation of traffic management system performance before and after AI implementation. For a color version of this figure, see: www.iste.co.uk/taneja/6gurban.zip*

7.6.2. *Analysis techniques: from descriptive to predictive*

A lot of different methods are used to look at transportation data, from simple detailed analytics to complex forecast modeling. Descriptive analytics gives us information about past patterns, such as rush-hour traffic, crash areas and car utilization rates. These findings help people understand how things are now and figure out what needs to be done to make things better. Diagnostic analytics goes one step further by finding out why trends are happening. For instance, looking at links between traffic jams and the weather can help managers come up with better ways to deal with them. AI and ML algorithms power predictive analytics, which makes predictions about the future based on data from the past and the present. Predicting traffic flow, car repair needs and customer demand is often done with tools such as time-series analysis, regression models and neural networks.

Vehicle ID	Predicted maintenance date	Actual maintenance date	Maintenance accuracy (%)	Downtime reduction (hrs)
V001	2025-02-15	2025-02-14	100	2
V002	2025-03-01	2025-03-03	95	3
V003	2025-01-28	2025-01-28	100	1
V004	2025-04-10	2025-04-12	90	4

Table 7.4. *Predictive maintenance for vehicles: performance indicators*

The results of a predictive maintenance model used on a fleet of cars can be seen in Table 7.4. It checks the expected maintenance dates against the real dates and finds that the maintenance dates were predicted very accurately (between 90% and 100% of the time). The table also shows that the number of times that cars had to be taken out for repair was cut down because they were serviced faster than planned. Preventative maintenance keeps fleets from breaking down when they are not supposed to and increases their availability, both of which are important for making transportation systems run more efficiently. The fact that the predictions were right and that there was less downtime shows that AI works to make vehicles more reliable and operations run more smoothly.

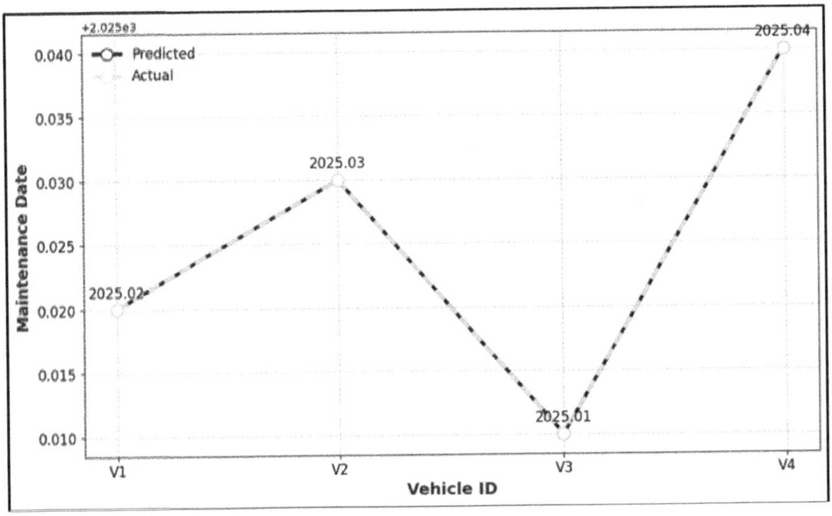

Figure 7.5. *Diagrammatic representation of predictive maintenance for vehicles: performance indicators. For a color version of this figure, see: www.iste.co.uk/taneja/6gurban.zip*

Predictive models let us make decisions ahead of time, which cuts down on delays and makes the system work better. The most advanced type, prescriptive analytics, uses optimization techniques to suggest specific things that should be done. AI-powered tools can, for example, suggest the best routes for public buses to take during rush hours or suggest changes to infrastructure to get rid of traffic jams.

The addition of DT technology improves these methods of analysis by letting them run models and test scenarios in real time (see Figure 7.5). Transportation managers can use a virtual setting to see how suggested changes would affect traffic. This makes sure that decisions are based on facts.

7.6.3. *Presentation of results: case studies and model outputs*

Case studies and visualizations that show the effects of AI and DT technologies are often used to show the results of data analysis. Predictive analytics are used in traffic control systems, which is an interesting case study. In a test project in Los Angeles, ML models looked at traffic data to predict traffic jams and change traffic lights on the fly. The results showed that journey times and pollution went down by a lot, which shows that data-driven solutions can work. DTs are also used to test self-driving cars, which is another example. Developers trained and tested self-driving algorithms by simulating different traffic situations in a virtual model of an urban setting. The results included more accurate object recognition and better movement in complicated settings.

Bus route	Predicted passenger demand (daily)	Actual passenger demand (daily)	Route optimization efficiency (%)	Operational cost reduction (%)
Route 1	350	340	5.7	10
Route 2	500	490	6.0	12
Route 3	600	610	3.5	8
Route 4	200	210	4.8	15

Table 7.5. *Passenger demand prediction and route optimization results*

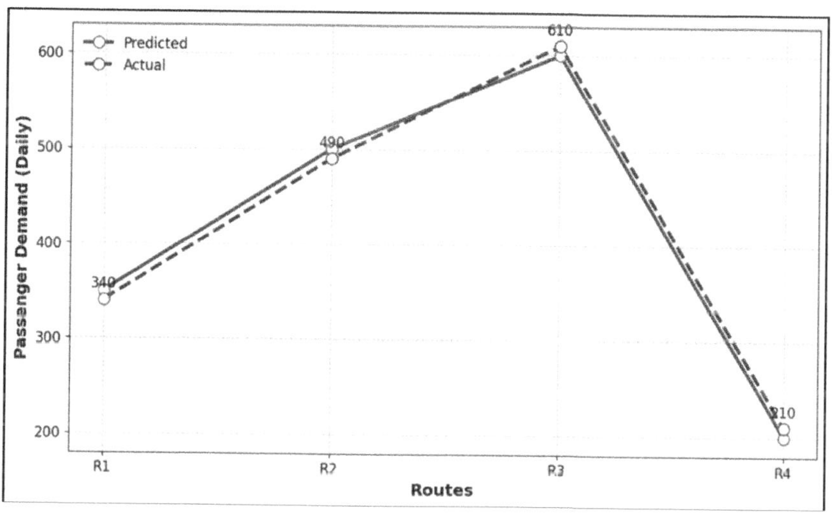

Figure 7.6. *Diagrammatic representation of passenger demand prediction and route optimization results. For a color version of this figure, see: www.iste.co.uk/taneja/6gurban.zip*

There is a comparison between the expected and real daily customer demand for different bus routes in Table 7.5. The table also shows how well optimization methods work on the route. It is based on expected demand, which helps change routes and plans to meet the needs of passengers. The results show a small difference between what was expected and what happened. The optimization savings for all routes were between 3.5% and 6%. The table also shows that running costs are going down, with some lines seeing drops of up to 15%. This means that public transport systems can improve service, make passengers happier and cut costs by using predictive analytics to guess what people will want.

Visualizations are a key part of telling stakeholders about the results. Dashboards that show real-time data give us information about how traffic moves, how well vehicles are doing and how many people are in each queue. Geographic Information System (GIS) maps show where there are a lot of accidents or traffic jams, which help planners decide where to focus their efforts. Data analysis has been used to make plans and paths better for public transportation. As shown in Figure 7.6, a case study from Singapore showed how AI algorithms could guess how many people would want to ride a bus and then change the plans to accommodate those people. Due to this, customer happiness went up and running costs went down. Overall, the fact that strong data collection, advanced analysis methods and clear results presentation all work together, show how AI and DT technologies can completely change smart transportation. These findings help everyone involved make smart choices that improve the safety, speed and long-term viability of urban transportation systems.

7.7. Integrating AI and DT for enhanced mobility

When AI and DT technologies are combined, they will likely change the way people travel and get around. For transportation systems to become more flexible, smart and efficient, they need to combine the forecasting power of AI with the real-time, data-driven insights that DTs offer.

7.7.1. *Synergistic effects of AI and DT on transportation efficiency*

Big datasets and complex pattern recognition of AI provide us with real-time knowledge about traffic flow, vehicle movement and infrastructure performance. AI may use DT digital replicas of the actual transportation system along with DTs to replicate traffic behavior and project future events in certain contexts. This helps us to make better decisions including determining the optimal paths for employees, adjusting traffic signal timings on demand and spotting and avoiding traffic congestion. By looking at previous patterns, the weather and real-time traffic data, AI can, in a huge metropolis, predict when traffic congestion is likely to develop.

The DT can then replicate how that traffic congestion might impact the surrounding roadways. With this type of foresight, traffic management systems and city planners can instantly adjust to reduce delays and prevent traffic congestion. By maximizing traffic flow, reducing route times and hence saving fuel usage, this cohesive approach serves over time to increase the overall efficacy of the transport system.

7.7.2. *Future directions: AI and DT in smart city frameworks*

Real-time data from buses, trams and trains can be combined with traffic data to make it easier for different types of transport to work together. This could mean changing bus lines or plans based on the current traffic situation. This would make public transportation more efficient generally and reduce the need for private cars. AI can also help handle parking spots by pointing drivers to open spots in real time and cutting down on the time they spend looking for parking. Long-term, AI and DT systems will be needed to manage how people move around in growing towns. As more people move into cities, travel networks will get more complicated, and people will want more efficient ways to get around. DTs powered by AI will help city planners model and build transport systems that can adapt to these changes. This will make sure that infrastructure changes as cities and populations grow. City governments will be better able to deal with problems such as traffic and environmental damage in the future if they build smart, flexible transport systems. Eventually, combining AI and DT technologies will be very important for making towns smart, sustainable and strong.

Key concepts	Technological impacts	Benefits	Challenges/considerations
Integration of AI's predictive power with digital twin's real-time simulation	Real-time data processing, predictive traffic models and route optimization	Reduced travel times, fuel consumption and improved traffic flow	Need for robust data security, real-time data accuracy
AI and digital twins used for traffic management and accident prevention	Predictive traffic analytics and real-time incident detection	Improved safety, reduced accidents and dynamic traffic management	Risk of over-reliance on automated systems and algorithmic biases
AI and digital twins in integrated urban mobility systems	Cross-platform integration with public transport, energy and waste	Sustainable, efficient and interconnected urban mobility	Regulatory complexities and privacy concerns in smart city data

Table 7.6. *Integrating AI and digital twin for enhanced mobility*

Table 7.6 summarizes the main ideas, technical effects, advantages and difficulties of combining DT technologies with AI in transportation. While addressing issues such as data security, algorithmic biases and the difficulties of applying these solutions across metropolitan systems, it emphasizes how these technologies may enhance traffic management, lower congestion and maximize routes.

7.8. Conclusion

Combining DT technology with AI is transforming smart mobility and providing fresh approaches to make it safer, more ecologically friendly and more efficient. When combined, these technologies provide a sophisticated, adaptable system capable of managing the many challenges arising in contemporary transport networks. Together, DTs' real-time models and capacity to forecast the future and AI's capacity to manage vast volumes of data and make choices in real time define how quickly and effectively transport systems may be developed. Working together, AI and DTs allow municipalities to enhance traffic flow, reduce congestion and simplify people's travel. Making roads safer also greatly depends on these technologies. DTs can replicate various scenarios to identify the best approaches to manage traffic; AI can forecast and stop collisions. Moreover, these technologies will be rather promising in the future for purposes other than just transportation. They will be key to building smart cities, connecting transportation systems with other city assets such as energy lines and trash management. It is not easy for transportation companies to use AI and DT technologies. Regarding ethics and policies specifically, this is true. Policymakers must handle a multitude of complex problems such as data privacy, AI algorithm bias, job loss resulting from automation and ensuring autonomous systems are liable. Dealing with these issues will help to ensure that the advantages of new technologies are shared equitably, maintained safely and continue for a long period. AI and DTs will become more important as communities expand and transport routes become more convoluted. If the right rules and laws are put in place, these technologies will help make transportation systems smarter, more environmentally friendly and more efficient. Policymakers, industry leaders and stakeholders can make sure that AI and DT technologies help make the future of transport safer, easier to get to and more environmentally friendly by being open to new ideas and aware of the risks that come with them.

7.9. References

Alam, K.M. and El Saddik, A. (2017). C2PS: A digital twin architecture reference model for the cloud-based cyber-physical systems. *IEEE Access*, 5, 2050–2062.

Aslani, M., Mesgari, M.S., Wiering, M. (2017). Adaptive traffic signal control with actor-critic methods in a real-world traffic network with different traffic disruption events. *Transportation Research Part C: Emerging Technologies*, 85, 732–752.

Bergs, T., Gierlings, S., Auerbach, T., Klink, A., Schraknepper, D., Augspurger, T. (2021). The concept of digital twin and digital shadow in manufacturing. *Proc. CIRP*, 101, 81–84.

Bhatti, G., Mohan, H., Singh, R.R. (2021). Towards the future of smart electric vehicles: Digital twin technology. *Renewable and Sustainable Energy Reviews*, 141, 110801.

Dang, H., Tatipamula, M., Nguyen, H.X. (2022). Cloud-based digital twinning for structural health monitoring using deep learning. *IEEE Transactions on Industrial Informatics*, 18(6), 3820–3830.

Dasgupta, S., Rahman, M., Lidbe, A.D., Lu, W., Jones, S. (2021). A transportation digital-twin approach for adaptive traffic control systems. *arXiv*. doi: 10.48550/arXiv.2109.10863.

Deng, M., Menassa, C.C., Kamat, V.R. (2021). From BIM to digital twins: A systematic review of the evolution of intelligent building representations in the AEC-FM industry. *Journal of Information Technology in Construction*, 26, 58–83.

Ford, N. and Wolf, C.M. (2020). Smart cities with digital twin systems for disaster management. *Journal of Management in Engineering*, 36(4), 04020027.

Fuller, A., Fan, Z., Day, C., Barlow, C. (2020). Digital twin: Enabling technologies challenges and open research. *IEEE Access*, 8, 108952–108971.

Futai, M.M., Bittencourt, T.N., Carvalho, H., Ribeiro, D.M. (2022). Challenges in the application of digital transformation to inspection and maintenance of bridges. *Structure and Infrastructure Engineering*, 18(10), 1581–1600.

Huang, Z., Shen, Y., Li, J., Fey, M., Brecher, C. (2021). A survey on AI-driven digital twins in industry 4.0: Smart manufacturing and advanced robotics. *Sensors*, 21(19), 6340.

Kumar, S.A., Madhumathi, R., Chelliah, P.R., Tao, L., Wang, S. (2018). A novel digital twin-centric approach for driver intention prediction and traffic congestion avoidance. *Journal of Reliable Intelligent Environments*, 4, 199–209.

Liu, Z., Meyendorf, N., Mrad, N. (2018). The role of data fusion in predictive maintenance using digital twin. In *44th Annual Review of Progress in Quantitative Nondestructive Evaluation*, Provo.

Lv, Z., Li, Y., Feng, H., Lv, H. (2021). Deep learning for security in digital twins of cooperative intelligent transportation systems. *IEEE Transactions on Intelligent Transportation Systems*, 23(9), 16666–16675.

Madan, B.S., Zade, N.J., Lanke, N.P., Pathan, S.S., Ajani, S.N., Khobragade, P. (2024). Self-supervised transformer networks: Unlocking new possibilities for label-free data *Panamerican Mathematical Journal*, 34(4), 194–210. doi: 10.52783/pmj.v34.i4.1878.

Mohammadi, N. and Taylor, J.E. (2017). Smart city digital twins. In *Proc. IEEE Symp. Comput. Intell. (SSCI)*, 1–5.

Qi, Q., Tao, F., Hu, T., Anwer, N., Liu, A., Wei, Y., Wang, L., Nee, A.Y.C. (2019). Enabling technologies and tools for digital twin. *Journal of Manufacturing Systems*, 58(Part B), 3–21.

Rathore, M.M., Shah, S.A., Shukla, D., Bentafat, E., Bakiras, S. (2021). The role of AI machine learning and big data in digital twinning: A systematic literature review challenges and opportunities. *IEEE Access*, 9, 32030–32052.

Sepasgozar, S.M.E. (2021). Differentiating digital twin from digital shadow: Elucidating a paradigm shift to expedite a smart sustainable built environment. *Buildings*, 11(4), 151.

Shahzad, M., Shafiq, M.T., Douglas, D., Kassem, M. (2022). Digital twins in built environments: An investigation of the characteristics applications and challenges. *Buildings*, 12(2), 120.

8

6G-enabled Digital Twin for Smart Transportation

With smart transport one of the key areas of focus, the launch of 6G technologies is expected to transform several spheres. A digital twin is a computerized replica of actual objects, systems or processes. Models, tracking and building improvement all depend on it as do transportation systems. This study discusses how digital twin technology and 6G networks may be coexisted to create smart transport. Over the next 10 years, the objective is to make transport systems safer, more efficient and more ecologically benign. We investigate how the extremely low latency, high speed and massive number of connections in 6G networks enable us to get real-time, data-driven insights on how transport operates in this research. Digital twins run on 6G networks and can manage vast volumes of data from infrastructure, cars and sensors. This allows us to replicate dynamically the traffic flow, automobile behavior and infrastructure health. These models may aid in city planning, prevent mishaps, coordinate maintenance and enable smart city usage of less energy. We also discuss how, in digital twin environments, artificial intelligence (AI) and machine learning (ML) could enable individuals to make better judgments. AI-driven prediction models may enable individuals to forward-plan for events such as traffic congestion, collisions and system failures by being included in digital twins enabled by 6G. This capacity to predict what will happen in real time enables us to design flexible transportation systems that can adapt to changing traffic situations, determine the optimum paths and allow self-driving vehicles to communicate with one another free from any conflicts. The research also explores the advantages and drawbacks of deploying digital twins permitted by 6G. It addresses, for instance, data privacy concerns, hacking challenges and the requirement of professionals in telecommunications, AI and urban planning cooperating together. Through this effort, we demonstrate how smart, connected and long-lasting mixing of 6G networks with digital twin technologies may entirely transform travel operations.

Chapter written by Prashant WAKHARE, Pritesh PATIL, Anuradha Amar BAKARE, Rajshri NIKAM, Vipan KUMAR, Yamini SOOD and Utku KOSE.

8.1. Introduction

Rapid changes in communication technology have produced improved and more linked networks. One major advance in this regard is 5G. But as technology develops, the need for faster, more reliable networks using less energy has resulted in the development of 6G technology. By the 2030s, companies all over are projected to be extensively using 6G. It provides quick data flow, a lot of connections and extremely little latency, which will provide new prospects in various spheres including transportation. Combining digital twin technologies with 6G offers an optimistic approach to improve smart transport systems. It reveals fresh approaches to make them better generally, more ecologically friendly and safer. A "digital twin" is a computerized replica of a physical world system or process. Acting as a live model, it replicates the characteristics and behaviors of the real object, therefore providing us with valuable knowledge about its workings. From manufacturing and aviation to healthcare and energy, digital twins are already being tracked, diagnosed and predicted upon in numerous disciplines. Digital twin technology can replicate how full transportation settings, vehicles and infrastructure function in terms of smart transportation. More careful monitoring, enhancing and simulating traffic flow, automobile performance and infrastructure condition of affairs are made possible by this replication. This helps individuals to make wiser use of resources and make choices. The backbone that digital twins in the transportation industry need to fully realize will be 6G networks. The extremely low latency and great stability of 6G will enable us to observe and obtain feedback straight away from both physical and virtual systems (Jones et al. 2020). This will enable the seamless interaction between connected elements and quick data transmission. For applications such as traffic management, smart city infrastructure and self-driving cars, where fast and efficient interaction is required to maintain everyone's safety and that systems function smoothly, this is particularly crucial. Combining digital twins with 6G provides great possibilities for transportation systems and might find application in many different locations. First, by simulating traffic flow, backed-off behavior and real-time visual appearance, it may assist with traffic management. Transportation companies can use this information to plan better routes, control traffic flow and stop crashes before they happen.

8.1.1. *Overview of 6G technology*

6G technology is the sixth version of wireless communication networks. It is meant to be much better than 5G by offering much faster speeds, ultra-low delay, better connection and more stable communication. Sixth-generation (6G) networks will combine many technologies, such as advanced artificial intelligence (AI), machine learning (ML), the Internet of Things (IoT) and new communication standards, to make the world smarter and more linked. They should be available to the public around the 2030s. 5G already supports real-time apps such as self-driving cars and treatments done from afar (Taslimasa et al. 2023).

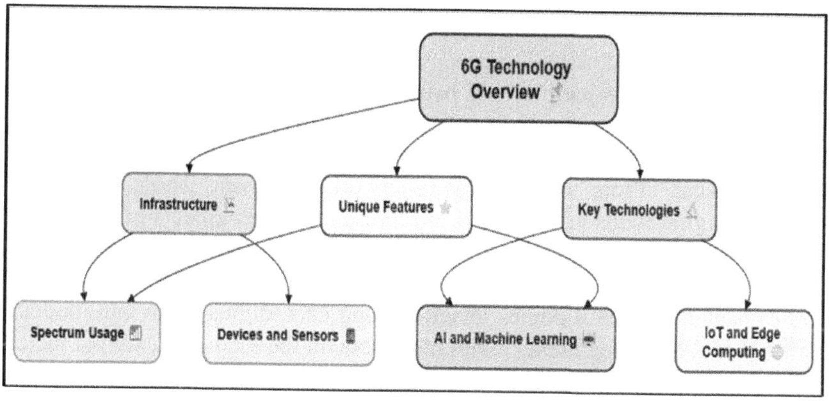

Figure 8.1. *The overview of 6G technology. For a color version of this figure, see: www.iste.co.uk/taneja/6gurban.zip*

6G, on the contrary, wants to support even more demanding use cases, pushing the limits of innovation and opening up new solutions for healthcare, transportation, smart cities and more. One of the best things about 6G is that it has very low latency. Round-trip delays should be as little as 1 millisecond or less. In real-time, mission-critical apps such as robotic surgery and self-driving cars, where even a fraction of a second of delay can be very bad, this amount of latency will make it possible. Figure 8.1 shows a hypothetical layout that shows the main parts and functions of the infrastructure for 6G technology. 6G will also be able to send data at speeds that are many times faster than current technologies. It could reach peak speeds of up to 1 terabit per second (Tbps). This huge bandwidth will make it possible to send huge amounts of data in virtual reality (VR), augmented reality (AR) and hologram communication, which will make it possible for people to have more engaging experiences than ever before (Yang et al. 2023).

8.1.2. *The concept of digital twins*

A digital twin is a computerized copy of a real thing, system or process that mimics how it works and behaves in real time by using sensors, data analysis and advanced modeling methods. Digital twins provide a living and interesting replica of the real-world version fit for tracking, investigation and enhancement. Digital twins originally emerged in industry as a means of increasing operating efficiency. Since then, it has permeated various disciplines such as transportation, engineering, urban design and healthcare. A digital twin is essentially a digital replica created precisely like the real world or process it stands for. Data is gathered from monitors included in the physical system or surroundings and sent to the digital twin for continuous monitoring (Brusa et al. 2023). The virtual model uses this data to replicate and project how the actual system would behave, therefore providing knowledge about its performance, any flaws and ways of improvement. These revelations help us make better judgments, maintain seamless operations of processes and prevent errors before they start. From cars to road networks to even whole transportation ecosystems, digital twins are modeled to represent various aspects of transportation (Xue et al. 2023). A digital twin of a smart city may, for example, replicate traffic flow, vehicle movements and infrastructure conditions to identify places needing repairs or backup. When it comes to self-driving cars, digital twins can model how the cars behave, how they interact with other cars on the road, and external factors to make sure they run safely and efficiently.

8.2. Literature review

8.2.1. *5G in smart transportation*

5G's fast data flow, very low delay and huge number of connections have made it a key technology for many real-time transportation uses. One of the most important places where 5G is making a big difference is in the creation of self-driving cars. Because 5G has low delay, it lets self-driving cars share info almost instantly with each other, with road infrastructure and with the cloud. Better communication lets cars make quick choices based on accurate information, which raises safety and lowers the risk of crashes. Along with self-driving cars, 5G also makes it easier to handle traffic. 5G-powered smart traffic systems can get information from connected cars and road sensors and process it to improve traffic flow and lessen congestion (Dong et al. 2022). Cities can handle roadworks, change traffic lights and guide drivers to less crowded roads by using real-time info on traffic conditions. This makes transportation networks work better. Adding 5G to vehicle-to-everything (V2X) communication systems has made it easier for cars, people and infrastructure to work together. This makes moving around cities safer and more efficient. V2X communication lets nearby cars or traffic management systems know right away about important events, such as a person crossing the street or a car suddenly slamming on the brakes. Also, 5G networks should help smart cities grow by making it easier for different types of transportation, such as buses, trains and bikes, to talk to each other in real time (Jafari et al. 2023). This connectivity makes mobility options that work well together, which improves the general transportation experience for people living in cities.

8.2.2. *Digital twin technology and its advancements*

Over the last several years, digital twin technology has advanced considerably and is now much superior at modeling, tracking and enhancing actual systems and processes. At first, digital twins were used in manufacturing, engineering and energy. Nowadays, they find use in many more sectors such as transportation, healthcare and agriculture, as they are so helpful for real-time data analysis and decision-making. One of the most significant advances is incorporating IoT cameras and data processing into digital twin architecture. This allows us to monitor constantly and provide comments in real time. These developments enable digital twins to faithfully mimic the condition of their physical counterparts. This makes system performance better and helps to forecast issues. Digital twins may indicate in industry when a machine will fail before it does (Liu et al. 2022). Smart cities may replicate traffic flow to assist in improved city planning. Including AI and ML into digital twin models has improved their predictive accuracy as well. Looking at the data produced by digital twins, AI systems may identify patterns, make real-time decisions and provide usable insights. This allows companies to operate more effectively, allocate their resources and be more proactive about maintenance. Another crucial shift is the use of digital twins in complex systems. These days, these systems can create simulations of whole ecosystems including electricity grids, transportation networks and healthcare systems (Ma et al. 2020). Digital twins, for instance, may be used in healthcare to replicate patient conditions, therefore guiding more individualized treatment approaches and improving clinical outcomes. Transportation is modeled through vehicle behavior and traffic system operation in cities using digital twins. This enables the identification of optimal routes and reduction of traffic.

8.2.3. *Digital twins in urban infrastructure*

Digital twins let city planners, engineers and other interested parties make virtual copies of real infrastructure such as roads, bridges, buildings and utility systems. This gives them useful information about how well these things work, how often they need upkeep and what risks might be involved. Transportation network control is one of the most important ways that digital twins are used in urban infrastructure (Mihai et al. 2021). Digital twins help towns improve traffic flow, lower congestion and make roads safer by modeling real-time traffic conditions, car movements and road conditions. For example, digital twins powering smart traffic management systems can change traffic lights on the fly based on real-time traffic data. This cuts down on delays and makes urban transportation more efficient. Not only are digital twins used for transportation, but they are also being used to control energy systems in towns. Digital twins of energy grids help improve how energy is distributed, predict when things will go wrong and make it easier to add green energy sources.

Table 8.1 shows a summary of the literature study that shows linked work, problems, future trends and research limits.

Approach	Challenges	Future Trends	Limitations
Integration of IoT and 5G for real-time traffic management	Interoperability between different digital twin systems	Seamless 6G integration for low-latency digital twins	High cost of deploying 6G networks and digital twins
Use of digital twins for autonomous vehicle simulations	High computational demand for real-time simulations	Increased AI and machine learning integration for smarter predictions	Limited availability of 6G infrastructure and support
Real-time monitoring of infrastructure using digital twins	Data privacy concerns due to sensitive transportation data	Wider adoption of autonomous vehicles in urban environments	Technical limitations in handling large-scale, real-time data
AI-driven traffic optimization with 5G networks (He et al. 2023)	Ensuring low latency in highly connected environments	Use of THz frequencies for ultra-fast communication	Challenges in maintaining data privacy and securing real-time data
Digital twin-based smart city planning and management	Integration of legacy transportation infrastructure with new technologies	Advanced digital twin simulations for entire city models	Interoperability issues between different digital twin models and technologies
6G for autonomous vehicle coordination	Scaling digital twin models to large, complex systems	Blockchain for enhanced data privacy and security	Data accuracy concerns due to inconsistent sensor readings
Real-time predictive maintenance with digital twins	Ensuring robust cybersecurity for transportation data	Expanded use of edge computing for real-time analytics	High energy consumption for running large-scale IoT networks
Machine learning algorithms for traffic prediction using IoT	Managing the massive amount of data from IoT devices	Ubiquitous IoT sensor deployment for better data collection	Difficulty in scaling digital twins across vast urban networks
Simulation of public transport systems with digital twins	Real-time decision-making in dynamic and unpredictable environments	AI-driven predictive traffic management	Network congestion and interference in dense urban areas
Smart parking management through digital twin technology (Guo et al. 2022)	Ensuring seamless communication between autonomous vehicles	Use of quantum computing for processing massive transportation data	Lack of global standards for data exchange and system integration

Approach	Challenges	Future Trends	Limitations
Use of edge computing with digital twins for faster decision-making	Meeting the power requirements of widespread IoT sensors	Collaborative smart city infrastructures powered by 6G	Limited computational power for processing massive datasets
Integration of blockchain for secure transportation data exchange	Regulation and standardization of data exchange protocols	Smart vehicle-to-vehicle (V2V) and vehicle-to-infrastructure (V2I) communication	Challenges in updating legacy transportation systems
Digital twin models for optimizing urban mobility networks	Dealing with data inconsistencies and inaccuracies	Advanced robotics for smart city maintenance and monitoring	Public skepticism about the integration of digital twins and 6G technology
Sensor networks and IoT for dynamic transportation monitoring (He et al. 2022)	Interference from network congestion in smart cities	Improved data integration and decision-making frameworks	Concerns over the environmental impact of widespread sensor deployment

Table 8.1. *Summary of literature review*

8.3. 6G technology overview

8.3.1. Key features of 6G networks

6G technology is a big step up from what came before it. It has abilities that will change the future of communication networks in big ways. One of the most interesting things about 6G is that it can offer very fast data rates, possibly as fast as 1 Tbps. With this rise in speed, huge amounts of data will be able to be sent, which will support complicated apps such as hologram conversation, VR and realistic AR. Because 6G has a high rate, these apps will be able to connect with each other in real time and provide a smooth user experience. One important thing about 6G networks is that they have very low latency, with round-trip delays of 1 millisecond or less (Hu et al. 2022). This decrease in latency is very important for mission-critical apps such as self-driving cars, smart transportation systems and remote healthcare, where even small delays can have big effects. Because of the low delay, decisions can be made in real time, and systems can react right away to changing surroundings. A huge number of gadgets should be able to connect to 6G, which will make the Internet of Everything (IoE) possible. With the power to join up to a million devices per square kilometer, 6G will link an unimaginable number of sensors, devices and tools, making an environment that is completely linked (Wu et al. 2021).

8.3.2. *Network architecture and communication protocols*

Although the framework of 6G networks will expand on the fundamental principles of past generations, it will also include some fresh elements to assist the more complex capabilities required by new applications. Fundamentally, 6G will run on an open, modular, scalable network with both centralized and distributed components. From high-speed mobile internet services to mission-critical applications such as self-driving vehicles and healthcare, this blended approach may accommodate various kinds of usage. One of the most significant new elements of 6G network architecture is combining edge computing with fog computing. These technologies enable handling of data closer to its source, therefore reducing latency and freeing processing capacity from big data centers. Real-time applications such as interaction between self-driving vehicles, where decisions must be taken in milliseconds (Du et al. 2023), would greatly benefit from this approach. Edge and fog computing will improve scaling and make the best use of resources by spreading processing resources across the network. To handle the extra data flow and complexity of the network, 6G networks will also use more modern communication methods. One of these protocols is the advanced use of AI and ML techniques to handle networks and assign resources in real time. With these smart protocols, the network will be able to organize itself, find the best settings and fix itself, which will make it faster, more reliable and safer. 6G will also use beamforming methods, such as huge MIMO (multiple-input, multiple-output), to improve signal strength and range, especially in cities where signal confusion is a problem. Below are mathematical equations that describe these core processes.

Step 1. Data Transmission Rate (Bandwidth Calculation)

The data transmission rate (R) can be calculated using Shannon's Capacity Theorem:

$$R = B * log2\left(1 + \frac{P}{N}\right)$$

where:

– R is the data rate in bits per second (bps);

– B is the bandwidth in Hz;

– P is the signal power;

– N is the noise power.

Step 2. Latency in Communication (End-to-End Latency)

The end-to-end latency L in the communication system can be expressed as:

$$L = L_{transmission} + L_{propagation} + L_{processing}$$

where:

– L_transmission is the time taken to transmit data,

Step 3. Network Throughput (Capacity of a Communication Channel)

The throughput T is defined by:

$$T = \frac{N}{L}$$

Step 4. Routing Optimization (Path Selection)

The optimal routing path P can be determined by minimizing the total cost function:

$$P_{opt} = arg\, min\, \Sigma\, (C_i)$$

Step 5. Data Packet Loss in Network

Packet loss probability P loss can be calculated using the following formula:

P_loss = (Number of lost packets) / (Total number of packets transmitted)

This equation helps in determining the reliability of the network, especially in highly dynamic environments such as autonomous vehicle communication.

Step 6. Energy Efficiency (Energy per Bit)

Energy efficiency E_b, or energy consumed per bit, is crucial for low-power networks:

$$E_b = \frac{(P_{transmission} * t_{transmission})}{R}$$

8.3.3. *Enhanced capabilities: speed, latency and reliability*

Big gains in speed, latency and stability mean that 6G technology will transform mobile networks and enable next-generation applications. This incredibly fast transmission rate will enable high-bandwidth applications such as VR, realistic AR and 3D visual communication to become widespread. 6G's fast speeds will enable users to work better because these applications must transmit massive volumes of data immediately, therefore providing more seamless and interesting experiences (Bao et al. 2021). Along with higher speeds, 6G will significantly improve delay. 6G networks will be able to handle real-time, mission-critical apps where even small delays can have big effects thanks to round-trip delays of 1 millisecond or even less. Self-driving cars will be able to talk to each other, infrastructure and control systems in real time, which will make them safer and better able to respond. Furthermore, 6G's low delay will help remote medical applications such as telesurgery and real-time monitoring, letting doctors connect with patients and tools in almost real time. Figure 8.2 shows the improved features of 6G technology, mainly the faster speeds, lower delay and higher dependability.

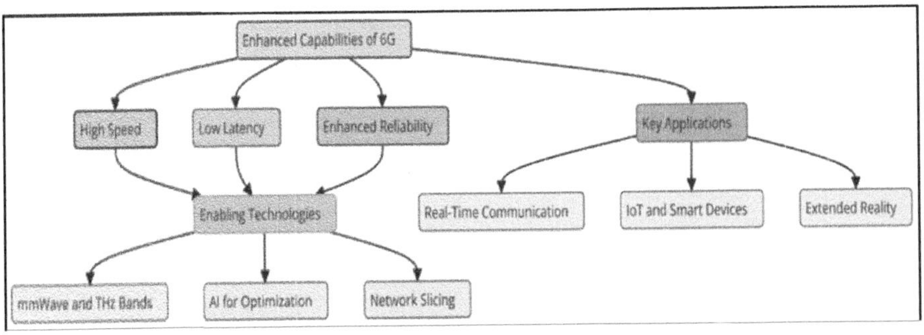

Figure 8.2. *Enhanced capabilities: speed, latency and reliability. For a color version of this figure, see: www.iste.co.uk/taneja/6gurban.zip*

Another important improvement that 6G brings is reliability. With improvements in error correction methods, beamforming techniques and smart network management, 6G will make sure that the communication system is very stable and can keep important apps running without any problems (Tran-Dang et al. 2022). In fields such as industrial robotics, self-driving cars and emergency management, where downtime or lost connections can have bad results, this level of dependability is very important.

8.3.4. *Role of AI, ML and IoT in 6G for transportation*

Particularly in the transportation sector, the IoT, AI and ML will all be quite crucial for creating and operating 6G networks. Using 6G's high speed and minimal latency, these technologies will enable smart, efficient and self-driving systems to make transportation safer, more effective and a better traffic management tool. Making transportation networks run better will depend on AI and ML algorithms considering the enormous volumes of data generated by IoT devices in sensors, equipment and vehicles. By means of traffic signal timing, accident detection in real time and traffic congestion prediction, these AI-driven insights help to enhance the flow of traffic by means of which traffic congestion is lessened. By gathering and evaluating data from their surroundings in real time, self-driving vehicles will also be taught how to safely negotiate difficult urban environments using ML algorithms. The IoT will be the backbone of the 6G-connected transportation environment because millions of devices and sensors are incorporated into buildings, traffic systems and vehicles. These IoT sensors will compile and transmit information on items such as traffic patterns, road conditions and automobile speed.

– Step 1: Data collection from IoT sensors:

The real-time data D(t) can be modeled as an integral over time:

$$D(t) = \int (t0\ to\ t1) f(x, y, z, \ldots) dt$$

– Step 2: Data preprocessing and feature extraction using ML:

Feature extraction is then performed to identify key attributes that can be used for predictions (e.g. traffic congestion patterns, road conditions).

Data preprocessing is typically a linear transformation of the collected data:

$$X_{processed} = \int (D) f(D) dD$$

– Step 3: ML model training:

After preprocessing, ML models are trained to predict traffic patterns, vehicle behavior or infrastructure health based on historical data. The goal is to train the model to optimize real-time decision-making.

$$L = \int (x0\ to\ x1) \left(f_{model(x)} - y\right)^2 dx$$

– Step 4: Prediction and decision-making (AI optimization):

Real-time optimization can be modeled as a decision-making function D_opt that minimizes a cost function C:

$$D_{opt} = \int (T) \left(\Sigma(i = 1\ to\ n) C_{i(t)}\right) dt$$

– Step 5: Real-time communication and feedback loop using 6G:

Real-time feedback can be expressed as an integral of the difference between expected and actual outcomes:

$$\Delta F(t) = \int (t0\ to\ t1)\left(f_{expected(t)} - f_{actual(t)}\right)dt$$

– Step 6: System refinement and continuous learning

The system continually learns and refines itself based on the incoming data and feedback. This ensures that the AI model adapts over time to improve predictions, optimize decisions and make the transportation system more efficient.

Continuous learning can be represented by an integral update rule for model parameters θ:

$$\theta_{new} = \int (D)\nabla_\theta L(\theta)dD$$

where:

– θ_new represents the updated model parameters;

– ∇_θ L(θ) is the gradient of the loss function with respect to the parameters θ;

– D is the dataset used for learning.

8.4. Digital twin concept for smart transportation

8.4.1. Definition and components of a digital twin

A "digital twin" is a copy or virtual version of a real thing, system or process that acts and has the same properties as the real thing in real time. It copies physical systems digitally using data from sensors, devices and other sources. This lets them be monitored, analyzed and improved in real time. In a digital twin setup, the physical system and its digital copy are always exchanging data with each other. This lets a simulation of the system's processes happen all the time.

The key components of a digital twin include:

– Physical entity: the thing, system or process in the real world that is being watched. This could be anything from the movement of a car to a whole traffic system or infrastructure such as roads and bridges.

– Sensors and data collection: these are built-in sensors that measure things such as temperature, speed, direction and the state of the surroundings. This information is sent to the digital twin so that it can be processed in real time.

– Data model and analytics: advanced analytics, ML and AI techniques are used to process the collected data and give information about how well the physical system is working. This model is always being changed to show how the real system is right now.

– Simulation and visualization tools: digital twins usually come with visualization tools that make it easy for users to see, analyze and interact with the data in the system. This helps people who make decisions improve processes and run models to see what problems might occur.

– Feedback loop: a digital twin has a feedback mechanism built in so that model data can be used to make real-time changes to the physical system that make it work better or lessen the chance of problems occurring.

8.4.2. *Application of digital twins in transportation systems*

Digital twin technology can be used in many ways in the transportation industry to make things safer, more efficient and more environmentally friendly. In transportation systems, digital twins create a virtual copy of real-world assets such as cars, infrastructure and traffic networks. This lets decisions and improvements be made in real time based on data. By combining data from sensors, cameras and cars, digital twins make it possible to watch and simulate traffic in real time. This computer model helps the people in charge of traffic predict traffic jams, find accidents and find the best times for traffic lights to make traffic move better. Digital twins can help come up with ways to reduce traffic jams, speed up travel and make roads safer by modeling different traffic situations.

8.4.3. *Real-time monitoring and simulation in transportation networks*

Real-time monitoring and modeling underlie the digital twin concept in transportation systems, which offer great advantages for safety, optimization and future prediction ability. By continuously updating them and running models based on real-world data, digital twins enable transport systems to change with the times. This helps the systems to operate more effectively in general. Digital twins use data from IoT sensors installed inside automobiles, infrastructure and the surroundings to monitor the real-time state of transportation networks. Important information regarding traffic, weather, vehicle behavior and road structure is provided by these cameras. Constant data collecting and analysis allows digital twins to create a virtual replica of the present state of the system. This helps those in transportation to make rapid, wise judgments. Digital twins are among the finest things, as they let one examine many outcomes and scenarios in real time. For example, a digital twin of a traffic system may indicate how route restrictions, weather variations or accident occurrence might affect the traffic flow overall. This lets transportation officials come up with proactive plans to stop or lessen problems, such as changing traffic lights, rerouting vehicles or sending out emergency services. Figure 8.3 shows real-time tracking and modeling methods used to improve the performance and efficiency of transport networks.

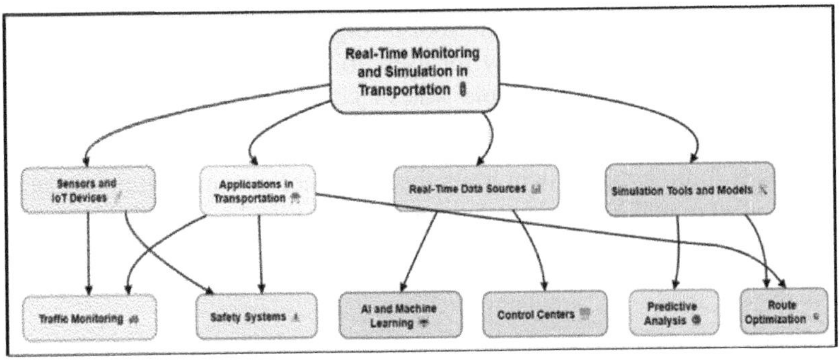

Figure 8.3. *Real-time monitoring and simulation in transportation networks. For a color version of this figure, see: www.iste.co.uk/taneja/6gurban.zip*

Digital twins can guess what will happen in the future using ML algorithms and data from the past and information being fed in real time. For instance, digital twins can predict trends of traffic jams, the need for road repair or how self-driving cars will behave in different situations. With this ability to predict the future, transport systems can plan their operations more efficiently, cutting down on delays and making them safer. Digital twins make it easier for different parts of the transport network to work together.

8.5. Result and discussion

Adding digital twins that can connect to 6G networks to smart transport systems makes them much safer, more environmentally friendly and more efficient. 6G networks allow for real-time data sharing, very low delay and for huge numbers of devices to join. This makes it possible for digital twins to successfully model and watch transportation networks. This makes it possible for dynamic traffic control, predictive repair and the coordination of self-driving cars, which leads to less traffic, better safety and better use of resources.

Evaluation parameter	Value (6G)	Value (5G)	Improvement (%)
Latency (ms)	1	10	90
Data transfer speed (Gbps)	100	10	900
Number of connected devices (million)	1,000	100	900
Traffic flow efficiency (%)	95	85	11.76

Table 8.2. *Network performance evaluation*

The network performance evaluation in Table 8.2 clearly shows the differences between 6G and 5G. It shows that 6G greatly improves key performance factors that are important for real-time applications and smart transportation. Figure 8.4 shows some important differences between 6G and 5G technologies, showing how speed and delay have improved.

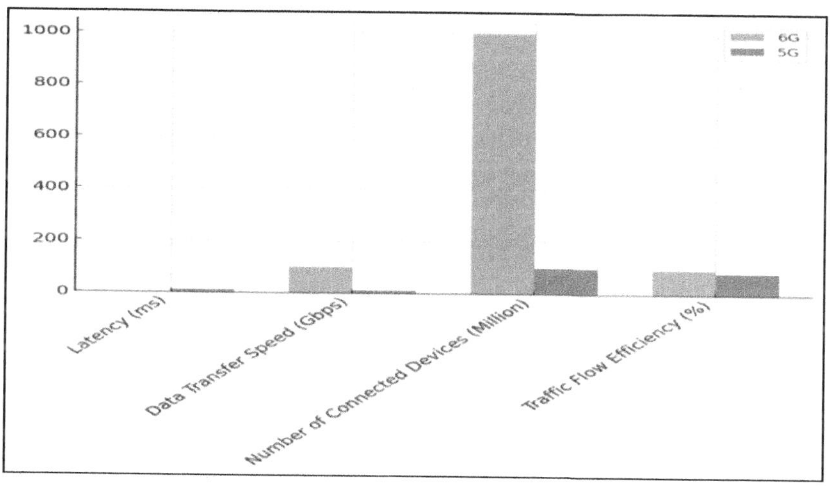

Figure 8.4. *Comparison of 6G and 5G metrics. For a color version of this figure, see: www.iste.co.uk/taneja/6gurban.zip*

Latency is one of the most noticeable changes for the better. 6G networks have 90% less delay than fifth-generation networks, dropping from 10 milliseconds to just 1 millisecond. Figure 8.5 shows a trend study that shows how the performance of 6G and 5G technologies has changed over time.

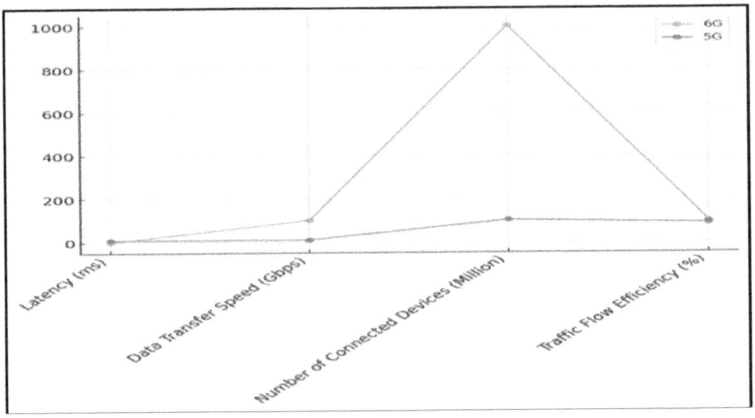

Figure 8.5. *Trend analysis of 6G and 5G performance. For a color version of this figure, see: www.iste.co.uk/taneja/6gurban.zip*

This is very important for situations where decisions need to be made right away, such as in self-driving cars, smart traffic systems and emergency response situations. Less delay means that people can talk and respond more quickly, which makes transportation networks safer and more efficient. The speed at which data is sent has also greatly improved. Figure 8.6 shows how 6G is better than 5G in a number of ways, such as speed, delay and capacity.

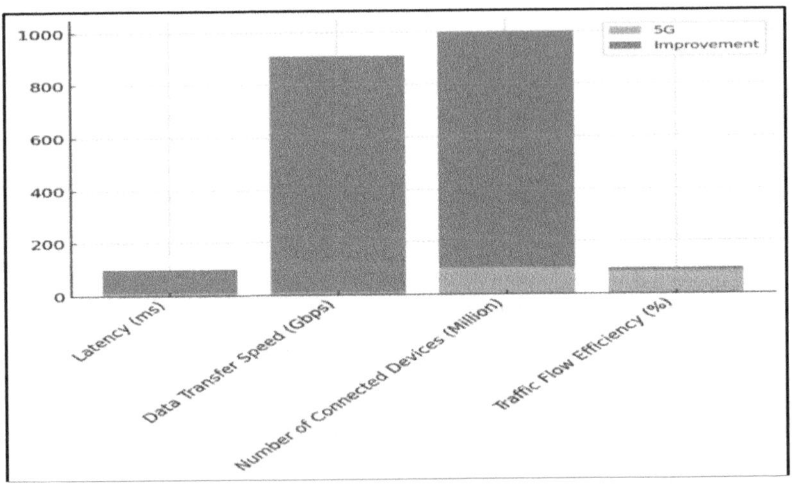

Figure 8.6. *6G improvements over 5G across metrics. For a color version of this figure, see: www.iste.co.uk/taneja/6gurban.zip*

In 6G, speeds can reach up to 100 Gbps, up from 10 Gbps in 5G. This is a 900% rise. This huge increase in data transfer speeds makes it possible to send large amounts of data without any problems. This is important for uses such as streaming HD videos, tracking traffic in real time and creating realistic VR experiences. This feature makes sure that transport networks can handle the huge amounts of data that sensors, cars and equipment produce. 6G also supports up to 1,000 million devices, 10 times as many as 5G's 100 million. This means that a lot more devices can be linked. For the IoE to work, billions of connected objects, from cars to smart infrastructure, must be able to talk to each other and work together to make a smart, connected transportation environment.

Evaluation parameter	Value (6G)	Value (5G)	Improvement (%)
Model accuracy (%)	98	90	8.89
Real-time data sync time (ms)	1	5	80
Predictive maintenance accuracy (%)	95	80	18.75
System scalability (%)	98	85	15.29

Table 8.3. *Model accuracy and performance evaluation.*

Table 8.3 shows that 6G is much better than 5G when it comes to modeling accuracy, syncing data in real time, predictive maintenance and system scalability. These are all very important for making digital twins work well in smart transportation. The graph in Figure 8.7 shows how the performance of 6G and 5G differs in terms of speed, delay and capacity.

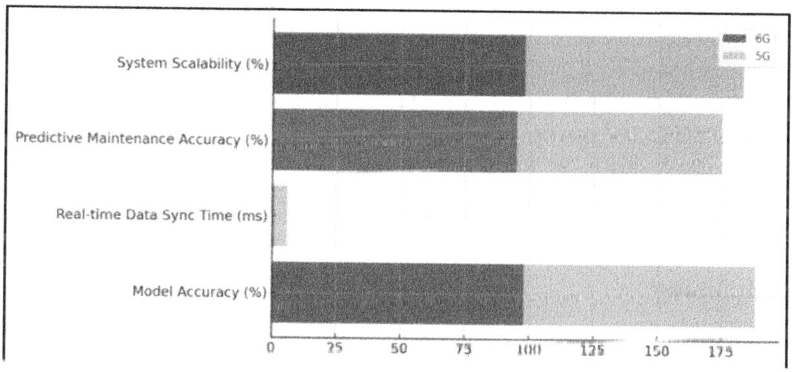

Figure 8.7. *6G vs 5G performance metrics comparison. For a color version of this figure, see: www.iste.co.uk/taneja/6gurban.zip*

The accuracy of models goes up from 90% in 5G to 98% in 6G, which is an 8.89% rise. Better studies and predictions of real-world transportation systems come from more accurate models. This improvement is important because it makes real-time traffic control and decision-making more effective. The higher accuracy also makes digital twins work better by making sure that the virtual models are more like the real systems. Figure 8.8 shows how key speed measures have improved over time with 6G compared to 5G.

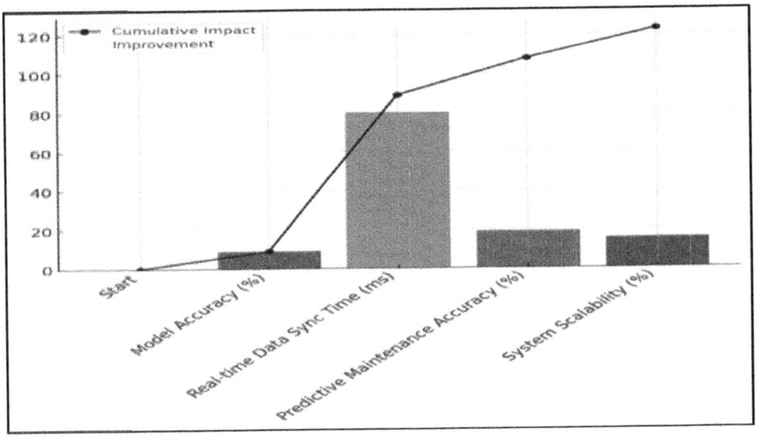

Figure 8.8. *Cumulative improvement of 6G over 5G. For a color version of this figure, see: www.iste.co.uk/taneja/6gurban.zip*

This lets resources and processes be used more efficiently. In terms of synchronizing data in real time, 6G is a huge step forward. Synchronization time drops from 5 milliseconds to just 1 millisecond with 6G, which is an 80% decrease. This very low delay is very important for real-time processes, which need to make rapid changes based on data that is changing all the time, such as how traffic flows or how cars behave. The accuracy of predictive maintenance goes up by 18.75%, from 80% in 5G to 95% in 6G. This improvement makes it easier to predict when a system will break down, so fixes can be made quickly and transport networks are less likely to be interrupted.

8.6. Conclusion

Putting 6G technology and digital twin systems together is a completely new way to improve smart transport networks. With 6G's very low delay, fast data transfer and huge connection, digital twins can work better, allowing for real-time exercises, planned upkeep and higher safety standards in transportation systems. The fact that 6G can handle the constant flow of data from IoT devices makes it possible for digital twins to show exact, changing pictures of things such as roads, cars and traffic control systems. This makes it possible to make better decisions, handle traffic better, cut down on traffic jams and make urban transportation more efficient overall. Furthermore, 6G's mix of edge computing, AI, IoT and digital twins makes the transportation environment more connected, quick and smart, thus enhancing their value. Although the opportunities are fantastic, several issues still need to be resolved before digital twins and 6G can operate without incident. Technical issues must be resolved; these include the necessity of robust network architecture, real-time data handling capability and the capacity of many technologies to interact. Since transport systems transmit and receive a lot of private data in real time, the issues of data privacy and security are also major ones. Also, investments and changes to facilities are needed to make sure that both 6G networks and digital twin technologies are used on a large scale, especially in cities with complicated transportation systems.

8.7. References

Bao, L., Wang, Q., Jiang, Y. (2021). Review of digital twin for intelligent transportation system. In *Proceedings of the 2021 International Conference on Information Control, Electrical Engineering and Rail Transit (ICEERT)*, Lanzhou, 30 October–1 November. IEEE, Piscataway, NJ, 309–315.

Brusa, E., Dagna, A., Delprete, C., Gentile, R. (2023). An orchestration method for integrated multi-disciplinary simulation in digital twin applications. *Aerospace*, 10, 601.

Dong, P., Zhao, J., Liu, X., Wu, J., Xu, X., Liu, Y., Wang, S., Guo, W. (2022). Practical application of energy management strategy for hybrid electric vehicles based on intelligent and connected technologies: Development stages, challenges, and future trends. *Renew. Sustain. Energy Rev.*, 170, 112947.

Du, H., Leng, S., He, J., Xiong, K., Zhou, L. (2023). Digital twin empowered cooperative trajectory planning of platoon vehicles for collision avoidance with unexpected obstacles. *Digit. Commun. Netw.*, 2352–8648.

Guo, J., Bilal, M., Qiu, Y., Qian, C., Xu, X., Choo, K.K R. (2022). Survey on digital twins for Internet of Vehicles: Fundamentals, challenges, and opportunities. *Digit. Commun. Netw.* 2352–8648.

He, C., Luan, T.H., Lu, R., Su, Z., Dong, M. (2022). Security and privacy in vehicular digital twin networks: Challenges and solutions. *IEEE Wirel. Commun.*, 30, 154–160.

He, W., Mao, J., Song, K., Li, Z., Su, Y., Wang, Y., Pan, X. (2023). Structural performance prediction based on the digital twin model: A battery bracket example. *Reliab. Eng. Syst. Saf.*, 229, 108874.

Hu, Z., Lou, S., Xing, Y., Wang, X., Cao, D., Lv, C. (2022). Review and perspectives on driver digital twin and its enabling technologies for intelligent vehicles. *IEEE Trans. Intell. Veh.*, 7, 417–440.

Jafari, M., Kavousi-Fard, A., Chen, T., Karimi, M. (2023). A review on digital twin technology in smart grid, transportation system and smart city: Challenges and future. *IEEE Access*, 11, 17471–17484.

Jones, D., Snider, C., Nassehi, A., Yon, J., Hicks, B. (2020). Characterising the digital twin: A systematic literature review. *CIRP J. Manuf. Sci. Technol.*, 29, 36–52.

Liu, J., Zhang, L., Li, C., Bai, J., Lv, H., Lv, Z. (2022). Blockchain-based secure communication of intelligent transportation digital twins system. *IEEE Trans. Intell. Transp. Syst.*, 23, 22630–22640.

Ma, J., Chen, H., Zhang, Y., Guo, H., Ren, Y., Mo, R., Liu, L. (2020). A digital twin-driven production management system for production workshop. *Int. J. Adv. Manuf. Technol.*, 110, 1385–1397.

Mihai, S., Davis, W., Hung, D., Trestian, R., Karamanoglu, M., Barn, B., Prasad, R., Venkataraman, H., Nguyen, H. (2021). A digital twin framework for predictive maintenance in industry 4.0. In *Proceedings of the HPCS 2020: 18th Annual Meeting*, Barcelona.

Taslimasa, H., Dadkhah, S., Neto, E.C.P., Xiong, P., Ray, S., Ghorbani, A.A. (2023). Security issues in Internet of Vehicles (IoV): A comprehensive survey. *Internet Things*, 22, 100809.

Tran-Dang, H., Krommenacker, N., Charpentier, P., Kim, D.S. (2022). The Internet of Things for logistics: Perspectives, application review, and challenges. *IETE Tech. Rev.* 39, 93–121.

Wu, Y., Zhang, K., Zhang, Y. (2021). Digital twin networks: A survey. *IEEE Internet Things J.*, 8, 13789–13804.

Xue, W., Wang, Z., Zheng, R., Mei, X., Yang, B., Nakano, K. (2023). Fail-safe behavior and motion planning incorporating shared control for potential driver intervention. *IEEE Trans. Intell. Veh.*, 8, 3884–3897.

Yang, Z., Li, L., Gu, F., Ling, X. (2023). Dependable and reliable cloud-based architectures for vehicular communications: A systematic literature review. *Int. J. Commun. Syst.*, 36, e5457.

9

Digital Twins Supercharges Efficiency-Unlocking the Power of Industry 5.0

The revolutionary technology of Virtual Reality (VR) and Augmented Reality (AR) is shaping Industry 5.0. Exploring AR and VR and understanding its usefulness in the present context is the main objective of this chapter. This chapter helps us understand the usefulness of VR and AR to the eventual users. VR and AR can help an organization achieve growth and help in sustainability by converging on the mission and vision of the organization, therefore gaining the advantage by leveraging prototyping and refining suitable innovation before obliging for physical production. Pretesting any ideas and developing products before determining the acceptability in the market before launch is one of the benefits derived from AR and VR. Also, customization of products for different users becomes possible. AR and VR enhance training and take it to another level. Discovering the potential of these digital twins in the metaverse and their application in various industries, this chapter is a systematic review of published research papers.

This chapter tries to understand the digital twins, AR and VR, and their actual application in Industry 5.0, discussing the benefits derived and challenges faced. This chapter also explores the future potential of AR and VR in the context of sustainable future. The immeasurable benefits discussed here regard the understanding of VR and AR and their role in building smart Industry 5.0

9.1. Introduction

Significant changes can be noted in the industrial domain; the focus has shifted to producing innovative quality products within a shorter period (Phuyal et al. 2020). Modern manufacturing companies are in the process of adopting technology mainly

Chapter written by T. Shirley DEVAKIRUBAI.

to meet the needs of the current generation. Adopting new technology helps the business to reduce barriers and maintain standards in producing quality products (Eswaran and Raju Bahubalendruni 2022). The focus of Industry 5.0 is a human-positioned technology-oriented production (Wang et al. 2024). The context of Industry 5.0 is to develop an all-encompassing, innovative production process encouraging innovation and human skills for sustainable production (Hamza Zafar et al. 2024). These advancements in the metaverse include augmented reality (AR) and virtual reality (VR), together called the digital twins (Jin and Ryu 2025). Usage of these AR and VR is varied in fields such as entertainment, games, training and manufacturing (Astrologo et al. 2024).

Industrial interaction between the physical and virtual world is possible with the intervention of AR and VR; an immersive experience gives a real-world experience (Yin et al. 2023). Industry 5.0 is more of a human-focused approach entwined with technology compared to Industry 4.0; the main focus was on technology (Cónego et al. 2024). A significant focus of Industry 5.0 is a human-centered approach; VR is mostly used for training employees in the industrial setting (Jalilvand et al. 2024). VR is not a simulation; it is visualizing the real situation in an immersive environment (Alcácer and Cruz-Machado 2019). Envisioning of the real design in a controlled setting is possible through VR (Riesener et al. 2024). Artificial intelligence (AI) generates the immersive experience, and VR provides a form for the AI generation (Jin and Ryu 2025). VR enables the industry to provide training to employees with enabled features such as collaboration, simulation and a risk training environment (Lund et al. 2023). With VR, the users' physical movements control the immersive experience, and VR provides clear guidance to the users (Nenna et al. 2023). VR technology enables the users to get immersed and gain a newer experience with the manipulated environment (Wen and Gheisari 2021). VR enables the user to have a detailed analysis of the product coupled with maintained quality; it creates a synergy between the real and the factual world (Kohtala and Steinert 2021). There are innumerable benefits derived from VR such as better training, with distant control, and a riskless training environment that can be created with VR (Dianatfar et al. 2025). During the product design stage, companies can save time and money with precision when business opts for VR (Guo et al. 2025). Interaction with the immersive world and having a three-dimensional experience are the main advantages derived from VR (Sudiarno et al. 2024).

AR gives a realistic experience by overlaying digital images to create a live experience (Martinsen et al. 2023). AR gives a realistic experience to the users to perform intricate activities (Eswaran and Raju Bahubalendruni 2024). Enhancing user experience by digitally overlaying three-dimensional objects with interaction is possible through AR (Singh et al. 2024b). AR usage in the manufacturing industry has become indispensable with its increased usage in assembly (Marino et al. 2024). Training of employees is successful with AR (Daling et al. 2023). It changes digital lexes into real life-like immersive experiences and creates a metaverse for the embodied environment to interact with the virtual environment (Yong et al. 2025). Understanding and training on the job are easy with AR, as the virtual environment overlays the real world. AR enhances efficiency with fewer errors (Mompeu et al. 2024). Training for dangerous jobs can be efficiently done with AR (Gong et al. 2024).

The industrial arena is changing, now shifted to Industry 5.0, prioritizing human-centered technology and sustainability. A big impact is created by the metaverse technology of AR and VR, the digital twins, a connection between the real and the digital world. VR is a powerful tool for providing immersive training in a risk-free environment for better collaboration with accurate simulations. Cost and time are reduced in the designing stage. An intricate task is simplified with AR, enabling on-the-job training more efficient and errorless. Together, these technologies contribute to a better workforce in high-risk industries. The convergence of Industry 5.0 ideologies with digital twins such as AR and VR is molding the industries by fostering innovation, increasing intricate skills and promoting sustainable practices. Integration optimizes efficiency and quality by creating an engaging and safe work environment, marking a noteworthy change in Industry 5.0.

9.2. Review of literature

Bridging the gap to connect the real and the virtual world is the role of digital twins (Ke et al. 2019). Digital twins also replicate the real world through digital content and three-dimensional to build processes, systems, strategies or real content in a digital world (Tang et al. 2023). Using digital twins assists in easy job performance as the worker need not shift from the manual panel to the digital outlay as it is available before them (Hsieh and Smith 2024). With AR, the user learning experience increases manifold, as there is an immediate change in the perspective of the viewer to get training (Sharma et al. 2022). AR is a significant module of the metaverse, having the potential to connect the real and the digital world. Virtual objects are embodied in the real world, giving a better immersive experience (Muruganantham and Kumar 2024). Digital twin-enabled prototyping permits the workers to deploy and use the virtual and actual materials; this aids in identifying likely mistakes and remodeling the design as a marketable product (Wang et al. 2015). The immersive training experience is enhanced with a digital twin as an actual and engaging experience for the trainees, enabling customized training experience with outcome-based training (Deng et al. 2023). These technologies are repeatedly being used to enhance productivity, improve production processes and distance collaboration among group members (Logeswaran et al. 2024). AR and VR are used in intricate welding technology (Veningston and Rajendran 2024). This technology has gained prominence, as it integrates the metaverse with devices and ensures smooth adaption by users mixing the real and the virtual environment; it is immersive, easily usable, less priced and can be used extensively (Murala and Panda 2023). Perception of the real world with the virtual components enhances the user's understanding of the real world (Marto et al. 2022). Safety, increased productivity and quality are the main reasons for using AR and VR in many industries (Schiavi et al. 2022). The potentiality of the digital twins is a transformative converging of the real and the virtual world. Noteworthy benefits such as effective job performance, better learning comprehension, errorless prototyping and improved productivity are achieved. Replication of the real world with overlaying digital elements empowers the users to have immersive, interactive and cost-effective results. Seamless user adaption and extensive usage of these technologies in the metaverse aid in intricate job performance. Despite all of the derived benefits in the usage of AR and VR in Industry 5.0, the research on the long-term impact of AR and VR is limited. This research explores the future of AR and VR and its impact on enhancing Industry 5.0.

9.3. Research questions

– How do VR and AR technologies enable enhanced prototyping and innovation in Industry 5.0, and what is their impact on product development cycles?

– To what extent do VR and AR technologies support product customization and personalization for diverse user needs in Industry 5.0?

– How do VR and AR technologies revolutionize training and development programs in Industry 5.0, and what are their effects on workforce competency and efficiency?

9.4. VR and AR prototyping and innovation in Industry 5.0

Organizations can develop a framework to enhance the prototyping system for better product development (Tay et al. 2001). Rapid prototyping is gaining prominence in the manufacturing industry; this reduces cost and errors in the product life cycle (Helge Bøhn 1997). New product development has to carefully identify the loopholes for any risks associated with the prototyping (Liao et al. 2010). New product development with the involvement of customers can increase the new product prototyping success (Tih et al. 2016). Using prototypes reduces the cost and time spent on development and processes (Liu et al. 2013). Businesses can develop more models for developing ideas in trial and error methods with prototypes (Oh 1995). AR-enabled prototyping reduces resource wastage, and assembling a product in accurate and instinctive ways is possible (Pang et al. 2006). Accuracy with AR is achieved with this technology, enabling restoring a product without pasting or joining (Seixas et al. 2018). It manipulates the real and virtual parts for trial and error and modifies the same for commercialization with prototyping (Wang et al. 2015). Efficient virtual experimentation of various variables with VR enhances business success (Branca et al. 2024). Creating a design in a predictable, active and interaction way aids in building quality design (Pektaş and Özgüç 2011).

Figure 9.1. *Image showing product designing through AR and VR. For a color version of this figure, see: www.iste.co.uk/taneja/6gurban.zip*

Visualizing the prototype before the actual creation reduces costly mistakes and unwanted repetitions (Choi and Samavedam 2001). Prototyping optimizes the production process, enabling production quality, maintaining and controlling it (Fasuludeen Kunju et al. 2022). AR platform provides a clear and in-built environment for better assembling and control (Pang et al. 2006). Prototypes are built focusing on the consumer needs to create new opportunities in the new age (Song et al. 2024). Businesses focus on changing consumer needs and competition to maintain uniqueness (Falchetti et al. 2021). Organizations can achieve cost-effectiveness by implementing digital-enabled prototyping (Su et al. 2025). Innovative strategies are employed by firms to face competition and succeed in the market (Wu et al. 2025). Innovation and sustainability go hand in hand, highlighting quality with sustainability emphasizing research, mainly prototyping and customization (Gajdzik et al. 2024) Prototyping is a significant component of innovation, enabling sustainability at the core of Industry 5.0 (Dokter et al. 2023).

The critical role of prototyping in modern business development is important in the context of Industry 5.0, stressing innovation and sustainability. By implementing prototype frameworks, businesses can drastically reduce costs, improve product development and curtail errors in the product lifecycle. Mixing the customer feedback into the designing stage of the prototype process increases product success and confirms the product's suitability with the changing consumer needs. AR and VR technology adoption amplifies and transfigures the prototyping process, with precision, efficient usage of available resources and better designs. Virtual development minimizes mistakes and optimizes production, enabling quality and control. Convergence consumer-enabled prototypes and adapt to the evolving market demands directed toward competitive advantage. Collaborating sustainability and innovation with prototyping at its center is necessary for piloting through the complexity of modern marketing. Prototyping is not just a process in product development; it is the fundamental aspect of innovation and the core to building a successful and sustainable business in the context of Industry 5.0.

9.5. VR and AR technologies in product customization and personalization

VR and AR are changing the Industry 5.0 landscape for product customization and personalization. Industry 5.0 is a human-centric approach; high-end technologies are used for efficient customization and a better user experience. VR and AR core components play a major role in offering an immersive, interactive environment enabling businesses and consumers to engage in dynamic, real-time product customization. Integrating AR and VR for creating new designs, manufacturing and promotional processes, companies create a customer-driven environment. A paradigm shift is noticed in consumer behavior; consumer preferences have evolved drastically, and businesses are meeting these needs with the aid of technology such as AR and VR (Zhou et al. 2023).

Figure 9.2. *Showing prototyping and product designing. For a color version of this figure, see: www.iste.co.uk/taneja/6gurban.zip*

These technologies enable product customization focusing on individual needs and preferences (Ettis and Sellami 2025). Cost-effective plans are created with AR and VR-enabled engineering processes (Siedler et al. 2021). Nowadays, customer satisfaction is difficult to achieve by traditional mass production and mass marketing (Lan et al. 2025). Technology-enabled product customization increases brand loyalty and customer engagement (Lin et al. 2017).

Figure 9.3. *Immersive experience for customers. For a color version of this figure, see: www.iste.co.uk/taneja/6gurban.zip*

Immersive experience enables the customers to have an interactive environment focusing on specific needs for product customization and personalization (Geissler et al. 2024). Customer experience, customer engagement and customer satisfaction are improved with the technology-enabled product personalization (Patel 2024). Limitless options coupled with immersive and interactive technology attract customers to have strong business engagement (Sridharan and Kumar 2024). AR and VR provide personalized experiences to customers (Singh et al. 2024a). They provide a personalized shopping experience with an interactive and immersive experience converging the digital and real world (Wong et al. 2024). Designing the product for the evolving needs of the customers and getting information on user specifications help in creating unique products that satisfy individual needs (Sihi 2018). AR and VR integrate sustainability for a sustainable Industry 5.0 (Contini et al. 2025). VR and AR are reshaping Industry 5.0, changing the marketing landscape and increasing personalization and customer-centered. Concentrating on a human-based approach, VR and AR give an immersive and interactive environment for better customer engagement in real time. Converging varied customer needs and demands and creating unique products for specific needs with cost effectiveness are the major benefits to be achieved. Businesses should embrace VR and AR to personalize customer preference, thus increasing brand loyalty, customer satisfaction and engagement. Giving multiple choices and seamlessly integrating the digital and physical world, business can gain more customers and create a long-lasting relationship. AR and VR are a data-driven approach, imbibing the core principles of Industry 5.0. These are not just technologies; they are the catalyst for a customized and personalized Industry 5.0 future.

9.6. VR and AR technologies changing training and development

Industry 5.0 is changing traditional training and development, into a more immersive, interactive and tailored experience, thus increasing the worker's efficiency and competency. Simulations are provided by overlaying and simplifying the complex process, which is the key to the success of training and development. Traditional methods of learning are not sufficient for giving a wholesome experience to the workers. AR and VR provide an interactive experience, increasing training effectiveness (Lin et al. 2024). Training programs develop the cognitive aspects of the workforce and increase training effectiveness (Nguyen et al. 2025). Training can be enhanced using AR and VR (Hajjami and Park 2024). These technologies help the organization by providing proper training to the workforce (Mendes Monteiro et al. 2025). Personalized training with the engagement of the employees can be achieved with the use of this technology (Enstroem and Bhawna 2025). Increased data retention, efficiency and better quality are the benefits achieved through AR and VR training (Kamwa et al. 2025). Immersive training experience enhances safe training practices and decreases possible accidents among trainees (Hussain et al. 2024).

Figure 9.4. *Training employees. For a color version of this figure, see: www.iste.co.uk/taneja/6gurban.zip*

Training the employees for highly skilled jobs is easier (Song and Nam 2025). Training in an immersive and interactive environment enhances training efficiency and effectiveness. Personalized training catering to individual capability reduces the barriers of traditional training methods. Overlaying real-world information into the digital world enhances hands-on training, full engagement and skill retention. Training in an immersive environment reduces cost. Training in AR and VR environments can be done in a remote setting. Personalized training catering to individual needs and learning capability enhances training effectiveness, leading to better understanding and increased knowledge retention. AR and VR training is safe, reducing hazards and creating fewer errors and accidents. Trainees can get better training with fewer errors in real time. Workplace safety issues are addressed with AR and VR training. Training in an immersive world increases the confidence of the trainees and equips them with skills necessary for Industry 5.0.

Category	
Prototyping	– Virtual experimentation, visualization and manipulation of designs, reduced costs and errors through effective utilization of AR and VR (Choi and Samavedam 2001; Branca et al. 2024). – AR increases accuracy and efficiency for assembling and effective resource management (Pang et al. 2006; Seixas et al. 2018). – Integrating customer feedback in prototyping leads to increased product success and market adaptability (Song et al. 2024). – Digital prototyping is effective as it reduces costs (Su et al. 2025).
Product customization and personalization	– VR and AR create immersive, real-time product customization and experiences, meeting evolved consumer preferences (Zhou et al. 2023; Geissler et al. 2024). – AR and VR technologies improve customer engagement, brand loyalty and satisfaction (Lin et al. 2017; Patel 2024). – Enables data-driven, personalized product designs (Sihi 2018). – Creates a better connection between business and consumer (Sridharan and Kumar 2024). – AR and VR increase sustainability in industry 5.0 (Contini et al. 2025).
Training and development	– VR and AR create immersive, interactive and personalized training environments, improving worker competency and efficiency (Lin et al. 2024; Nguyen et al. 2025). – Provides realistic simulations and hands-on experiences, enabling better skill retention and reduced errors (Hussain et al. 2024; Kamwa et al. 2025). – AR and VR provide personalized training (Enstroem and Bhawna 2025). – Facilitates remote training and improves workplace safety (Song and Nam 2025).

Table 9.1. *Latest findings in implementation of AR and VR in Industry 5.0*

9.7. Conclusion

Understanding AR and VR in the context of Industry 5.0 highlights the multifaceted transformation in industrial operations. Optimizing training and development, creating prototypes and curating personalized products, these technologies play a significant role in creating a better future. Industry 5.0, a humane approach driven by technology, is providing immersive environments with the help of AR and VR, bridging the gap between the physical and virtual world and amplifying the innovation and skills of humans. A risk-free training environment with stimulations enhances the training experience with safety. Personalized training with remote access reduces the challenges of traditional training methodologies.

Organizations can potentially gain a more competent and skilled workforce. Prototyping is enhanced with AR and VR; innovative models are curated. Virtual conceptualization, creation and manipulation help in product development. Cost reduction, fewer errors and more product development can be achieved. They create products with customer insights and feedback. With personalized products to meet customer demands, organizations can gain a competitive advantage. Brand loyalty and customer engagement can be increased. Convergence of Industry 5.0 with AR and VR technology provides an efficient, sustainable and human-centric industrial environment. These are not mere technologies; they are the significant tool for a better sustainable Industry 5.0. AR and VR are the best technologies for enhancing and building a successful future.

9.8. References

Alcácer, V. and Cruz-Machado, V. (2019). Scanning the industry 4.0: A literature review on technologies for manufacturing systems. *Engineering Science and Technology*, 22(3), 899–919.

Astrologo, A.N., Nano, S., Klemm, E.M., Shefelbine, S.J., Dennerlein, J.T. (2024). Determining the effects of AR/VR HMD design parameters (mass and inertia) on cervical spine joint torques. *Applied Ergonomics*, 116, 104183. doi: 10.1016/j.apergo.2023.104183.

Branca, G., Marino, V., Resciniti, R. (2024). How do consumers evaluate products in virtual reality? A literature review for a research agenda. *Spanish Journal of Marketing - ESIC*, 28(3), 356–380. doi: 10.1108/SJME-07-2022-0153.

Choi, S.H. and Samavedam, S. (2001). Visualisation of rapid prototyping. *Rapid Prototyping Journal*, 7(2), 99–114. doi: 10.1108/13552540110386763.

Cónego, L., Pinto, R., Pinto, J., Gonçalves, G. (2024). Leveraging gamification in industry 5.0: Tailored solutions for workplace' employees. *Procedia Computer Science*, 232, 1769–1778. doi: 10.1016/j.procs.2024.01.175.

Contini, G., Grandi, F., Peruzzini, M. (2025). Human-centric green design for automatic production lines: Using virtual and augmented reality to integrate industrial data and promote sustainability. *Journal of Industrial Information Integration*, 44, 100801. doi: 10.1016/j.jii.2025.100801.

Daling, L.M., Tenbrock, M., Isenhardt, I., Schlittmeier, S.J. (2023). Assemble it like this! – Is AR- or VR-based training an effective alternative to video-based training in manual assembly? *Applied Ergonomics*, 110, 104021. doi: 10.1016/j.apergo.2023.104021.

Deng, Y., Wang, Z., Dong, L., Lei, Y., Dong, Y. (2023). Immersive innovations: An examination of the efficacy and evolution of virtual reality in human movement training. *Robotic Intelligence and Automation*, 43(5), 551–566. doi: 10.1108/RIA-05-2023-0072.

Dianatfar, M., Järvenpää, E., Siltala, N., Lanz, M. (2025). Template concept for VR environments: A case study in VR-based safety training for human–robot collaboration. *Robotics and Computer-Integrated Manufacturing*, 94, 102973. doi: 10.1016/j.rcim.2025.102973.

Dokter, G., Boks, C., Rahe, U., Jansen, B.W., Hagejärd, S., Thuvander, L. (2023). The role of prototyping and co-creation in circular economy-oriented innovation: A longitudinal case study in the kitchen industry. *Sustainable Production and Consumption*, 39, 230–243. doi: 10.1016/j.spc.2023.05.012.

Enstroem, R. and Bhawna, B. (2025). AI and VR: Shaping the next generation of adaptive learning and development programmes. In *The Future of HRM in a World of Persistent Virtual Reality*, Kumar, D., Suthar, N., Taherdoost, H., Madanchian, M. (eds). Emerald Publishing Limited, Leeds, 141–163. doi: 10.1108/978-1-83662-110-220251007.

Eswaran, M. and Raju Bahubalendruni, M.V.A. (2022). Challenges and opportunities on AR/VR technologies for manufacturing systems in the context of industry 4.0: A state of the art review. *Journal of Manufacturing Systems*, 65, 260–278. doi: 10.1016/j.jmsy.2022.09.016.

Eswaran, M. and Raju Bahubalendruni, M.V.A. (2024). AR/VR assisted integrated framework of autonomous disassembly system for industrial products. *Computers & Industrial Engineering*, 196, 110522. doi: 10.1016/j.cie.2024.110522.

Ettis, S.A. and Sellami, A. (2025). "I'll do it for myself": Enhancing customer value through online product customization experience. *Journal of Retailing and Consumer Services*, 82, 104143. doi: 10.1016/j.jretconser.2024.104143.

Falchetti, D., Cattani, G., Ferriani, S. (2021). Start with "Why," but only if you have to: The strategic framing of novel ideas across different audiences. *Strategic Management Journal*, 43(1), 130–159. doi: 10.1002/smj.3329.

Fasuludeen Kunju, F.K., Naveed, N., Anwar, M.N., Ul Haq, M.I. (2022). Production and maintenance in industries: Impact of industry 4.0. *Industrial Robot*, 49(3), 461–475. doi: 10.1108/IR-09-2021-0211.

Gajdzik, B., Siwiec, D., Wolniak, R., Pacana, A. (2024). Approaching open innovation in customization frameworks for product prototypes with emphasis on quality and life cycle assessment (QLCA). *Journal of Open Innovation: Technology, Market, and Complexity*, 10(2), 100268. doi: 10.1016/j.joitmc.2024.100268.

Geissler, D., Beiderbeck, D., Schmidt, S.L., Schreyer, D. (2024). Emerging technologies and shifting consumer motives: Projecting the future of the top-tier sports media product. *Technological Forecasting and Social Change*, 203, 123366. doi: 10.1016/j.techfore.2024.123366.

Gong, P., Lu, Y., Lovreglio, R., Yang, X., Deng, Y. (2024). Comparing the effectiveness of AR training and slide-based training: The case study of metro construction safety. *Safety Science*, 176, 106561. doi: 10.1016/j.ssci.2024.106561.

Guo, W., Liu, Y., Li, Y. (2025). Precision mechanical manufacturing and product appearance VR design based on environmental thermal energy control. *Thermal Science and Engineering Progress*, 57, 103124. doi: 10.1016/j.tsep.2024.103124.

Hajjami, O. and Park, S. (2024). Using the metaverse in training: Lessons from real cases. *European Journal of Training and Development*, 48(5/6), 555–575. doi: 10.1108/EJTD-12-2022-0144.

Hamza Zafar, M., Langås, E.F., Sanfilippo, F. (2024). Exploring the synergies between collaborative robotics, digital twins, augmentation, and industry 5.0 for smart manufacturing: A state-of-the-art review. *Robotics and Computer-Integrated Manufacturing*, 89, 102769. doi: 10.1016/j.rcim.2024.102769.

Helge Bøhn, J. (1997). Integrating rapid prototyping into the engineering curriculum – A case study. *Rapid Prototyping Journal*, 3(1), 32–37. doi: 10.1108/13552549710169264.

Hsieh, T.-C. and Smith, S. (2024). An innovative AR-assisted self-adjusting digital twin for speed control of a servomechanism. *Computers & Industrial Engineering*, 193, 110328. doi: 10.1016/j.cie.2024.110328.

Hussain, R., Sabir, A., Lee, D.-Y., Zaidi, S.F.A., Pedro, A., Abbas, M.S., Park, C. (2024). Conversational AI-based VR system to improve construction safety training of migrant workers. *Automation in Construction*, 160, 105315. doi: 10.1016/j.autcon.2024.105315.

Jalilvand, I., Jang, J., Gopaluni, B., Milani, A.S. (2024). VR/MR systems integrated with heat transfer simulation for training of thermoforming: A multicriteria decision-making user study. *Journal of Manufacturing Systems*, 72, 338–359. doi: 10.1016/j.jmsy.2023.11.007.

Jin, S.V. and Ryu, E. (2025). Unraveling the dynamics of digital equality and trust in AI-empowered metaverses and AI-VR-convergence. *Technological Forecasting and Social Change*, 210, 123877. doi: 10.1016/j.techfore.2024.123877.

Kamwa, L.I.D., Paes, D., Feng, Z., Mander, S., Datoussaid, S., Descamps, T., Rahouti, A., Lovreglio, R. (2025). Video see-through augmented reality fire safety training: A comparison with virtual reality and video training. *Safety Science*, 184, 106714. doi: 10.1016/j.ssci.2024.106714.

Ke, S., Xiang, F., Zhang, Z., Zuo, Y. (2019). A enhanced interaction framework based on VR, AR and MR in digital twin. *Procedia CIRP*, 83, 753–758. doi: 10.1016/j.procir.2019.04.103.

Kohtala, S. and Steinert, M. (2021). Leveraging synthetic data from CAD models for training object detection models – A VR industry application case. *Procedia CIRP*, 100, 714–719. doi: 10.1016/j.procir.2021.05.092.

Lan, S., Jiang, Y., Guo, T., Li, S., Yang, C., Edwin Cheng, T.C., Sethanan, K., Tseng, M.-L. (2025). Personalized product design and user review and experience analysis: A data-driven hybrid novel approach. *Computers & Industrial Engineering*, 202, 110939. doi: 10.1016/j.cie.2025.110939.

Liao, Y., Liao, K., Hutchinson, R. (2010). A conceptual framework for prototyping outsourcing in new product development: A knowledge-based view. *Journal of Manufacturing Technology Management*, 21(1), 122–138. doi: 10.1108/17410381011011515.

Lin, Y., Yu, S., Zheng, P., Qiu, L., Wang, Y., Xu, X. (2017). VR-based product personalization process for smart products. *Procedia Manufacturing*, 11, 1568–1576. doi: 10.1016/j.promfg.2017.07.297.

Lin, P.-Y., Chen, T.-C., Lin, C.-J., Huang, C.-C., Tsai, Y.-H., Tsai, Y.-L., Wang, C.-Y. (2024). The use of augmented reality (AR) and virtual reality (VR) in dental surgery education and practice: A narrative review. *Journal of Dental Sciences*, 19(Supplement 2), S91–S101. doi: 10.1016/j.jds.2024.10.011.

Liu, B., Campbell, R.I., Pei, E. (2013). Real-time integration of prototypes in the product development process. *Assembly Automation*, 33(1), 22–28. doi: 10.1108/01445151311294621.

Logeswaran, K., Savitha, S., Suresh, P., Prasanna Kumar, K.R., Gunasekar, M., Rajadevi, R., Dharani, M.K., Jayasurya, A.S. (2024). Unifying technologies in Industry 4.0. In *Topics in Artificial Intelligence Applied to Industry 4.0*, Ragab AL-Refaey, M., Tyagi, A.K., AL-Malaise AL-Ghamdi, A.S., Kukreja, S. (eds). John Wiley and Sons, New York. doi: 10.1002/9781394216147.ch7.

Lund, G.K., Ortova, M., Syversen, A.G. (2023). Using VR technology in the pre-onboarding of temporary employees in a Norwegian SME. *Procedia CIRP*, 120, 320–325. doi: 10.1016/j.procir.2023.08.057.

Marino, E., Barbieri, L., Bruno, F., Muzzupappa, M. (2024). Assessing user performance in augmented reality assembly guidance for industry 4.0 operators. *Computers in Industry*, 157–158, 104085. doi: 10.1016/j.compind.2024.104085.

Martinsen, M., Zhou, Y., Dahlquist, E., Yan, J., Kyprianidis, K. (2023). Positive climate effects when AR customer support simultaneous trains AI experts for the smart industries of the future. *Applied Energy*, 339, 120988. doi: 10.1016/j.apenergy.2023.120988.

Marto, A., Gonçalves, A., Melo, M., Bessa, M. (2022). A survey of multisensory VR and AR applications for cultural heritage. *Computers & Graphics*, 102, 426–440. doi: 10.1016/j.cag.2021.10.001.

Mendes Monteiro, J., Torres, D., Ramos, A.L., Pimentel, C. (2025). The use of virtual reality as e-training tool for dies' changeover in stamping presses: A case study on automotive industry. *International Journal of Lean Six Sigma*, 16(2), 442–460. doi: 10.1108/IJLSS-02-2023-0041.

Menin, A., Torchelsen, R., Nedel, L. (2022). The effects of VR in training simulators: Exploring perception and knowledge gain. *Computers & Graphics*, 102, 402–412. doi: 10.1016/j.cag.2021.09.015.

Mompeu, G., Danglade, F., Mérienne, F., Guillet, C. (2024). Methodology for augmented reality-based adaptive assistance in industry. *Computers in Industry*, 154, 104021. doi: 10.1016/j.compind.2023.104021.

Murala, D.K. and Panda, S.K. (2023). The role of immersive reality (AR/VR/MR/XR) in metaverse. In *Metaverse and Immersive Technologies*, Chandrashekhar, A., Saheb, S.H., Panda, S.K., Balamurugan, S., Peng, S.-L. (eds). Taylor & Francis, Abingdon. doi: 10.1002/9781394177165.ch6.

Muruganantham, G. and Kumar, B.D. (2024). Augmented reality: Shaping the metaverse. In *The Metaverse Dilemma: Challenges and Opportunities for Business and Society*, Krishnan, C., Behl, A., Dash, S., Yadav, P.D. (eds). Emerald Publishing Limited, Leeds. 33–52. doi: 10.1108/978-1-83797-524-220241003.

Nenna, F., Zanardi, D., Gamberini, L. (2023). Enhanced interactivity in VR-based telerobotics: An eye-tracking investigation of human performance and workload. *International Journal of Human-Computer Studies*, 177, 103079. doi: 10.1016/j.ijhcs.2023.103079.

Nguyen, L., Murphy, K., Andrews, G. (2025). Design and development of a gamified cognitive training program targeting executive functions for older adults. *Entertainment Computing*, 52, 100892. doi: 10.1016/j.entcom.2024.100892.

Oh, D. (1995). The role of prototyping in a bottom-up approach to systems development: The "ideal". *Campus-Wide Information Systems*, 12(4), 12–18. doi: 10.1108/10650749510104917.

Pang, Y., Nee, A.Y.C., Khim Ong, S., Yuan, M., Youcef-Toumi, K. (2006). Assembly feature design in an augmented reality environment. *Assembly Automation*, 26(1), 34–43. doi: 10.1108/01445150610645648.

Patel, K. (2024). Revolutionizing customer experience: Integrating blockchain with AR and VR in retail. In *Augmenting Retail Reality, Part B: Blockchain, AR, VR, and AI*, Verma, B., Mittal, A., Raman, M., Sindhav, B. (eds). Emerald Publishing Limited, Leeds, 1–22. doi: 10.1108/978-1-83608-708-320241003.

Pektaş, Ş.T. and Özgüç, B. (2011). Virtual prototyping for open building design. *Open House International*, 36(4), 46–56. doi: 10.1108/OHI-04-2011-B0005.

Phuyal, S., Bista, D., Bista, R. (2020). Challenges, opportunities and future directions of smart manufacturing: A state of art review. *Sustainable Futures*, 2, 100023. doi: 10.1016/j.sftr.2020.100023.

Riesener, M., Schukat, E., Curiel-Ramirez, L.A., Schäfer, N., Valdez-Heras, A. (2024). Development of a VR-based digital factory planning platform for dynamic 3D layout editing. *Procedia CIRP*, 130, 419–426. doi: 10.1016/j.procir.2024.10.109.

Schiavi, B., Havard, V., Beddiar, K., Baudry, D. (2022). BIM data flow architecture with AR/VR technologies: Use cases in architecture, engineering and construction. *Automation in Construction*, 134, 104054. doi: 10.1016/j.autcon.2021.104054.

Seixas, M.L., Assis, P.S., Figueiredo, J.C.D., Pinto, M.A., Paula, D.G.C. (2018). The use of rapid prototyping in the joining of fractured historical silver object. *Rapid Prototyping Journal*, 24(3), 532–538. doi: 10.1108/RPJ-09-2016-0148.

Sharma, A., Mehtab, R., Mohan, S., Mohd Shah, M.K. (2022). Augmented reality – An important aspect of Industry 4.0. *Industrial Robot*, 49(3), 428–441. doi: 10.1108/IR-09-2021-0204.

Siedler, C., Glatt, M., Weber, P., Ebert, A., Aurich, J.C. (2021). Engineering changes in manufacturing systems supported by AR/VR collaboration. *Procedia CIRP*, 96, 307–312. doi: 10.1016/j.procir.2021.01.092.

Sihi, D. (2018). Home sweet virtual home: The use of virtual and augmented reality technologies in high involvement purchase decisions. *Journal of Research in Interactive Marketing*, 12(4), 398–417. doi: 10.1108/JRIM-01-2018-0019.

Singh, B., Kaunert, C., Vig, K., Gautam, R. (2024a). Revolutionizing customers shopping experience via augmented-virtual reality in retail business: Whirling dreams toward transforming retail industry reality. In *Augmenting Retail Reality, Part B: Blockchain, AR, VR, and AI*, Verma, B., Mittal, A., Raman, M., Sindhav, B. (eds). Emerald Publishing Limited, Leeds, 23–37. doi: 10.1108/978-1-83608-708-320241005.

Singh, P., Sharma, M., Daim, T. (2024b). Envisaging AR travel revolution for visiting heritage sites: A mixed-method approach. *Technology in Society*, 76, 102439. doi: 10.1016/j.techsoc.2023.102439.

Song, C.S. and Nam, J.-H. (2025). Machine learning-based optimal value calculation for welding variables in AR training. *International Journal of Naval Architecture and Ocean Engineering*, 17, 100652. doi: 10.1016/j.ijnaoe.2025.100652.

Song, X., Wei, Z., Bao, Y. (2024). Prototype strategy, market big data and identification of latent customer needs: An organizational learning perspective. *Industrial Management & Data Systems*, 124(10), 2939–2964. doi: 10.1108/IMDS-11-2023-0836.

Sridharan, A. and Kumar, S. (2024). The impact of metaverse on businesses. In *The Metaverse Dilemma: Challenges and Opportunities for Business and Society*, Krishnan, C., Behl, A., Dash, S., Yadav, P.D. (eds). Emerald Publishing Limited, Leeds, 13–30. doi: 10.1108/978-1-83797-524-220241002.

Su, Z., Ali, M., Lin, F., Tan, Y., Liao, W.-H., Wong, H. (2025). Pilot capability evaluation of a modular laser diode-based prototype for beam focusing detection and calibration in laser processing. *Precision Engineering*. doi: 10.1016/j.precisioneng.2025.03.013.

Sudiarno, A., Dewi, R.S., Widyaningrum, R., Ma'arij, A.M.D., Supriatna, A.Y. (2024). Investigating the future study area on VR technology implementation in safety training: A systematic literature review. *Journal of Safety Science and Resilience*, 5(2), 235–248. doi: 10.1016/j.jnlssr.2024.03.005.

Tang, Y.M., Kuo, W.T., Lee, C.K.M. (2023). Real-time mixed reality (MR) and Artificial Intelligence (AI) object recognition integration for digital twin in Industry 4.0. *Internet of Things*, 23, 100753. doi: 10.1016/j.iot.2023.100753.

Tay, F.E.H., Khanal, Y.P., Kuen Kwong, K., Cheng Tan, K. (2001). Distributed rapid prototyping – A framework for Internet prototyping and manufacturing. *Integrated Manufacturing Systems*, 12(6), 409–415. doi: 10.1108/EUM0000000006106.

Tih, S., Wong, K.-K., Lynn, G.S., Reilly, R.R. (2016). Prototyping, customer involvement, and speed of information dissemination in new product success. *Journal of Business & Industrial Marketing*, 31(4), 437–448. doi: 10.1108/JBIM-09-2014-0182.

Veningston, K. and Rajendran, D.K. (2024). VR and AR in welding technologies. In *Automation in Welding Industry*, Moinuddin, S.Q., Saheb, S.H., Dewangan, A.K., Cheepu, M.M., Balamurugan, S. (eds). John Wiley and Sons, New York. doi: 10.1002/9781394172948.ch8.

Wang, X., Ong, S.K., Nee, A.Y.C. (2015). Real-virtual interaction in AR assembly simulation based on component contact handling strategy. *Assembly Automation*, 35(4), 376–394. doi: 10.1108/AA-02-2015-012.

Wang, B., Zheng, L., Wang, Y., Fang, W., Wang, L. (2024). Towards the industry 5.0 frontier: Review and prospect of XR in product assembly. *Journal of Manufacturing Systems*, 74, 777–811. doi: 10.1016/j.jmsy.2024.05.002.

Wen, J. and Gheisari, M. (2021) VR-Electricians: Immersive storytelling for attracting students to the electrical construction industry. *Advanced Engineering Informatics*, 50, 101411. doi: 10.1016/j.aei.2021.101411.

Wong, B.K.M., Law, F.L., Tan, C.I. (2024). Modern consumerism and retailing: The metaverse bound. In *Augmenting Retail Reality, Part A: Blockchain, AR, VR, and the Internet of Things*, Verma, B., Mittal, A., Raman, M., Sindhav, B. (eds). Emerald Publishing Limited, Leeds, 143–166. doi: 10.1108/978-1-83608-634-520241020.

Wu, X., Chen, X., Wang, X. (2025). With whom to be distinctive? Examining the impact of innovation narrative distinctiveness from the category prototype vs. category exemplar on firm performance. *Technovation*, 143, 103210. doi: 10.1016/j.technovation.2025.103210.

Yin, Y., Zheng, P., Li, C., Wang, L. (2023). A state-of-the-art survey on augmented reality-assisted digital twin for futuristic human-centric industry transformation. *Robotics and Computer-Integrated Manufacturing*, 81, 102515. doi: 10.1016/j.rcim.2022.102515.

Yong, J., Wei, J., Lei, X., Wang, Y., Dang, J., Lu, W. (2025). Intervention and regulatory mechanism of multimodal fusion natural interactions on AR embodied cognition. *Information Fusion*, 117, 102910. doi: 10.1016/j.inffus.2024.102910.

Zhou, F., Zhang, N., Wang, N., Mou, J. (2023). Design affordance in VR and customization intention: Is customer inspiration a missing link? *Technological Forecasting and Social Change*, 192, 122594. doi: 10.1016/j.techfore.2023.122594.

10

Role of AI and Digital Twin in Industry 5.0

This chapter discusses the crucial contribution of the Internet in revolutionizing industry via AI (Artificial Intelligence) and digital twin (DT) technologies for human-centric, sustainable and efficient industrial systems of Industry 5.0. AI also improves decision-making by incorporating intelligent automation, real-time analytics and predictive modeling, whereas DT offers virtual replicas of physical systems and helps connect the physical and digital worlds. Together, they catalyze innovations in smart manufacturing, personalized production, energy optimization and human–machine collaboration. Finally, the chapter lists the enabling technologies such as Internet of Things (IoT), edge/cloud computing and 5G/6G communications that facilitate AI-DT integration. While the potential for transformation is significant, challenges remain, including technical complexity, data privacy issues, high implementation costs and ethical dilemmas, requiring advanced research and robust frameworks to address. Mitigating these limitations is fundamental to Industry 5.0, which forecasts highly personalized, localized production system designs and green processes using frontier technologies, including quantum computing. This synthesis positions AI and DT as pillars of industrial evolution in upcoming years, providing agility and robustness to ever-changing global business environments.

10.1. Introduction

Industry 5.0 is the transition from Industry 4.0 to incorporate changes in manufacturing systems and industrial processes. While Industry 4.0 focuses on automation, digitization and various cyber-physical systems, Industry 5.0 seeks to bring humans, supported by artificial intelligence (AI), robotics and digital twin (DT) systems, into the spotlight. It aims at achieving the best of mechanization, on the one hand, and the innovation, flexibility and problem-solving capabilities of the manual employee, on the other hand.

Chapter written by Harashleen KOUR, Shubham GUPTA and Osamah Ibrahim KHALAF.

DT technology, on the contrary, a virtual representation of physical systems, enables predictive modeling, real-time monitoring and dynamic feedback loops. AI and DT together build the fundamental basis of intelligent manufacturing systems whereby operational efficiency is mixed with custom-tailored and sustainable means of production.

The integration of AI and DT in Industry 5.0 tackles some of the most pressing challenges such as resource optimization, risk evaluation in real-time and enhanced human–machine cooperation. Together they permit manufacturers to form adaptive and resilient systems while supporting a worldwide push towards greener, healthier industrial ecosystems (Campero-Jurado et al. 2020). With the advances in enabling technologies such as IoT, cloud computing and 5G/6G communication, the scope for integration of AI and DT in Industry 5.0 is vast and transformative, as shown in Figure 10.1. This chapter elaborates on the principal concepts, applications and synergies of the technologies, in addition to their role in assessing the future of smart and environmentally sustainable industries.

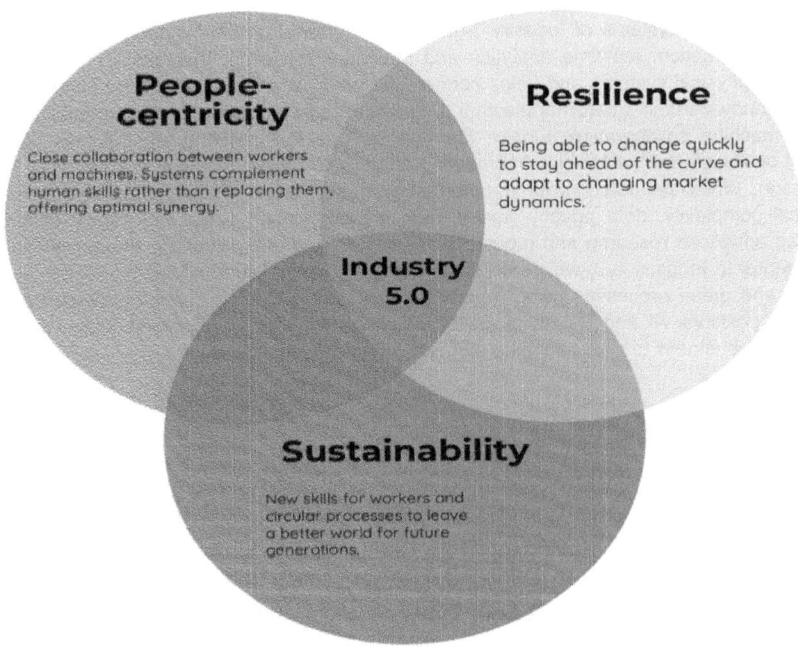

Figure 10.1. *Foundation pillars of Industry 5.0. For a color version of this figure, see: www.iste.co.uk/taneja/6gurban.zip*

10.2. Importance of AI and DT in Industry 5.0

AI and DT technologies act as stringent enablers of Industry 5.0 in pursuit of the three major goals – human centricity, sustainability and increasing production efficiency. Together, these technologies form a collegiate framework that directs innovation, fosters resilience and interoperable value across various industries. AI contributes greatly to Industry 5.0, by augmenting human abilities, supporting decision-making for all levels of human tasks through intelligent automation and introducing adaptability to learning in complex environments. AI-powered systems can analyze gigantic amounts of data in real time and offer valuable information that can enrich operational performance and enhance the productivity of available resources, whereas a DT is a virtual facsimile of a physical asset, process, or system that acquaints real-time monitoring, simulation and optimization. In the context of Industry 5.0, DTs serve as a connection that meshes the existences of both the physical and digital worlds, providing an inclusive understanding of industrial processes (Ait-Alla et al. 2021). By designing a virtual environment for experimentation and analysis, DTs empower manufacturers to test innumerable scenarios, predict outcomes and implement sustainable solutions without unruly physical operations, and DT technologies, when integrated, offer the highest performances ever so far on which the Industry 5.0 aspirations rest. AI enhances the capabilities of DTs for analytical and predictive endeavors and wields more precise simulation and data-driven decision on the part of DTs.

10.3. Fundamentals of AI and DT in Industry 5.0

AI and DT represent fundamental technologies in Industry 5.0; they facilitate the seamless integration of human–machine collaboration. Together, these innovations drive personalized, efficient and sustainable industrial solutions. Together, they drive personalized, efficient and sustainable industrial solutions.

10.3.1. *AI in Industry 5.0*

The Human-Centric Industry 5.0 moves away from the automation-focused approach of Industry 4.0 and emphasizes human-centered, resilient and sustainable values at its core, all made possible with the help of AI. Unlike Industry 4.0 focuses primarily on autonomous systems and digitalization, Industry 5.0 emphasizes a partnership between humans and intelligent systems to foster productivity, novelty and societal welfare.

AI in Industry 5.0 fully enhances human proficiencies rather than competing with them. AI systems will empower workers to perform equitable tasks without much difficulty but with quality, work speed and safety. Advanced machine learning models and natural language processing algorithms enable close cooperation between people and machines, wherein workers can, in real time, steer the intelligent systems (Asokan et al. 2022). For example, machines known as AI-powered collaborative robots operate alongside humans within a manufacturing setting, bringing the flexibility and dexterity of humans in combination with the swift and precise actions of machines.

AI is fundamental to sustainability, a key component of Industry 5.0. It can reduce resource waste, energy consumption and environmental impact by leveraging predictive analytics and optimization. Getting AI to deliver returns means continuously monitoring AI performance and engaging AI-driven intelligent capabilities for maximized sustainability gain and learning curve acceleration. Also, Industry 5.0 with AI boosts resilience through real-time monitoring, predictive maintenance and adaptive responses to disruptions. Machine learning models examine sensor data from industrial machinery to predict failures before they occur, reducing downtime and operational risks (Vyskočil et al. 2023). In addition, AI bolsters cybersecurity, identifying and responding to advanced cyberattacks to maintain the integrity and reliability of networked industrial systems.

To summarize, the holistic AI revolution of Industry 5.0 will not just stay fit for automation. Things such as decision support, optimization and customization will begin to emerge. It is here that the intelligent systems, empowered by AI, will be used to analyze vast amounts of real-time data to enable predictive insights, operational streamlining and adaptation to dynamic changes in the systems. AI empowers multiple operating modalities for the power industry by fusing machine intelligence with human productivity in a layered collaborative ecosystem.

10.3.2. *DT technology in Industry 5.0*

DT technology is a key component in the advancement of Industry 5.0, facilitating the smooth integration of both physical and digital realms. With the ability to recreate physical systems, processes or products virtually, DT technology supposes practically seamless operations optimization, improved decision-making and the enabling of a human-centered, sustainable and resilient industrial ecosystem. A major contribution of DT technology to Industry 5.0 is its emphasis on sustainability. DTs facilitate accurate energy management, resource optimization and emission reduction by modeling the environmental consequences of industrial processes (Bork et al. 2023). For instance, in the manufacturing industry, DT models can evaluate and reduce material waste, enhance energy efficiency and aid in the creation of eco-friendly products. These features support the Industry 5.0 goal of establishing a sustainable and circular economy.

A DT consists of three essential components: the physical entity, the digital model and the communication infrastructure. The physical entity refers to the object or process that exists in the real world, while the digital model is the representation that exists in the virtual realm and, for the most part, creates itself from measurements made on relevant parameters using data collected by sensors. The communication infrastructure represents the data exchange method between the physical and digital realms that allows for constant online synchronization and updates.

DTs' structural framework is an Industry 5.0 perspective emphasizing the multilayered architecture and functional elements. This model has a different layer for each purpose to empower intelligent operation and better decision-making, as well as a sustainable industrial ecosystem.

10.3.2.1. *Data layer*

The data layer constitutes the essential foundation of the DT framework, encompassing a diverse array of datasets that provide crucial input for advanced analysis and decision-making:

– Employee data: (which captures workforce-related information) includes skills, performance metrics and resource allocation.

– Machine data: records real-time machine performance, operational status and maintenance needs, designed to enhance reliability and uptime.

– Material data: tracks the availability, consumption and flow of materials; this ensures resource optimization.

– Rule data: incorporates operational policies, compliance standards and automated decision-making rules to maintain process consistency.

– Environmental data: monitors factors such as energy usage, emissions and ecological impact, aligning with sustainable practices.

Although this layer serves as a comprehensive repository of raw data, it facilitates the subsequent transformation into actionable intelligence. However, the effectiveness of this transformation depends on the quality and integration of the underlying data sources.

10.3.2.2. *Model layer*

The model layer serves as a conduit between unrefined data and applicable uses. It classifies industrial processes into two major types: discrete industry and process industry:

– Discrete industry represents sectors (such as automotive or electronics) that are marked by distinct production units.

– Process industry pertains to continuous production settings, which include chemical, pharmaceutical and food processing industries.

By integrating these segments, the layer enables the modeling, simulation and optimization of different (and heterogeneous) industrial use cases.

That said, the complexity of these processes can be problematic, as they usually require more nuanced approaches. While they serve different purposes, both classifications are vital components of any successful industrial activity.

10.3.2.3. *Application layer*

The application layer wraps the tangible results and decision-support power of DTs:

– Smarter plans and production schedules: it enables efficient resource allocation and workflow management.

– Material allocation management: it is a critical step in ensuring just-in-time delivery and effective inventory management.

– Production parameters optimization: it improves process efficiency and product quality by adjusting operational variables.

– Equipment maintenance: it uses predictive and preventive strategies to reduce downtime; in contrast, fault prediction and maintenance analyzes trends in real time to predict when a fault will occur, allowing a proactive response to the problem.

– Product quality tracking: while product quality tracking tracks quality parameters, it is very important for compliance and customer satisfaction.

The layered framework as shown in Figure 10.2 shows DTs aligned with Industry 5.0, creating data-driven intelligence and human–machine cooperation (Di Meglio et al. 2024). Its goal is to develop adaptable, sustainable and efficient manufacturing ecosystems.

Yet, the resulting foundation fuels both modernization and competitiveness within industrial domains through the attainment of granular data insights, the deployment of advanced modeling and the use of practical applications.

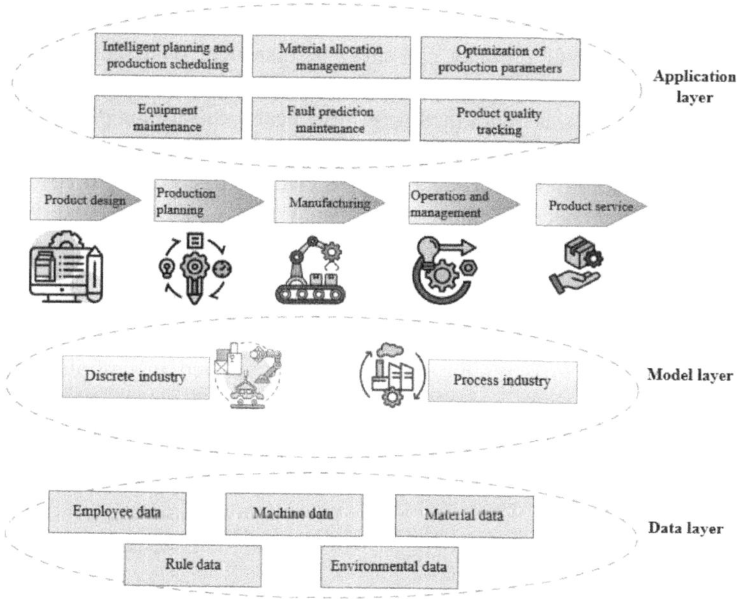

Figure 10.2. *Digital twins in Industry 5.0. For a color version of this figure, see: www.iste.co.uk/taneja/6gurban.zip*

DTs also enable hyper-personalization in Industry 5.0 by creating simulations and tailor-making products to suit individual preferences. Advanced DT platforms integrate customer preferences, behavioral data and real-time feedback to create bespoke products and services. In the healthcare sector, for example, DT technology models patient physiology to design personalized treatment plans, monitor disease progression and forecast outcomes. This is how Industry 5.0 exemplifies the ability to blend a human-centric design with advanced analytics.

A second key use of DT technology is for the empowerment of workers. DT simulates complex environments for immersive training, simulating such scenarios that work with multiplayers, which gives workers advanced skills and functionality knowledge. Augmented reality (AR)/virtual reality (VR) interfaces powered with DT provide more intuitive access to complex data that helps workers make better decisions and manage complex systems.

10.3.3. *Integration of AI with DT*

DTs are constantly updated virtual replicas of physical systems, which leverage complex algorithms to interpret real-time data, forecast system performance and enable the optimization of all processes in diverse scenarios (Männle et al. 2023). Through AI, these virtual replicas can analyze historical data, adjust to various environmental changes and offer insights that can be used for informed decision-making. In sectors such as manufacturing, healthcare and urban planning, where AI-based DTs are used to predict maintenance needs, optimize resource usage and inform customized solutions, this integration is critical. In addition to AI, DTs also get better and better because they are updated and can be synced with new information.

Such a combination not only enhances operational efficiency by informing immediate, on-the-ground decision-making but also promotes sustainability and resiliency by allowing for strategic foresight to be applied in complex, dynamic environments.

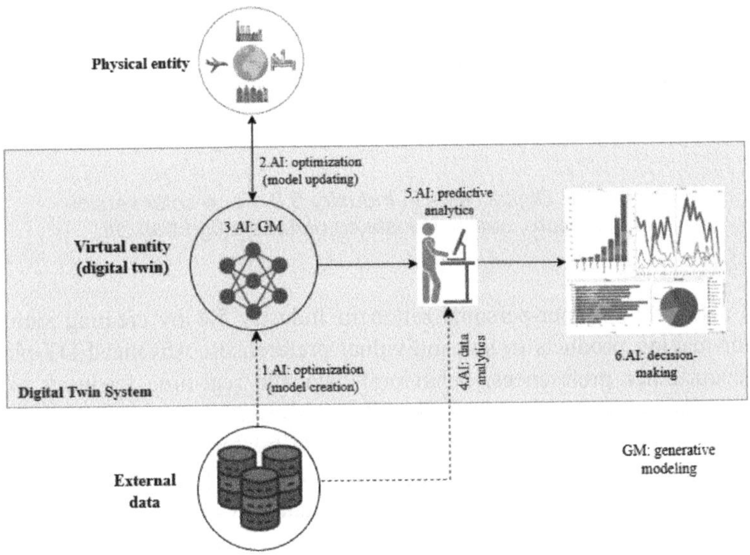

Figure 10.3. *Digital twin system. For a color version of this figure, see: www.iste.co.uk/taneja/6gurban.zip*

Figure 10.3 shows the DT system (shown as a blue rectangle) with an interface to a physical entity and external data. Its structural architecture makes it possible to highlight the various contributions that AI can offer for optimizing the outcomes of a DT system. These contributions are highlighted from 1.AI to 6.AI.

The union of AI and DT technology is opening a path for great change in Industry 5.0, dissolving the lines between intelligent automation and real-time analytics.

10.3.3.1. *Real-time analytics and intelligent automation*

AI-powered DTs support real-time analytics from very large datasets with physical assets to uncover actionable insights (Mortlock et al. 2022). The insights are useful for intelligent automation, where machines learn autonomously to adjust enhancing efficiency, waste reduction or productivity improvement. AI predictive algorithms tuning DTs might detect a maintenance event well in advance to reduce downtime and operational costs.

10.3.3.2. *Feedback systems for optimization*

AI models, when aligned with DT technology, make resilient feedback systems that further enhance the operational performance of systems and processes. Such feedback systems can continually develop simulations and predictive models by learning from historical as well as real-time data to ensure peak performance (Castellani et al. 2021). AI-powered feedback loops allow DTs to adjust to changes in the environment and evolving business needs, building robustness and agility.

The fusion of AI with DT has opened the path for co-op churning of the human and machine for a mixed reality environment in which operators can converse with the AI smart DTs for data-supported decision-making. As a result, this collaboration supports Industry 5.0 in complementing human work while using developed technology for sustainable economic growth.

10.4. Applications of AI and DT in Industry 5.0

The application of AI and DT within the Industry 5.0 arena marks a shift of paradigm, giving birth to innovation and providing a seamless partnership among state-of-the-art technologies and human-centric objectives. These technologies, by fusing the physical and virtual domains using intelligent, data-driven insights, enable industries to optimize their operations, achieve sustainability and develop personalized solutions.

10.4.1. *Smart manufacturing*

Smart manufacturing (SM) is a technology-driven approach that involves monitoring production processes using machines connected to the Internet (Boumsisse et al. 2024). SM aims to automate tasks and find prospects for improving manufacturing performance through data analysis:

1. **Predictive maintenance using AI-enabled DTs:** predictive maintenance using AI-enabled DTs in innovative SM in Industry 5.0 synergizes AI and DT technologies to an unrivaled level of efficiency and accuracy. Predictive

maintenance is one such integration that uses an AI-enabled DT to continuously monitor and analyze the integrity and working condition of the machinery. This digital copy uses actual working information to anticipate dependent failures, therefore indicating ways for preventative action. These virtual replicas use real-time data to predict potential failures and recommend proactive interventions. One such example is the use of sensors monitoring the evolvement of manufacturing equipment to process and send data to DT, which performs its functions through AI algorithms to detect anomalies reflective of parts wearing out. By predicting and preventing equipment failure, companies will reduce downtime drastically and prolong the life span of their machines while better allocating their resources. This will have the added effect of increasing operational efficiency while federalizing uninterrupted production – an important determinant of competitiveness.

2. **Production line monitoring and optimization through DT simulations:** AI-enhanced DT simulations are developed for real-time monitoring and optimization of production line operation. They give the virtual model a sense of the bottlenecks, inefficiencies and other areas worth enhancing by trailing multiple scenarios and taking stock of each of their possible outcomes (Bajic et al. 2023). For instance, a DT can evaluate the impact of tweaked process parameters so that the manufacturer can make data-supported decisions without stopping production online. This sped-up production enables an overwhelming time-to-market, waste and assurance of quality. Relying on AI's prediction capabilities, manufacturers can make what are known as real-time adjustments to changing demands, operationalizing flexibility and resilience in Industry 5.0 systems.

10.4.2. *Personalized and adaptive production*

1. **Customizing manufacturing processes based on real-time DT insights:** Industry 5.0 demands a personalized yet AI- and DT-based approach in the fundamental transformation process. DTs provide total insights into a manufacturing process in real time and hence allow for the personalization of a product to meet consumer needs. For instance, according to a recent automobile manufacturing report, DTs collect and correlate the data arising from customer feedback, design specifications and production metrics to provide specified vehicles (Gamboa-Rosales and López-Robles 2023). The continuous feedback loop between the physical environment and the virtual environment ensures every product satisfies customer expectations, resulting in satisfaction and loyalty.

2. **AI-driven adaptability for user-centric designs:** AI enhances the adaptability of manufacturing systems by analyzing data collected through DTs and suggesting improvements in design to be user-centric in nature. These include ergonomics, aesthetics and functional requirements meeting the diversity of customer requirements. Using insights from AI, manufacturers can adapt production

processes to meet emergent personalized solutions just in time for product delivery without loss of efficiency. This adaptability is the heart of Industry 5.0 because it keeps the manufacturing human-centric while reaping the benefits of new-age technologies.

10.4.3. *Energy optimization and sustainability*

1. **AI and DT collaboration for real-time energy consumption monitoring:** the synergy of AI and DTs allows for the measurement of energy consumption in real time, which is one of the important aspects of sustainable manufacturing. The DTs, therefore, create real-time flexibility for manufacturers to visualize and analyze energy consumption patterns through their integration with IoT sensors across varied stages of the manufacturing process (Minerva et al. 2022). In turn, AI processes this information to identify opportunities for addressing inefficiencies, improving energy distribution and suggesting sustainable practices.

2. **Sustainability metrics optimization in Industry 5.0 environments:** the quintessence of Industry 5.0 is sustainable development. And AI-enabled DTs will go a long way towards achieving that. The DTs have been enabled such that one can continuously monitor the key sustainability metrics – carbon emissions, water use and material waste, besides assuring the real-time monitoring of these values. AI tools further enhance this ability in modeling alternative ways of production and the sustainability impact of these methods. For instance, AI can model the environmental benefits of using alternative sources of energy or in circular economy practices. This data-driven modeling ability allows businesses to align operations in adherence to global policies on sustainability while achieving profitability.

10.4.4. *Worker safety and human–machine collaboration*

1. **AI-powered DT models for real-time risk assessment:** with Industry 5.0, worker safety has become a key issue, and AI-enabled DTs are very innovative solutions for real-time risk assessment. These DTs simulate job environments, anticipate potential risks of work and have preventive strategies. In high-risk sectors, for example, DTs might analyze sensor data and visualize unsafe situations such as equipment failure or emissions of toxic materials (Tavakoli et al. 2024). AI algorithms will analyze the risks and define the claimed level of risk for any expected occurrences, ordering them based on their seriousness and possibility, providing a base for instant actions. Such an advanced system enhances worker safety, allowing companies to solve problems proactively.

2. **Enhancing human–machine collaboration using AI-augmented DT systems:** humans and machines working together is a key characteristic of

Industry 5.0, for which AI and DT integration is crucial. DTs serve as intermediaries to translate information from physical assets into real-time insights and actionable data for human operators. A good example of this is in robotic assembly lines, whereby DTs can assign jobs to workers in the most optimal manner, based on what they could learn from the employee's resumé and machine performance analysis. AI algorithms can also enhance this collaboration by showing where one worker has more assignments than the other. In sum, this is a scenario in which human workers cohere with AI tools in a networked structure that enables Industry 5.0 – a place where human excellence is adorned with technological augmentation as opposed to being replaced by technological agency.

10.5. Enabling technologies for AI and DT in Industry 5.0

In Industry 5.0, the integration of AI and DT technologies is supported by several imperative enabling technologies that collectively improve manufacturing processes, increase efficiency and foster sustainability. The following is a detailed overview of these enabling technologies.

10.5.1. *IoT for data acquisition*

The IoT represents the backbone of data acquisition systems for DT models, forming the main channel through which real-world objects communicate with their virtual twins. Machines, infrastructure and other physical assets use IoT sensors in enormous quantities to acquire data from environmental conditions, operational parameters and performance metrics. Such real data collection keeps the DT models updated and accurate in reflecting the status of their physical twins.

IoT's capability for real-time data streaming is exceptionally crucial for integrating AI. Continuous data flow into AI algorithms permits timely dynamics for decision-making, predictive analytics or real-time insight. For instance, predictive maintenance technologies use IoT sensors to oversee the condition of an industrial machine and can then send real-time alerts in case anomalies are detected. This unhindered data flow makes the whole process better and more efficient for Industry 5.0 systems by fostering a more cohesive bond between AI and DT frameworks.

Furthermore, the recent developments in IoT protocols such as the MQTT (Message Queuing Telemetry Transport) and CoAP (Constrained Application Protocol) have already further enhanced the processes in data acquisition (San et al. 2023). These lightweight protocols enable fuel-efficient, low-latency communications via IoT devices, which enable rapid data transmission to cloud or edge computing platforms for further analysis and storage.

10.5.2. *Edge computing and cloud computing*

In conjunction with AI and DT, edge and cloud computing are essential in supporting the computational and storage requirements. Edge computing meets the need for low latency in data processing at the source. Edge devices analyze and filter data locally before it gets transmitted to centralized systems, which lightens the load on central systems while being able to provide real-time response systems (Bakon et al. 2022). This capability comes in especially handy for applications where immediate decision-making applications arise, like those used in autonomous vehicles or industrial robots.

On the contrary, this brings to bear another unique advantage that cloud computing proffers: scalability in storing and analyzing the big bulk data originating from the DTs. Sophisticated cloud platforms can provide huge computation objects for the incorporation of AI algorithms into complex simulations, scenario planning or predictive analytics. For example, cloud-based DTs can provide modeling for whole manufacturing plants from a global perspective and remote operational controls.

The synergy between edge and cloud computing enables a hybrid approach to optimized system efficiency. Along the lines of time-critical missions, edge devices take care of deterministic operations, while cloud computing stores and processes acquired historical data that is sometimes complex (Zheng et al. 2024). Emerging technologies such as fog computing further bridge the gap between edge and cloud computing, creating a seamless continuum for AI and DT operations.

10.5.3. *Advanced communication technologies (5G/6G)*

The successful working of AI and DT systems demands steady and low-latency communication, which can be facilitated with advanced communication technologies such as 5G and 6G. 5G technology provides ultra-reliable low-latency connectivity and improved mobile broadband and makes it possible to send data from IoT devices and DT models almost instantly. This is vital for remote surgery, smart grids and real-time monitoring of supply chains.

Looking ahead, 6G is likely envisioned as the system that will create a completely different dimension of scalability for AI-DT systems with virtually unlimited data transfer speeds and readability. With submillisecond latency and terabit-per-second data rates, 6G will create intelligent networks with tens of billions of devices communicating unobtrusively with one another (Zhang et al. 2024). In addition, 6G combined with AI-enabled network administration will also ensure optimal resource allocation while allowing adaptive behavior of the system.

Advanced communication technologies also play a significant role in enabling massive Machine-Type Communications (MTCs), permitting large clusters of IoT devices to work simultaneously. This allows for scalability in Industry 5.0 without compromising speed or reliability.

10.5.4. *Cybersecurity for AI-DT systems*

The ideal functioning of AI and DT systems will rely on constant and low-latency communication; thus, advanced technologies of communication such as 5G and 6G might provide just those attributes. With 5G technology, ultra-reliable low-latency connectivity and improved mobile broadband will allow the almost instantaneous transmission of data from IoT devices and DT models. This is necessary for remote surgery, smart grids and real-time monitoring of supply chains.

Blockchain technology ensures increased security in AI-DT systems through decentralized and tamper-proof data exchange (Lawrence et al. 2024). Each transaction or data transfer is cryptographically secured, which guarantees traceability and authentication. Similarly, advanced encryption techniques such as homomorphic encryption enable the processing of data in its encrypted form, reducing risk during computations.

Another challenge set before Industry 5.0 cybersecurity frameworks is IoT devices that need to be secured, as those are frequently the weakest link in the security chain. AI-enabled intrusion detection systems can monitor and report suspicious activity in the traffic flowing through the network. Zero-trust architecture entails granting access to critical resources based on the principle of need to know.

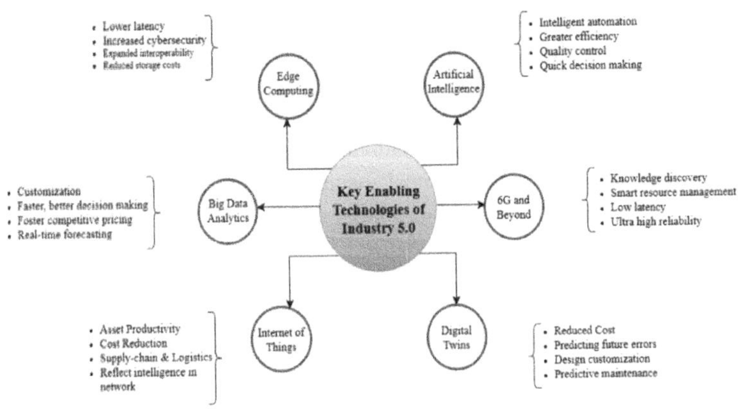

Figure 10.4. *Key enabling technologies of Industry 5.0. For a color version of this figure, see: www.iste.co.uk/taneja/6gurban.zip*

A successful merger of IoT, edge and cloud computing, advanced communications technologies and updated cybersecurity frameworks, as shown in Figure 10.4, has laid down the enabling foundations for AI and DT in Industry 5.0.

10.6. Challenges and limitations

Industry 5.0 envisions the inevitable combination of human creative minds and collective work processes with technologies such as AI and DTs to create a higher-performing and more sustainable industrial world. But this lofty aspiration would come loaded with hurdles and canceling roadblocks (Davidopoulou and Ouranidis 2022). The technical, data privacy, cost and ethics challenges that hinder the seamless integration and use of AI- and DT-based systems in Industry 5.0 are analyzed in this section.

10.6.1. *Technical challenges*

Integrating these systems with others across the cyber-physical system for Industry 5.0 remains one of the main challenges when deploying AI and DT solutions in the industry. The continuum between the real world and the digital realm to deploy such systems is often the seamless synchronization between the physical and virtual environment. Given that legacy systems vary in terms of industries, the interoperability of such systems could pose problems as the formats, standards and protocols used by legacy systems differ.

The customization required to make the AI models, DT frameworks and the existing infrastructure compatible is overwhelming and makes it complex and time-consuming to integrate.

Scalability is another major technical hurdle. AI and DT systems have a great challenge of handling real-time data, since the production line, especially high-throughput production lines, would generate data on a massive scale with high precision and real-time speed. Displacing this demand on computational resources creates bottlenecks in system capacity.

In addition, the rising complexity of production processes requires AI and DT systems to be scalable enough to offer disruption-free workflow (Decardi-Nelson et al. 2024). Edge computing and hybrid cloud architecture offer potential solutions, but further research and in-depth development are required for deployment on a larger scale

10.6.2. *Data privacy and security concerns*

Integration complexity is one of the most essential challenges in the operationalization of AI and DT in Industry 5.0. Such deployment requires the perfect synchronization of physical and virtual worlds. Differences in the formats, standards and protocols used by different industries in legacy systems pose a key obstacle to interoperability. Custom implementation for the AI model, the DT framework and the legacy infrastructure must be guaranteed through code, which can lead to a longer time to market and more complexity.

Data protection is the other concern. Compliance with data protection regulations, such as the General Data protection Regulation (GDPR) of the European Union is necessary (Yaqub and Alsabban 2023). These laws impose strict data handling practices, which include stringent access and auditability and companies could face legal penalties and erosion of public trust for any failures. As a result, they are held to work out a balance between efficient utilization of data and operating within the scope of stringent laws surrounding data use.

10.6.3. *Cost and implementation barriers*

The usability of AI and DT systems in Industry 5.0 involves huge initial setup costs. The development and deployment of these technologies call for huge financial resources, including hardware, software and infrastructure expenses. With these costs, small- and medium-sized enterprises have always found a blocker for the technology: the limitation of adoption on a wider scale. In addition, the incremental return on investment is not always explicit; therefore, stakeholders will be reluctant to invest.

Other challenges relate to skillset requirements for re-adapting the workforce. The thrust of Industry 5.0 speaks of collaborative interaction between humans and machines, so workers must have specialized competencies to operate, take care of and optimize AI and DT systems (Li et al. 2020). Upskilling programs are exhaustive as well as time-consuming and therefore placed as burdens onto any organization, particularly those with a large heterogeneous workforce. The further compound problem remains the serious lack of trained professionals in the field of AI and DTs, which has worsened and slowed down the pace of the drive towards adoption.

10.6.4. *Ethical considerations*

As automation is increasingly being woven into the fabric of our lives, Industry 5.0 is faced with some truly daunting ethical dilemmas about how to balance technological advancement with human-centered principles. One of those challenges is that vast quantities of human workers cannot be displaced by automated methods, leading to unemployment and greater social inequity. Although Industry 5.0 may herald an era focused on collaborative robotics and human–machine interaction, the need continues to move beyond mere automation, as systems should be designed to complement rather than replace human decision-making and creativity.

The ethical background of how AI-enabled automation impacts society is another issue. This will include the ingrained biases within the AI algorithms that result in certain decisions being discriminatory from the outset. Transparency, fairness and accountability within the AI models need to gain public trust while eradicating unintended societal consequences (Ben Youssef and Mejri 2023). In addition to this, it is a consideration of the extent to which the very establishment where automation is on the rise causes psychological harm, job insecurity and reduced levels of job satisfaction among employees, compromising the core purposes of Industry 5.0.

10.7. Future trends and research directions

With regard to future trends and research directions regarding Industry 5.0, the study demonstrates the transformational powers of emerging technologies such as AI, DTs and IoT that induce intelligent, sustainable and human-centric manufacturing ecosystems. Some of the key trends and directions are included in the following sections.

10.7.1. *AI and DT for hyper-personalization*

The convergence of AI and DT technologies will revolutionize the hyper-personalization of manufacturing. Unlike traditional mass production, Industry 5.0 envisions systems where the manufacture of products is based on very individual characteristics. AI, with its capability for reaching vast datasets, enables the discovery of unique customer requirements. Coupled with DTs for providing real digital replicas of physical assets, this combination allows for a departure into individual-specific system operations in manufacturing. Such systems can dynamically adjust production processes in real time, based on customer preferences, environmental conditions and resource availability.

For example, AI-DT systems can fine-tune designs, materials and means of manufacture to present a customized product while optimizing for efficiency and sustainability. Research in this area investigates ways of exceeding AI algorithms for predictive analytics, works on enhancing DT models for real-time simulations and ensures adaptive manufacturing systems that also remain resource-efficient and resilient.

10.7.2. *Autonomous and decentralized manufacturing ecosystems*

The integration of AI-DT leads to Industry 5.0, which is a kick-start to an autonomous and decentralized manufacturing ecosystem. These ecosystems function as entirely independent production networks that allow for decision and control decentralization across many nodes. AI algorithms enable machines and systems to make decisions with minimal or no human involvement, whereas DTs provide a near-perfect flow of data across the network. Such a decentralized implementation offers a flexible, scalable and resilient means by which manufacturing systems are much stronger and able to withstand disruptions. To select a few examples, in decentralized ecosystems, the case of a non-performing production node is able to queue reaching the neighboring nodes for task reallocation, so that overall activity is uninterrupted. Discussion on implementing advanced AI models for decentralized (dekkos) decision-making, as well as strong DT frameworks, enabling real-time coordination and communication in these ecosystems, remain early research studies. Interoperability, data security and energy efficiency are key points of emphasis in bringing this vision to life.

10.7.3. *Integration with emerging technologies*

The future of AI and DT systems will be their seamless integration with new technologies. Quantum computing has a great potential to improve the computational power of AI-DT systems, which can be used to solve highly complex optimization problems and to facilitate time-consuming simulations. Quantum algorithms can help AI models process large datasets more efficiently using fewer computational resources, potentially allowing for real-time decision-making in rapidly changing environments. Likewise, innovative sensors and materials will transform DT systems. High-precision sensors for the generation of precise data for real-time simulations are complemented by smart materials that enable a self-healing and adaptive feature, embedded in physical assets. These developments herald the emergence of the next generation of DT systems, attuned to higher degrees of accuracy, responsiveness and predictive capability. Adopting quantum mechanics and nanostructured materials advances current AI-DT systems through the improvement of its operational and functional efficiency while also focusing on the generation of quantum AI models, new flexible sensor technologies and novel smart materials.

10.7.4. *Evolving standards and frameworks*

To be in keeping with the rapid proliferation of AI and DT technologies in Industry 5.0, the development of standard frameworks is imperative. These standards should guarantee the interoperability, integrity and consistency of the diverse systems and industries. Common protocols and rules are important to allow smooth communication between AI models and DT systems in many of the deep, complex spaces of manufacturing. Furthermore, policy and regulatory advancement is required to address the ethical, legal and social implications of AI-DT applications. An example could suggest typical frameworks to address data privacy, cybersecurity and accountability in making autonomous systems relatively risk-free. Proactive approaches are required wherein policymakers and industry leaders meet and promulgate rules for creative innovations that incorporate safety and fairness. Current research is directing efforts towards the development of flexible scalable standards catering to future technologies while establishing broader international cooperation and convergence.

Summarily, the future of AI and DT in Industry 5.0 builds upon the hyper-personalization directive, autonomous manufacturing advances, integration with emerging technologies and the evolution of standards and policies. Continued research and innovation in these sectors will drive the transformation of manufacturing systems to be efficient, sustainable and resilient to market demands in a world that is rapidly changing.

10.8. Case studies and real-world implementations

Case studies and real-world implementations of AI and DT in Industry 5.0 illustrate how these technologies are successfully applied in addressing complex challenges, facilitating improvement and enhancing innovation. Some selected examples in key industries are as follows.

10.8.1. *Automotive manufacturing*

AI is hugely responsible for revolutionizing the automotive industry using predictive maintenance and energy optimization, hence reducing operational inefficiency and operational cost. Through predictive maintenance, with AI support, manufacturers can predict the chances of equipment failure before it happens by evaluating real-time data that is collected from the devices themselves. While, for its part, the DT completely and precisely duplicates physical assets today virtually, permitting engineers to carry out simulations under a variety of scenarios and loads. For instance, automotive giants such as BMW and Tesla deploy AI-DT systems to monitor production lines to detect anomalies in the equipment and schedule maintenance proactively. This strategy introduces minimal unplanned downtime and improved utilization over a piece of equipment's lifetime.

Figure 10.5 shows the interaction between physical space ("Smart Machine") and virtual space ("Digital Twin") in the cloud-based interconnected environment.

In physical space, it uses actuators, health monitoring and adaptive actuation for real-time sensory data collection and dynamic operation. This data is processed and sent to the Virtual Space that uses 3D modeling data mining and computational simulations to optimize system performance. These feedback loops allow for constant synchronization between the physical and virtual domains for predictive maintenance, informed decision-making and optimized performance. This integration serves as a quintessential example of how DTs improve the efficiency and reliability of the cyber-physical realizations of processes that are so vital to the core fundamentals of Industry 5.0.

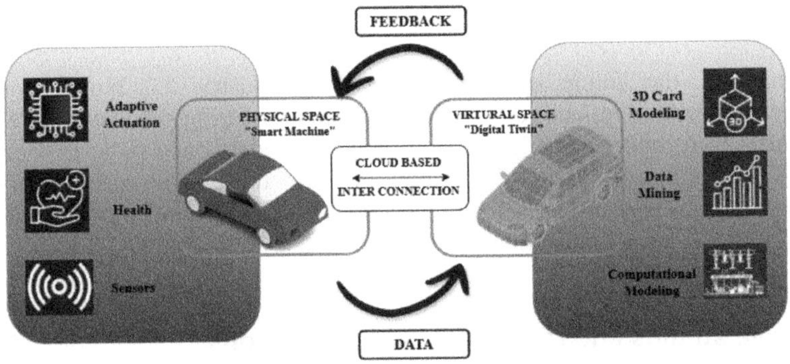

Figure 10.5. *Automotive manufacturing. For a color version of this figure, see: www.iste.co.uk/taneja/6gurban.zip*

Energy optimization is yet another game changer. AI-DT systems study the patterns of energy consumption to determine the wasteful use of energy and suggest corrective measures. Ford, for instance, has deployed AI at its plants to better manage energy consumption, achieving a substantial decrease in energy costs by optimizing HVAC (heating, ventilation, and air conditioning) systems, lighting and production schedules. Such practices lower production costs for automotive manufacturers and also provide sustainability and global environmental protection goals.

10.8.2. *Smart factories*

AI and DTs cross-pollute into smart factories, which highlights the ongoing monitoring and decision-making of production in real time. These systems provide deep visibility into manufacturing processes that allow dynamic adjustments to maximize output. Siemens, for example, deploys AI-DT systems at its Amberg plant, where production steps are digitally tracked. The sensors on the machines collect data for the AI algorithms to identify inefficiencies and determine what the road ahead might look like.

DTs in smart factories bring together the virtual and physical worlds. Manufacturers use simulation to help validate new designs and processes before (and while) they disrupt production workflows. This ability reduces risks and costs in accelerating innovation. Moreover, AI-DT systems facilitate real-time feedback loops, allowing managers to quickly react to shifts in demand or disruptions in the supply chain. This agility not only increases productivity but also enables customization at scale, fulfilling different client requirements.

10.8.3. *Sustainable industries*

AI-DT systems are now also being applied to maintain a good image of the organization as they implement green manufacturing and reduce waste. Hence, DTs are broad ecosystem-based production processes that make it possible to monitor consumption and ecological impacts. This information is processed through AI algorithms that suggest processes for saving energy and reducing waste.

One good example would be Schneider Electric using AI-DT technologies to realize carbon neutrality throughout its operations. The company has considerably reduced greenhouse gas emissions through effective monitoring of energy consumption and optimizing renewable integration. With DTs, Procter and Gamble is reducing water consumption at all its plants by establishing high-water-using areas and taking corrective measures. While improving environmental stewardship, these campaigns also drive cost savings, as, indeed, going forward, sustainability and profitability are not mutually independent principles.

AI-DT systems are also of great significance to circular economy models. Tracking product lifecycles serves to make designs for easy disassembly and better recycling, which would lead to less waste. Moreover, this development converges with global initiatives like that of the United Nations Sustainable Development Goals (SDGs), further establishing the utmost relevance in emphasizing sustainability practices in the industrial environment.

10.9. Conclusion

AI and DT technologies are increasingly being explored and integrated to realize the vision of Industry 5.0 characterized by human-centricity and sustainability efficiency of operations. These technologies help enable predictive modeling, real-time analytics, dynamic decision-making and moreover, creating systemic adaptability and resilience across industries. AI's innovative automation and decision support complement human intelligence, seamlessly connecting the physical and digital worlds through DTs for comprehensive modeling and optimization, fostering sustainability and efficiency in industry and society. These support SM, personalized production, energy optimization and improved collaboration between humans and machines. Nevertheless, obstacles including technical complexity, data privacy, ethical concerns and implementation costs remain. How these barriers are addressed through advanced research, emerging technologies such as quantum computing solutions, and the evolution of standardized frameworks will determine the future shape of Industry 5.0. In conclusion, the integration of AI and DT will revolutionize industrial ecosystems into interconnected productive networks, leading to efficiency, sustainability and innovation in a constantly evolving society.

10.10. References

Ait-Alla, A., Kreutz, M., Rippel, D., Lütjen, M., Freitag, M. (2021). Simulated-based methodology for the interface configuration of cyber-physical production systems. *International Journal of Production Research*, 59(17), 5388–5403 doi: 10.1080/00207543.2020.1778209.

Asokan, D.R., Huq, F.A., Smith, C.M., Stevenson, M. (2022). Socially responsible operations in the Industry 4.0 era: Post-COVID-19 technology adoption and perspectives on future research. *International Journal of Operations & Production Management*, 42(13), 185–217. doi: 10.1108/IJOPM-01-2022-0069.

Bajic, B., Suzic, N., Moraca, S., Stefanović, M., Jovicic, M., Rikalovic, A. (2023). Edge computing data optimization for smart quality management: Industry 5.0 perspective. *Sustainability*, 15(7), 1–19. doi: 10.3390/su15076032.

Bakon, K., Holczinger, T., Süle, Z., Jaskó, S., Abonyi, J. (2022). Scheduling under uncertainty for Industry 4.0 and 5.0. *IEEE Access*, 10, 74977–75017. doi: 10.1109/ACCESS.2022.3191426.

Ben Youssef, A. and Mejri, I. (2023). Linking digital technologies to sustainability through industry 5.0: A bibliometric analysis. *Sustainability*, 15(9). doi: 10.3390/su15097465.

Bork, D., Ali, S.J., Dinev, G.M. (2023). AI-enhanced hybrid decision management. *Business and Information Systems Engineering*, 65(2), 179–199, doi: 10.1007/s12599-023-00790-2.

Boumsisse, I., Benhadou, M., Haddout, A. (2024). Exploring the potential synergies between industry 5.0 and green lean six sigma for sustainable performance: A new dimension of operational excellence. *Evolutionary Studies in Imaginative Culture*, 8, 1242–1259. doi: 10.70082/esiculture.vi.1442.

Campero-Jurado, I., Márquez-Sánchez, S., Quintanar-Gómez, J. (2020). Smart helmet 5.0 for industrial Internet of Things using artificial intelligence. *Sensors*, 20(21), 1–27. doi: 10.3390/s20216241.

Castellani, A., Schmitt, S., Squartini, S. (2021). Real-world anomaly detection by using digital twin systems and weakly supervised learning. *IEEE Transactions on Industrial Informatics*, 17(7), 4733–4742. doi: 10.1109/TII.2020.3019788.

Davidopoulou, C. and Ouranidis, A. (2022). Pharma 4.0-artificially intelligent digital twins for solidified nanosuspensions. *Pharmaceutics*, 14(10). doi: 10.3390/pharmaceutics14102113.

Decardi-Nelson, B., Alshehri, A.S., Ajagekar, A., You, F. (2024). Generative AI and process systems engineering: The next frontier. *Computers & Chemical Engineering*, 187, 1–72. doi: 10.1016/j.compchemeng.2024.108723.

Di Meglio, A., Massarotti, N., Nithiarasu, P. (2024). A physics-driven and machine learning-based digital twinning approach to transient thermal systems. *International Journal of Numerical Methods for Heat & Fluid Flow*, 34(6), 2229–2256. doi: 10.1108/HFF-10-2023-0616.

Gamboa-Rosales, N.K. and López-Robles, J.R. (2023). Evolving from Industry 4.0 to Industry 5.0: Evaluating the conceptual structure and prospects of an emerging field. *Transinformação*, 35, 1–13. doi: 10.1590/2318-0889202335e237319.

Lawrence, N.P., Kumar Damarla, S., Woo Kim, J., Tulsyan, A., Amjad, F., Wang, K., Chachuat, B., Min Lee, J., Huang, B., Gopaluni, R.B. (2024). Machine learning for industrial sensing and control: A survey and practical perspective. *Control Engineering Practice*, 145, 1–48. doi: 10.1016/j.conengprac.2024.105841.

Li, X., Wang, B., Liu, C., Freiheit, T., Epureanu, B.I. (2020). Intelligent manufacturing systems in COVID-19 pandemic and beyond: Framework and impact assessment. *Chinese Journal of Mechanical Engineering (English Edition)*, 33(1). doi: 10.1186/s10033-020-00476-w.

Männle, D., Pohlmann, J., Monji-Azad, S., Hesser, J., Rotter, N., Affolter, A., Lammert, A., Kramer, B., Ludwig, S., Huber, L., Scherl, C. (2023). Artificial intelligence directed development of a digital twin to measure soft tissue shift during head and neck surgery. *PLoS One*, 18(8), 1–12. doi: 10.1371/journal.pone.0287081.

Minerva, R., Awan, F.M., Crespi, N. (2022). Exploiting digital twins as enablers for synthetic sensing. *IEEE Internet Computing*, 26(5), 61–67. doi: 10.1109/MIC.2021.3051674.

Mortlock, T., Muthirayan, D., Yu, S.Y., Khargonekar, P.P., Abdullah Al Faruque, M. (2022). Graph learning for cognitive digital twins in manufacturing systems. *IEEE Transactions on Emerging Topics in Computing*, 10(1), 34–45. doi: 10.1109/TETC.2021.3132251.

San, O., Pawar, S., Rasheed, A. (2023). Decentralized digital twins of complex dynamical systems. *Science Reports*, 13(1), 1–15. doi: 10.1038/s41598-023-47078-9.

Tavakoli, P., Yitmen, I., Sadri, H., Taheri, A. (2024). Blockchain-based digital twin data provenance for predictive asset management in building facilities. *Smart and Sustainable Built Environment*, 13(1), 4–21. doi: 10.1108/SASBE-07-2023-0169.

Vyskočil, J., Douda, P., Novák, P., Wally, B. (2023). A digital twin-based distributed manufacturing execution system for Industry 4.0 with AI-powered on-the-fly replanning capabilities. *Sustainability (Switzerland)*, 15(7), 1–27. doi: 10.3390/su15076251.

Xu, Q., Yue, T., Ali, S., Arratibel, M. (2024). Pretrain, prompt, and transfer: Evolving digital twins for time-to-event analysis in cyber-physical systems. *IEEE Trans. Softw. Eng.*, 50(6), 1464–1477. doi: 10.1109/TSE.2024.3388572.

Yaqub, M.Z. and Alsabban, A. (2023). Industry-4.0-enabled digital transformation: Prospects, instruments, challenges, and implications for business strategies. *Sustainability*, 15(11). doi: 10.3390/su15118553.

Zhang, Z., Liu, Y., Peng, Z., Chen, M., Xu, D., Cui, S. (2024). Digital twin-assisted data-driven optimization for reliable edge caching in wireless networks. *IEEE Journal on Selected Areas in Communications*, 1–15. doi: 10.1109/JSAC.2024.3431575.

Zheng, P., Yang, J., Lou, J., Wang, B. (2024). Design and application of virtual simulation teaching platform for intelligent manufacturing. *Science Reports*, 14(1), 1–19. doi: 10.1038/s41598-024-62072-5.

List of Authors

Sachin AHUJA
Computer Science & Engineering
University Institute of Engineering
Chandigarh University
Mohali
India

Logapadmini B.
Department of Information Technology
Hindustan Institute of Technology and Science
Bay Range Campus
Padur
Chennai
India

C.V. Suresh BABU
Department of Information Technology
Hindustan Institute of Technology and Science
Bay Range Campus
Chennai
India

Ritesh Gangasingh BAIS
MGMs College of Engineering
Nanded
India

Anuradha Amar BAKARE
Department of Polytechnic
Dr. Vishwanath Karad MIT World Peace University
Pune
India

Pradnya BORKAR
Department of CSE
Symbiosis Institute of Technology
Nagpur Campus
Symbiosis International (Deemed University)
Pune
India

T. Shirley DEVAKIRUBAI
Madras Christian College
Chennai
India

Sartajvir Singh DHILLON
Computer Science & Engineering
University Institute of Engineering
Chandigarh University
Mohali
India

Anupma GUPTA
Department of Electronics and
Communication Engineering
Chandigarh University
Punjab
India

Shubham GUPTA
Model Institute of Engineering
and Technology
Jammu
India

Mohammad Alamgir HOSSAIN
Department of Computer Science
College of Computer Science &
Information Technology
Jazan University
Saudi Arabia

G. ILANKUMARAN
Alagappa Institute of Management
Alagappa University
Karaikudi
India

A. IYAPPAN
International Institute of Business Studies
Bangalore
India

Tripuraneni JAGGAIAH
International Institute of Business Studies
Bangalore
India

Manjushri JOSHI
Department of Polytechnic
Dr. Vishwanath Karad MIT World
Peace University
Pune
India

Jasneet KAUR
Computer Science & Engineering
University Institute of Engineering
Chandigarh University
Mohali
India

Mandeep KAUR
School of Computer Science Engineering
and Technology
Bennett University
Greater Noida
India

Osamah Ibrahim KHALAF
Al-Nahrain University
Al-Nahrain Renewable Energy
Research Center
Baghdad
India

Utku KOSE
Department of Computer Engineering
Suleyman Demirel University
Turkey

Harashleen KOUR
Model Institute of Engineering
and Technology
Jammu
India

Abhishek KUMAR
Dept of CSE
Chandigarh University
Punjab
India

Vipan KUMAR
Department of Electronics
and Communication Engineering
Sri Sai College of Engineering
and Technology
Badhani
India

Suresh Vishnudas LIMKAR
Department of Computer Science &
Engineering
Central University of Jammu
India

Sulakshana MALWADE
Department of Computer Engineering
DVK World Peace University School of Polytechnic and Skill Development
Pune
India

Rajshri NIKAM
Anantrao Pawar College of Engineering and Research
Pune
India

Mariya OUAISSA
Cadi Ayyad University
Marrakech
Morocco

Mariyam OUAISSA
Chouaib Doukkali University
El Jadida
Morocco

Pritesh PATIL
Department of Information Technology
AISSMS Institute of Information Technology
Pune
India

Srinibas PATTANAIK
Computer Science & Engineering
University Institute of Engineering
Chandigarh University
Mohali
India

C. Kishor Kumar REDDY
Department of Computer Science and Engineering
Stanley College of Engineering and Technology for Women
India

Vibhuti REHALIA
Department of Electrical Engineering
Sri Sai College of Engineering and Technology
Badhani
India

Jainender SHARMA
Department of Civil Engineering
Sri Sai University
Palampur
India

SHIKHA
Department of Electrical Engineering
Sri Sai University
Palampur
India

Bhanu Partap SINGH
Institute of Engineering and Technology
Chitkara University
Punjab
India

T. Monika SINGH
Department of Computer Science and Engineering
Stanley College of Engineering and Technology for Women
India

Lav SONI
Institute of Engineering and Technology
Chitkara University
Punjab
India

Yamini SOOD
Department of Computer Science and Engineering
Sri Sai University
Palampur
India

Pasham SOWMYA
Department of Computer Science and Engineering
Stanley College of Engineering and Technology for Women
India

Ashu TANEJA
Institute of Engineering and Technology
Chitkara University
Punjab
India

Kimmi VERMA
Department of Computer Science
and Engineering
ABES Engineering College
Ghaziabad
India

Alessandro VINCIARELLI
Computational Social Intelligence
(Computing Science)
University of Glasgow
Scotland
UK

Prashant WAKHARE
Department of Information Technology
AISSMS Institute of Information
Technology
Pune
India

Index

P, R

S, T

U, V, W

Other titles from

iSTE

in

Computer Engineering

2025

CHIKH Azeddine
Systemic Approach to Categorizing and Modeling Requirements

2024

CHAKRABORTY Rajdeep, GHOSH Anupam, KUMAR MANDAL Jyotsna, CHOUDHURY Tanupriya, CHATTERJEE Prasenjit
Smart Edge Computing: An Operation Research Perspective
(International Perspectives in Decision Analytics and Operations Research Set – Volume 2)

HOMÈS Bernard
Fundamentals of Software Testing (2nd edition, revised and updated)

JERBI Abdessalem
Discrete-Event Simulation: Concepts and Production in Arena

PRADHAN Devasis, KUMAR SAHU Prasanna, MYO TUN Hla, CHATTERJEE Prasenjit
Artificial and Cognitive Computing for Sustainable Healthcare Systems in Smart Cities
(International Perspectives in Decision Analytics and Operations Research Set – Volume 3)

2023

CHOUDHURY Tanupriya, KHANNA Abhirup, CHATTERJEE Prasenjit, UM Jung-Sup, BHATTACHARYA Abhishek
Blockchain Applications in Healthcare: Innovations and Practices
(International Perspectives in Decision Analytics and Operations Research Set – Volume 1)

PAI G A Vijayalakshmi
A Textbook of Data Structures and Algorithms 1: Mastering Linear Data Structures
A Textbook of Data Structures and Algorithms 2: Mastering Nonlinear Data Structures
A Textbook of Data Structures and Algorithms 3: Mastering Advanced Data Structures and Algorithm Design Strategies

2022

HOMÈS Bernard
Advanced Testing of Systems-of-Systems 1: Theoretical Aspects
Advanced Testing of Systems-of-Systems 2: Practical Aspects

MEHTA Shikha, TIWARI Sanju, SIARRY Patrick, JABBAR M.A.
Tools, Languages, Methodologies for Representing Semantics on the Web of Things

SIDHOM Sahbi, KADDOUR Amira
Systems and Uses of Digital Sciences for Knowledge Organization
(Digital Tools and Uses Set – Volume 9)

ZAIDOUN Ameur Salem
Computer Science Security: Concepts and Tools

2021

DELHAYE Jean-Loïc
Inside the World of Computing: Technologies, Uses, Challenges

HARDIN Thérèse, JAUME Mathieu, PESSAUX François,
VIGUIÉ DONZEAU-GOUGE Véronique
Concepts and Semantics of Programming Languages 1: A Semantical Approach with OCaml and Python
Concepts and Semantics of Programming Languages 2: Modular and Object-oriented Constructs with OCaml, Python, C++, Ada and Java

MKADMI Abderrazak
Archives in The Digital Age: Preservation and the Right to be Forgotten (Digital Tools and Uses Set – Volume 8)

TOKLU Yusuf Cengiz, BEKDAŞ Gebrail, NIGDELI Sinan Melih
Metaheuristics for Structural Design and Analysis
(Optimization Heuristics Set – Volume 3)

2020

DARCHE Philippe
Microprocessor 1: Prolegomenes – Calculation and Storage Functions – Models of Computation and Computer Architecture
Microprocessor 2: Core Concepts – Communication in a Digital System
Microprocessor 3: Core Concepts – Hardware Aspects
Microprocessor 4: Core Concepts – Software Aspects
Microprocessor 5: Software and Hardware Aspects of Development, Debugging and Testing – The Microcomputer

DUVAUT Patrick, DALLOZ Xavier, MENGA David, KOEHL François,
CHRIQUI Vidal, BRILL Joerg
Internet of Augmented Me, I.AM: Empowering Innovation for a New Sustainable Future

LAFFLY Dominique
TORUS 1 – Toward an Open Resource Using Services: Cloud Computing for Environmental Data
TORUS 2 – Toward an Open Resource Using Services: Cloud Computing for Environmental Data
TORUS 3 – Toward an Open Resource Using Services: Cloud Computing for Environmental Data

LAURENT Anne, LAURENT Dominique, MADERA Cédrine
Data Lakes
(Databases and Big Data Set – Volume 2)

OULHADJ Hamouche, DAACHI Boubaker, MENASRI Riad
Metaheuristics for Robotics
(Optimization Heuristics Set – Volume 2)

SADIQUI Ali
Computer Network Security

VENTRE Daniel
Artificial Intelligence, Cybersecurity and Cyber Defense

2019

BESBES Walid, DHOUIB Diala, WASSAN Niaz, MARREKCHI Emna
Solving Transport Problems: Towards Green Logistics

CLERC Maurice
Iterative Optimizers: Difficulty Measures and Benchmarks

GHLALA Riadh
Analytic SQL in SQL Server 2014/2016

TOUNSI Wiem
Cyber-Vigilance and Digital Trust: Cyber Security in the Era of Cloud Computing and IoT

2018

ANDRO Mathieu
Digital Libraries and Crowdsourcing
(Digital Tools and Uses Set – Volume 5)

ARNALDI Bruno, GUITTON Pascal, MOREAU Guillaume
Virtual Reality and Augmented Reality: Myths and Realities

CARDON Alain
Beyond Artificial Intelligence: From Human Consciousness to Artificial Consciousness

HOMAYOUNI S. Mahdi, FONTES Dalila B.M.M.
Metaheuristics for Maritime Operations
(Optimization Heuristics Set – Volume 1)

JEANSOULIN Robert
JavaScript and Open Data

PIVERT Olivier
NoSQL Data Models: Trends and Challenges
(Databases and Big Data Set – Volume 1)

SEDKAOUI Soraya
Data Analytics and Big Data

SALEH Imad, AMMI Mehdi, SZONIECKY Samuel
Challenges of the Internet of Things: Technology, Use, Ethics
(Digital Tools and Uses Set – Volume 7)

SZONIECKY Samuel
Ecosystems Knowledge: Modeling and Analysis Method for Information and Communication
(Digital Tools and Uses Set – Volume 6)

2017

BENMAMMAR Badr
Concurrent, Real-Time and Distributed Programming in Java: Threads, RTSJ and RMI

BOUHAÏ Nasreddine, SALEH Imad
Internet of Things: Evolutions and Innovations
(Digital Tools and Uses Set – Volume 4)

HÉLIODORE Frédéric, NAKIB Amir, ISMAIL Boussaad, OUCHRAA Salma, SCHMITT Laurent
Metaheuristics for Intelligent Electrical Networks
(Metaheuristics Set – Volume 10)

MA Haiping, SIMON Dan
Evolutionary Computation with Biogeography-based Optimization
(Metaheuristics Set – Volume 8)

PÉTROWSKI Alain, BEN-HAMIDA Sana
Evolutionary Algorithms
(Metaheuristics Set – Volume 9)

PAI G A Vijayalakshmi
Metaheuristics for Portfolio Optimization: An Introduction using MATLAB®
(Metaheuristics Set – Volume 11)

REYES-GARCIA Everardo
The Image-Interface: Graphical Supports for Visual Information
(Digital Tools and Uses Set – Volume 3)

REYES-GARCIA Everardo, BOUHAÏ Nasreddine
Designing Interactive Hypermedia Systems
(Digital Tools and Uses Set – Volume 2)

SZONIECKY Samuel, BOUHAÏ Nasreddine
Collective Intelligence and Digital Archives: Towards Knowledge Ecosystems
(Digital Tools and Uses Set – Volume 1)

2016

BLUM Christian, FESTA Paola
Metaheuristics for String Problems in Bio-informatics
(Metaheuristics Set – Volume 6)

DEROUSSI Laurent
Metaheuristics for Logistics
(Metaheuristics Set – Volume 4)

DHAENENS Clarisse, JOURDAN Laetitia
Metaheuristics for Big Data
(Metaheuristics Set – Volume 5)

LABADIE Nacima, PRINS Christian, PRODHON Caroline
Metaheuristics for Vehicle Routing Problems
(Metaheuristics Set – Volume 3)

LEROY Laure
Eyestrain Reduction in Stereoscopy

LUTTON Evelyne, PERROT Nathalie, TONDA Alberto
Evolutionary Algorithms for Food Science and Technology
(Metaheuristics Set – Volume 7)

MAGOULÈS Frédéric, ZHAO Hai-Xiang
Data Mining and Machine Learning in Building Energy Analysis

RIGO Michel
Advanced Graph Theory and Combinatorics

ZELM Martin, DOUMEINGTS Guy, MENDONÇA Joao Pedro
Enterprise Interoperability: in the Digitized and Networked Factory of the Future

2015

BARBIER Franck, RECOUSSINE Jean Luc
COBOL Software Modernization: From Principles to Implementation with the BLU AGE® Method

CHEN Ken
Performance Evaluation by Simulation and Analysis with Applications to Computer Networks

CLERC Maurice
Guided Randomness in Optimization
(Metaheuristics Set – Volume 1)

DURAND Nicolas, GIANAZZA David, GOTTELAND Jean-Baptiste, ALLIOT Jean-Marc
Metaheuristics for Air Traffic Management
(Metaheuristics Set – Volume 2)

MAGOULÈS Frédéric, ROUX François-Xavier, HOUZEAUX Guillaume
Parallel Scientific Computing

MUNEESAWANG Paisarn, YAMMEN Suchart
Visual Inspection Technology in the Hard Disk Drive Industry

2014

BOULANGER Jean-Louis
Formal Methods Applied to Industrial Complex Systems
Formal Methods Applied to Complex Systems: Implementation of the B Method

EXPOSITO Ernesto, DIOP Codé
Smart SOA Platforms in Cloud Computing Architectures

GARDI Frédéric, BENOIST Thierry, DARLAY Julien, ESTELLON Bertrand, MEGEL Romain
Mathematical Programming Solver based on Local Search

KRICHEN Saoussen, CHAOUACHI Jouhaina
Graph-related Optimization and Decision Support Systems

LARRIEU Nicolas, VARET Antoine
Rapid Prototyping of Software for Avionics Systems: Model-oriented Approaches for Complex Systems Certification

LAURAS Matthieu, ZELM Martin, ARCHIMÈDE Bernard, BÉNABEN Frédérick, DOUMEINGTS Guy
Enterprise Interoperability: Interoperability for Agility, Resilience and Plasticity of Collaborations

OUSSALAH Mourad Chabane
Software Architecture 1
Software Architecture 2

QUESNEL Flavien
Scheduling of Large-scale Virtualized Infrastructures: Toward Cooperative Management

RIGO Michel
Formal Languages, Automata and Numeration Systems 1: Introduction to Combinatorics on Words
Formal Languages, Automata and Numeration Systems 2: Applications to Recognizability and Decidability

SAINT-DIZIER Patrick
Musical Rhetoric: Foundations and Annotation Schemes

TOUATI Sid, DUPONT DE DINECHIN Benoit
Advanced Backend Code Optimization

2013

ANDRÉ Etienne, SOULAT Romain
The Inverse Method: Parametric Verification of Real-time Embedded Systems

BOULANGER Jean-Louis
Safety Management for Software-based Equipment

DELAHAYE Daniel, PUECHMOREL Stéphane
Modeling and Optimization of Air Traffic

FRANCOPOULO Gil
LMF — Lexical Markup Framework

GHEDIRA Khaled
Constraint Satisfaction Problems. CSP Formalisms and Techniques

GOVAERT Gérard, NADIF Mohamed
Co-Clustering: Models, Algorithms and Applications

LANDRAGIN Frédérick
Man–Machine Dialogue: Design and Challenges

LUCAS Laurent, LOSCOS Céline, REMION Yannick
3D Video: Models, From Capture to Diffusion

ROCHANGE Christine, UHRIG Sascha, SAINRAT Pascal
Time-Predictable Architectures

WAHBI Mohamed
Algorithms and Ordering Heuristics for Distributed Constraint Satisfaction Problems

ZELM Martin, VAN SINDEREN Marten, FERRAIRA PIRES Luis, DOUMEINGTS Guy
Enterprise Interoperability: Research and Applications in the Service-oriented Ecosystem

2012

ARBOLEDA Hugo, ROYER Jean-Claude
Model-Driven and Software Product Line Engineering

BLANCHET Gérard, DUPOUY Bertrand
Computer Architecture

BOULANGER Jean-Louis
Industrial Use of Formal Methods: Formal Verification
Formal Methods: Industrial Use from Model to the Code

CALVARY Gaëlle, DELOT Thierry, SÈDES Florence, TIGLI Jean-Yves
Computer Science and Ambient Intelligence

MAHOUT Vincent
Assembly Language Programming: ARM Cortex-M3 2.0: Organization, Innovation and Territory

MARLET Renaud
Program Specialization

SOTO Maria, SEVAUX Marc, ROSSI André, LAURENT Johann
Memory Allocation Problems in Embedded Systems: Optimization Methods

2011

BICHOT Charles-Edmond, SIARRY Patrick
Graph Partitioning

BOULANGER Jean-Louis
Static Analysis of Software: The Abstract Interpretation

CAFERRA Ricardo
Logic for Computer Science and Artificial Intelligence

KORDON Fabrice, HADDAD Serge, PAUTET Laurent, PETRUCCI Laure
Distributed Systems: Design and Algorithms
Models and Analysis in Distributed Systems

LORCA Xavier
Tree-based Graph Partitioning Constraint

RIDHA MAHJOUB A.
Progress in Combinatorial Optimization: ISCO2010

TRUCHET Charlotte, ASSAYAG Gerard
Constraint Programming in Music

VICAT-BLANC Pascale, GOGLIN Brice, GUILLIER Romaric,
SOUDAN Sébastien
Computing Networks: From Cluster to Cloud Computing

2010

AUBRUN Christophe, SIMON Daniel, SONG Ye-Qiong
Co-design Approaches for Dependable Networked Control Systems

AUDIBERT Pierre
Mathematics for Informatics and Computer Science

BABAU Jean-Philippe, BLAY-FORNARINO Mireille, CHAMPEAU Joël,
ROBERT Sylvain, SABETTA Antonino
Model Driven Engineering for Distributed Real-Time Systems: MARTE modeling, model transformations and their usages

BOULANGER Jean-Louis
Safety of Computer Architectures

SIGAUD Olivier, BUFFET Olivier
Markov Decision Processes in Artificial Intelligence

MONMARCHÉ Nicolas, GUINAND Frédérick, SIARRY Patrick
Artificial Ants

SOLNON Christine
Ant Colony Optimization and Constraint Programming

2009

FOURNIER Jean-Claude
Graph Theory and Applications: with exercises and problems

GUÉDON Jeanpierre
The Mojette Transform: theory and applications

JARD Claude, ROUX Olivier H.
Communicating Embedded Systems: Software and Design

LECOUTRE Christophe
Constraint Networks: Techniques and Algorithms

2008

BANÂTRE Michel, MARRON Pedro Jose, OLLERO Anibal, WOLITZ Adam
Cooperating Embedded Systems and Wireless Sensor Networks

MERZ Stephan, NAVET Nicolas
Modeling and Verification of Real-time Systems: Formalisms and Software Tools

PASCHOS Vangelis Th
Combinatorial Optimization and Theoretical Computer Science: Interfaces and Perspectives

WALDNER Jean-Baptiste
Nanocomputers and Swarm Intelligence

2007

BENHAMOU Frédéric, JUSSIEN Narendra, O'SULLIVAN Barry
Trends in Constraint Programming

JUSSIEN Narendra
A to Z of Sudoku

2006

BABAU Jean-Philippe, CHAMPEAU Joël, GÉRARD Sébastien
From MDD Concepts to Experiments and Illustrations – DRES 2006

HABRIAS Henri, FRAPPIER Marc
Software Specification Methods: An Overview Using a Case Study

MURAT Cécile, PASCHOS Vangelis Th
Probabilistic Combinatorial Optimization on Graphs

PANETTO Hervé, BOUDJLIDA Nacer
Interoperability for Enterprise Software and Applications: Proceedings of the Workshops and the Doctorial Symposium of the Second IFAC/IFIP I-ESA International Conference: EI2N, WSI, IS-TSPQ 2006

2005

GÉRARD Sébastien, BABAU Jean-Philippe, CHAMPEAU Joël
Model Driven Engineering for Distributed Real Time Embedded Systems

PANETTO Hervé
Interoperability of Enterprise Software and Applications: Workshops of the INTEROP-ESA 2005 International Conference (EI2N, WSI, ISIDI and IEHENA 2005)

Printed and bound by CPI Group (UK) Ltd, Croydon, CR0 4YY
13/09/2026
14961014-0002